Eurasia and India

Eurasia has assumed importance in the post-Soviet period and the peoples of Siberia have distinctive historical-cultural similarities with the Indian Himalayas due to common traditions and Buddhist culture. The Eurasianism of Russia brings it closer to India in historical-cultural, political and economic terms. Another important player in Eurasia is Kazakhstan, which has been highlighting the importance of Eurasianism. These relations provide an opportunity for India to engage in collaborative endeavours with the Eurasian countries. This book provides detailed analyses on the historical-cultural linkages between Eurasia (Buryatia, Khakassia, Tuva and Altai Republics of the Russian Federation) and India through history. It also examines the process of the revival of indigenous traditions in the region in the post-Soviet period, the importance of the Eurasian vector in Russia's and Kazakhstan's foreign policy, and the development of the Eurasian Economic Union and the implications this will have for India. Eminent academics and area specialists from Buryatia, Altai, Khakassia, Moscow, Kazakhstan and India have contributed to this book, which provides a firsthand view of the linkages between India and the Siberian region of India. *Eurasia and India* also includes rare photographs of the traces of Indian culture in Siberia. Offering a new understanding of the significant and strategic Indian ties to Eurasian states, this book will be of interest to academics studying Eurasian and Central Asian society and geopolitics, International Relations and South and Central Asian Studies.

K. Warikoo is Professor at the Centre for Inner Asian Studies, School of International Studies, Jawaharlal Nehru University, New Delhi. The author of several books on Kashmir, Central Asia and Afghanistan, he is the founding editor of *Himalayan and Central Asian Studies*, which was first published in 1997. His books *Xinjiang: China's North West Frontier* (2016), *Religion and Security in South and Central Asia* (2011) and *Himalayan Frontiers of India* (2009) were also published by Routledge.

Central Asia Research Forum

Series Editor: Shirin Akiner

For a full list of titles in this series, please visit www.routledge.com

Other titles in the series:

Leadership and Authority in Central Asia
The Ismaili community in Tajikistan
Otambek N. Mastibekov

National Identities in Soviet Historiography
The rise of nations under Stalin
Harun Yilmaz

Identity and Memory in Post-Soviet Central Asia
Uzbekistan's Soviet past
Timur Dadabaev

Migration and Identity in Central Asia
The Uzbek experience
Rano Turaeva

The Management of Public Services in Central Asia
Institutional transformation in Kyrgyzstan
David Scott

Xinjiang – China's Northwest Frontier
Edited by K. Warikoo

Sustainable Energy in Kazakhstan
Moving to cleaner energy in a resource-rich country
Edited by Yelena Kalyuzhnova and Richard Pomfret

Eurasia and India
Regional Perspectives
Edited by K. Warikoo

Eurasia and India
Regional Perspectives

Edited by K. Warikoo

LONDON AND NEW YORK

First published 2018
by Routledge
2 Park Square, Milton Park, Abingdon, Oxon OX14 4RN

and by Routledge
711 Third Avenue, New York, NY 10017

Routledge is an imprint of the Taylor & Francis Group, an informa business

© 2018 selection and editorial material, K. Warikoo; individual chapters, the contributors

The right of the editor to be identified as the author of the editorial material, and of the authors for their individual chapters, has been asserted in accordance with sections 77 and 78 of the Copyright, Designs and Patents Act 1988.

All rights reserved. No part of this book may be reprinted or reproduced or utilised in any form or by any electronic, mechanical, or other means, now known or hereafter invented, including photocopying and recording, or in any information storage or retrieval system, without permission in writing from the publishers.

Trademark notice: Product or corporate names may be trademarks or registered trademarks, and are used only for identification and explanation without intent to infringe.

British Library Cataloguing-in-Publication Data
A catalogue record for this book is available from the British Library

Library of Congress Cataloging-in-Publication Data
A catalog record for this book has been requested

ISBN: 978-1-138-04800-3 (hbk)
ISBN: 978-1-315-17045-9 (ebk)

Typeset in Times New Roman
by Apex CoVantage, LLC

Contents

List of figures vii
Contributors viii
Preface ix
Acknowledgements xii

1 Introduction 1
   DEVENDRA KAUSHIK

2 Historical and cultural role of Indian Mitra and
   Maitreya cults in the uniting process of Eurasia 13
   SERGEY LEPEKHOV

3 The Vedic constants of historical and cultural kinship
   of the peoples of Siberia and India 21
   I. A. ZHERNOSENKO

4 Eurasia and India: historical-cultural linkages 34
   K. WARIKOO

5 Fine arts and music: the cultural links of Southern
   Siberia and India 58
   M. V. DORINA

6 Heritage in Central Asia: the case of nomads 66
   BAATR U. KITINOV

7 Nikolai Roerich and Eurasia: the ambivalent horizon line 78
   RASHMI DORAISWAMY

8 Shamanism in Eurasia 88
   V. N. TUGUZHEKOVA

9 The Eurasian factor in Russian foreign policy:
   implications for India   93
   TATIANA SHAUMYAN

10 The Eurasian vector of Kazakhstan's policy: relevance
   for India   101
   FATIMA KUKEYEVA

11 Eurasianism and Kazakhstan's foreign policy   111
   ANGIRA SEN SARMA

12 International transport corridors of Eurasia: history,
   problems and prospects   126
   MARINA BALDANO

13 Eurasian regional economic cooperation: opportunities
   and challenges   134
   GATIKRUSHNA MAHANTA

   Bibliography   156
   Index   160

Figures

3.1	Birch plank of the *Book of Veles*	23
3.2	Model of Arkaim	25
3.3	Arkaim	26
3.4	*Belovodye* White Water River Ak-Kem	31
3.5	Karakolsky culture	32
4.1	Offerings made at birch trees (Buryatia)	38
4.2	Danil Mamyev, Altaian Shamanka and Prof. K. Warikoo performing fire ritual at Karakol Park, Gorno Altai	46
4.3	Swastika symbols spun in handwoven cloth in Altai	46
4.4	On the way to Sumeru Mount	47
4.5	Stone gate at the ruins of ancient temple near Yelman Stream, Gorno Altai	48
4.6	Ancient stones, Gorno Altai	49
4.7	Burgan Daa Buddhist Shrine, Chaa-Hol, Tuva	51
4.8	Mother Stone near Abakan, Khakassia	53
4.9	People pay reverence at the stone near Abakan, Khakassia, Russia	54
5.1	An Altaian-Khakassian flute *shoor*	62
5.2	A Buryatian flute *sur*	62
5.3	An Indian flute *bansuri*	62
6.1	Statue of Tsandan Jo wo in Egitui Datsan	72
6.2	Egitui Datsan	73

Contributors

Marina Baldano is Head, Department of History, Ethnology and Sociology, Institute for Mongolian, Buddhist and Tibetan Studies, Siberian Branch, Russian Academy of Sciences, Ulan Ude, Russia.

Rashmi Doraiswamy is Professor, Academy of International Studies, Jamia Millia Islamia, New Delhi.

M. V. Dorina teaches at N. F. Katanov Khakass State University, Abakan, Russia.

Devendra Kaushik is former Chairman, Maulana Abul Kalam Azad Institute of Asian Studies, Kolkata.

Baatr U. Kitinov is Associate Professor, Department of World History, People's Friendship University, Moscow, Russia.

Fatima Kukeyeva is Professor, Department of International Relations, Al-Farabi Kazakh National University, Almaty, Kazakhstan.

Sergey Lepekhov is Professor, Department of History, Ethnology and Sociology, Institute for Mongolian, Buddhist and Tibetan Studies, Siberian Branch, Russian Academy of Sciences, Ulan Ude, Russia.

Gatikrushna Mahanta is associated with Academy of International Studies, Jamia Millia Islamia, New Delhi.

Angira Sen Sarma is Assistant Professor, Academy of International Studies, Jamia Millia Islamia, New Delhi.

Tatiana Shaumyan is Professor, Institute of Oriental Studies, Russian Academy of Sciences, Moscow, Russia.

V. N. Tuguzhekova is Professor and Head, Khakass Research Institute of Language, Literature and History, Abakan, Khakassia, Russia.

K. Warikoo is Professor, Centre for Inner Asian Studies, School of International Studies, Jawaharlal Nehru University, New Delhi.

I. A. Zhernosenko is Associate Professor, Department of Culture and Communication Technologies, I. I. Polzunov Altay State Technical University, Barnaul, Russia.

Preface

With its huge territory, energy and other natural resources and growing economy, Eurasia has assumed importance in the post-Soviet period. The peoples of Siberia (Buryatia, Chita, Irkutsk, Tuva, Altai, the Urals, etc.) have distinctive historical-cultural similarities with the Indian Himalayas particularly due to common traditions and Buddhist culture. The Eurasianism of Russia, which is a Eurasian country due to its geographical situation, brings it closer to India in historical-cultural, political and economic terms.

Russia's Eurasianism is also determined by Siberia, which is endowed with rich energy reserves and untapped natural resources in the world. With its historical-cultural specificities, geo-cultural homogeneities stretching from the Urals to Vladivostok and abundant natural resources, Siberian region is poised to become an engine of Russia's future economic growth as well as a major trading partner of Asian economic giants like India. Siberia is considered as an important player because of the effectiveness of trans-national routes, inter-regional and intra-regional communication networks within Eurasia, and trans-national trade through railways, waterways and other means of transport and communication.

The recognition of the Asian factor in Russia's foreign policy is not only destined to balance its relations between the East and the West, but also consolidate Russia's Eurasian status. Another important player in Eurasia is Kazakhstan, which has been highlighting the importance of Eurasianism. This situation provides an opportunity to India for engaging in collaborative endeavours with the Eurasian countries. Russia has elevated its relations with China and India to the level of strategic partnership seeking to work for a multi-polar just and equitable world order. The establishment of the Collective Security Treaty (CST), the Eurasian Economic Union and the CIS Anti-terrorist Centre all point towards active Russian involvement in Eurasian affairs.

The vast Eurasian landmass is both a great challenge and opportunity not only for the peoples of Russia, Kazakhstan, Uzbekistan, Tajikistan and others inhabiting this region, but also to those living in its neighbourhood – India, China, Pakistan and Afghanistan in particular. The developments on this vast landmass known as the "heartland" have implications for its immediate and distant neighbours. There is a need to shift from the geopolitical game to a paradigm of geo-cultural and geo-economic cooperation. An intensified cooperation among the

Eurasian countries and their neighbours India, China and Iran will bring in much increased trade and economic cooperation besides reinvigorating the traditional historical cultural linkage between the peoples of Eurasia and India.

It is against this background that this book provides detailed analyses on the historical-cultural linkages between Eurasia (Buryatia, Khakassia, Altai and Tuva Republics of the Russian Federation) and India through history, importance of the Eurasian vector in Russian and Kazakhstan's foreign policy, development of the Eurasian Economic Union and implications for India. Eminent academics and area specialists from Buryatia, Altai, Khakassia, Moscow, Kazakhstan and India have contributed to this volume. This book provides a firsthand view of the linkages between India and the Siberian region which constitutes much of the Eurasian space. Besides, the rare photographs of the traces of Indian culture in Siberia make this book a unique one.

Chapter 1 brings out the relationship between Eurasia and India through history, citing archaeological and literary evidences. Analysing the works of noted Russian exponents of Eurasianism and Russo-Muslim cooperation, this chapter makes a case for closer regional cooperation on the basis of geo-economics rather than geopolitics. Chapter 2, written by a prominent Russian scholar of Buddhism from Buryatia, Sergey Lepekhov, explains the penetration of Buddhism into Mongolia, Central Asia and Buryatia, based on the Buddhist texts and practices prevalent in that region. He underlines the role played by Buddhism as the mediator and integrator in Eurasia, uniting the region of Central and East Asia into a cultural and civilisational integrity based on the Maitreya model of the interaction of both the secular and spiritual power.

In Chapter 3, noted Russian/Altaian culturologist I.A. Zhirnosenko presents rare evidence (supported by photographs of ancient sites and other objects) of the continued existence of ancient Aryan culture in the form of temples, altars, traditions of fire and sun worship, thereby throwing light on the Vedic origins of sacred knowledge of indigenous peoples in Siberia, Khakassia and Altai. In Chapter 4, K. Warikoo brings to light certain commonalities of traditions and beliefs still prevalent in Buryatia, Khakassia, Altai and Tuva Republics of Russian Federation and India, based on the author's field study in these areas. Whereas Buddhism, Shamanism and epic-heroism (*Geser*) have become important for the preservation and promotion of Buryat, Tuvan and Khakass ethno-cultural identity, a feeling of close geocultural and spiritual affinity between Tuva and Altai with India pervades in the region.

In Chapter 5, a well-known Khakass scholar in music and fine arts, M.V. Dorina explores the history of the development of music and fine arts in South Siberia (Khakassia and Altai), bringing to light the commonalities in terms of musical instruments and art works in India and this part of Eurasia. She has provided the historical evidence through photographs and other literary works. Chapter 6, written by Baatr U. Kitinov, an established Russian (Kalmyk) scholar of Buddhism provides a Eurasian view of the dissemination of Buddhism from India to Central Asia and Eurasia. He calls for revitalisation of Buddhism in Russia (Buryatia, Tuva and Kalmykia Republics) through the preservation and development of monuments, statues, written works/manuscripts and by organising events and so forth.

Chapter 7 by Rashmi Doraiswamy provides an insight into the inextricable links between the ideology of Eurasianism as propounded by Russian thinkers and the philosophy of Nicholas Roerich, who undertook several expeditions into Eurasia and India in pursuit of his vision. Doraiswamy analyses several paintings of Roerich, which hold a special place in the Eurasian thinking, as these explore the spiritual geography of Eurasia (Altai) and India (Himalayas). In Chapter 8, veteran scholar from Khakassia V.N. Tuguzhekova delves into the history of Shamanism in Eurasia and its revival following the disintegration of USSR. She details the recent initiatives taken up to scientifically examine and revive the Shamanist rituals and festivals in Khakassia and Tuva.

Chapter 9, written by the noted Russian scholar Tatiana Shaumyan, evaluates the Eurasian factor in contemporary Russia's foreign policy and its implications for India, bringing out the common perceptions and positions on various issues related to the geopolitics and geo-economics of Eurasia. She refers to the cultural and civilisational factors and historic ties between the Buddhists of Russian Siberia and the Baikal region with their co-religionists of India, Mongolia and Tibet. She dwells upon the general Russian view about the need to balance the Western and Eastern development vectors and to pay attention to development of the neglected Trans-Baikal region of Russia. Chapter 10 by a veteran scholar from Kazakhstan, Fatima Kukeyeva, provides an insight into the Eurasian vector of Kazakhstan, describing it important for Indian geopolitical, geo-economic and geocultural interests in Eurasia including Central Asia. She argues for strengthening the Eurasian vector of Russia and Kazakhstan to include India, which with its civilisational links to the region, and with its soft power approach could counterbalance China's increasing influence in the region.

In Chapter 11, Angira Sen Sarma, while tracing the genesis of Eurasianism, relates its revival in the post-Soviet era to the new urge for multi-polar world order, pluralism of value systems and traditionalism. The growing importance of Eurasianism in Kazakhstan's foreign policy is reflected in the emergence of Customs Union, Eurasian Economic Union and its multi-vector policy. In Chapter 12, the noted scholar based in Buryatia, Siberia, Marina Baldano examines the history, problems and prospects of international transport corridors of Eurasia. She calls for the development of North-South International Transport Corridor and also the Trans-Siberia Corridor to facilitate quicker and cheaper transportation of cargo across Eurasia and beyond. In Chapter 13, Gatikrushna Mahanta makes a critical analysis of the regional economic cooperation in Eurasia in the post-Soviet period, focussing on the formation and functioning of CAREC, Eurasian Economic Community, EurAsEc, Customs Union, Eurasian Economic Union and so forth. The author explores both the opportunities and challenges for Russia, Kazakhstan and India in this process.

Acknowledgements

I acknowledge with thanks all the contributors to this book, for sharing their expertise, knowledge and experience through their papers. I am particularly grateful to the Indian Council of Social Science Research, New Delhi, for providing some financial assistance to facilitate my field study in Altai region of Siberia, Russia in June 2015. I acknowledge with thanks the financial support from Jawaharlal Nehru University under its UPE-II Project programme for my field study in Tuva, Russia, in October–November 2016. I am also thankful to Dr. Irina Zhernosenko of Altay State Technical University, Barnaul, Russia; Mr. Danil Mamyev, Director, Karakol Ethno-Cultural Park, Gorno Altai Republic, Russia; Mr. Boris Amzarakov of Khakass Research Institute of Language, Literature and History, Abakan, Khakassia; Prof. Victor Kitov of the East Siberian State Academy of Culture and Arts, Ulan Ude, Buryatia; Dr. Marianna Kharunova, Director, Tuvan Institute of Humanitarian Studies, Republic of Tuva; and Prof. Fatima Kukeyva of Al Farabi Kazakhstan National University, Almaty, for extending their cooperation during my field studies in Altai, Khakassia, Buryatia and Tuva Republics of Russia and Kazakhstan, respectively.

1 Introduction

Devendra Kaushik

Eurasia is a vast land mass extending from the Caspian to western China, an area stretching from the Urals to the Great Mountain Arc in the west formed by the Altai, Tien Shan, the Pamir, the Hindukush and the Kopet Dagh running through the vast steppes and deserts in between. Russia, Central Asia and the Caucasian region naturally formed this great Eurasian land mass. However, the immediate neighbours – the Xinjiang region of China, Mongolia, Afghanistan and the north-west region of pre-independence India because of their close proximity and ethno-cultural ties – had been integrated with it, sometimes even to the extent of forming a common single state or empire. Close cultural and economic ties have existed between India and Central Asia, Caucasia and Russia from time immemorial. One can trace similarity between stone tools discovered in the north Indian territory of the Punjab and Kashmir and the tools excavated from the sites belonging to Gissar culture in Tajikistan. Harappan-type ceramics, seals and fragments of lazurites have been found on the southern bank of river Pyanj, a tributary of Amu Darya in Tajikistan. It seems the Harappan settlements received the supply of lazurites from the mines of Badakhshan in the Pamir region of Tajikistan. The relics discovered in Altyn-Tepe in Turkmenistan and Shortugai in Tajikistan indicate the existence of extensive trade in art and handicraft products between north-west India and Central Asia giving rise to interaction in the sphere of religion and culture as also in the development of material culture. These early contacts from the third and second millennia BC were further strengthened as a result of frequent transmigration of various ethnic groups from India and Central Asia. The inclusion of India and parts of Central Asia in a single state such as the Acheminian empire, followed by the state of Alexander the Great and the Selukids and the Graeco-Bactrian kingdom, the Kushan and the Mughal empires, is a well-known fact of history. Contacts with Central Asia were maintained during the reign of emperor Ashoka, whose state extended up to the border of that region. Various dynasties of the Central Asian Scythians, Huns and the Sakas ruled in north-west India.

India-Russia relations also go back to the remote past. In fact, they do not begin just with the journey of Afanasy Nikitin in the fifteenth century. They in fact can be traced back to the pre-historical epoch. The closeness in the field of culture and mythology point out to a common origin of the Indians and the Slavs as a result of a long period of their joint settlement in a common or a neighbouring territory. It is a well-known fact that among all the Indo-European languages, Sanskrit and Russian are the closest. The modern Russian language, so far as grammatical rules and syntax are concerned, strictly follows the great Indian grammarian Panini who lived in the sixth century BC. B. G. Tilak's scholarly work[1] *The Arctic Home in the Vedas* contains a mass of evidence showing that the ancestors of the Indo-Aryans and the Russian Slavs lived in proximity for a long time, giving rise to the striking similarity in language, mythology and religion. According to A. Asov,[2] Russian specialist of ancient literature and manuscripts, thousands of years before the rise of Kiev-Rus there existed a Vedic Rus professing Russian Vedas. This pre-Christian ancient Rus is characterised by Asov as a national variant of international Vedic culture, of which the Avestian and Vedic Indian cultures are the two other components. An exciting book titled *Rus Vedicheskaya*, authored by Yu. V. and Yu. G. Mizyn, was published in Moscow in 2004. In this book,[3] the authors express their opinion that their ancestors came from the north, descending from the Urals and the steppes in the Semirechie region and from there to India and Iran. The *Avesta* speaks of the region as *Aryanam Vaichak*, translated by President of Tajikistan Emam Ali Rehman in his book as the *Aryan Space*. B. G. Tilak[4] refers to this as *Airiana Vaejo* and its meaning given by him is the "Aryan paradise". A series of trade routes connected the Volga region with northern India via Trans Caucasia (Derbent, Baku and Shemaka) and Central Asia. Indian gold coins from the fourteenth century have been found in the Volga region near a village called Tenishevo, thus indicating a flourishing trade with the Golden Horde. In fact, a trade route between India and Russia had existed through Central Asia and the Caspian Sea since the tenth and eleventh centuries. There existed a rich trade in Kashmir shawls, which Indian traders carried to distant Moscow. There were arguments among scholars over naming the trade route from Kashmir across Central Asia through Xinjiang as the shawl route instead of the older nomenclature of the Silk Route. There were Armenian trading posts in India and in ancient Georgia. The Indian *Panchtantra* (didactic tales told through animals and birds) enjoyed great popularity in the region. An Indian fire temple existed at the Caspian coast near Baku, which used to be visited by Indian pilgrims throughout the nineteenth century.

The British colonial power was conscious of the Indian historical links with Central Asia and the Caspian region and did not hesitate to promote its strategic and geopolitical goals. During World War I, it sent a contingent of Indian soldiers under General Malleson based in Meshed in Iran, with the aim of preventing the Baku oil fields from falling into German hands. This military action in Central Asia and Trans Caucasia by British Indian authorities continued even after World War I. The British, however, failed to turn the tables against the Bolsheviks in the civil war following the 1917 October Revolution in Russia. The Malleson expedition, the execution of the Baku Soviet Commissars, the Bailey mission to Tashkent and the mission of Colonel Etherton to Kashgar point to the abortive British-Indian efforts justified on geopolitical reasons by involving colonial India into the "Great Game" in the Central Asian part of Eurasia.

Tilak's work *The Arctic Home in the Vedas*, which was published in 1903, enhanced the age of the Vedas from 2500 BC as mentioned in his previous work *Orion or Researches into the Antiquity of the Vedas* (published in 1893) on the basis of astronomical evidence corroborated by geological evidence. According to Tilak, the Vedas were composed in the Arctic region in the inter-glacial period. Another Indian classical scholar, the late Rahul Sankrityayan,[5] also had a long discussion in Moscow on this question with famous Russian archaeologist S. P. Tolostov. Rahul wanted to visit Central Asia during his stay in Leningrad, but could not do so as the Russian authorities did not permit him to go there. In their discussion, both of them agreed that the ancestors of the Slavs and the Indo-Aryans stayed somewhere in northern Russia, from where one branch migrated to India through Central Asia and Afghanistan and the other branch moved in the western direction, settling in Russia. In his two volumes of *History of Central Asia*[6] published in Hindi, Rahul gives more stress on similarities between the Slavic languages and Sanskrit, whereas Tilak's focus remained on Indo-Germanic and Indo-European cultural and linguistic closeness. Of course, the Aryans would not have gone further to Europe without their first camping on the Russian land. Rahul's work contains a long list of thousands of Sanskrit words with common Russian etymological roots.

Thus India has a long history of interaction with this Eurasian region which is in proximity to our land and continues to be of vital interest even in the present times. Obviously, we are more concerned than others that a revival in our vicinity of a "New Great Game" over its vast hydrocarbon and mineral resources is likely to destabilise the region, creating new challenges and threats to India. While trying to counteract various moves in this direction, we are also conscious that the region has a great potential for becoming a great hub of global stability and prosperity. This is possible only by creating a new edifice of peaceful regional cooperation and regional security through non-military and inclusive means together with other international actors having legitimate interest in the Eurasian region. The Shanghai Cooperation Organization meets these requirements, and India must actively participate in its activities by becoming its full member. This is all the more important in view of the US military withdrawal from Afghanistan. For the success of these efforts, it is necessary to build a national consensus on identifying these external and internal actors. The task of entrusting this work to a suitable agency/organization is equally important as also the defining of rules of the game. And this brings us to the questions of geopolitical and geostrategic interest of the players from inside and outside the region, the latter to include close neighbours only like Iran, China, India and Pakistan. It is impossible to think of Eurasia without Russia. Russia has a history of close relations with the Central Asian and the Caucasian region extending over a millennium. According to Lev Gumilev, already by the end of the twelfth century one could visualise Russia and the great steppe region as a single ethnographic region. Another prominent Russian historian, Robert Landa, wrote that 17 percent of the Russian nobility in the seventeenth century could trace back its ancestral lineage to the Golden Horde. In several Russian provinces most of the aristocratic families had Turkic surnames.

In the Volga-Ural region the Russians, Tartars and Bashkirs developed a common culture and lifestyle.

By the end of the nineteenth century Russia had already become a polyethnic, poly-confessional country, having a population of eighteen million Muslims that was equal to the number of Muslims in the Ottoman Empire. Of course, there were some armed clashes, the prolonged war with Turkey from the sixteenth to the eighteenth centuries over Crimea and the forty-seven-year-war with the Chechens stand in marked contrast with the more or less bloodless annexation of Kazakhstan and Central Asia (with the lone exception of the battle of Geok-Tepe against the Turkmens). The bloody war with Turkey and the Chechens was not because of religion but was motivated by Moscow's determination to gain access to the Black and Caspian Seas in order to eliminate the threat from the south. Russians moved with great caution in their relations with the Central Asians. They largely relied upon the Tartars of Kazan as representatives of European enlightenment in Turkestan. The consequences of merger of Central Asia in the Russian state were both negative and positive. On the negative side, it was the absence of self-rule and the civil administration and consolidation of feudalism in Khiva and Bukhara. On the positive side, it was characterised by end of internecine feudal wars, construction of the railroad and the abolition of slavery. On the whole notwithstanding the annexationist colonial aim of Tsarism, the merger of Russia with Central Asia had in point of history an objectively progressive character. It was impossible for the weak feudal Khanates of Central Asia to stay independent while sandwiched between the two capitalist powers of Europe that were engaged in a fierce struggle for market, annexation of colonies and division of the world into colonial empires.

British geographer Halford Mackinder[7] viewed the Russian Eurasian empire as a unique institution as it represented a remarkable "correlation between natural environment and political organisation . . . unlikely to be altered by any possible social revolution". Pre-Soviet Russian geographer Colonel Vanyukov justified Russian incorporation of Central Asia as "Return of the Slavs to the neighbourhood of their pre-historic home" where they would meet "kindred people". Vanyukov mentioned that for a long time the Cossacks had been marrying the daughters of the Caucasian mountaineers. He observes, "we are not Englishmen who in India do their utmost to avoid mingling with the natives, our strength in contrary lies in the fact that up to the present time we have assimilated the subject race, mingling affably with them". The *Vostochniki* represented by philosopher V.S.V. Solovyov, poet Andre Belly, and Alexander Block, and historian V.V. Bartold projected Russia's cultural mission in the orient. Prince Ukhtomski dreamt of the "fusion of Slavic-Turanian blood and emergence of a new border people of half-European and half Asian stock". Historian G.V. Vernadski wrote, "the Russian state is an Eurasian state and all separate nationalities of Eurasia must feel and recognise that it is their state". *Vostochniki* viewed Eurasia as a geopolitical entity brought about by a cultural process of "genetic mutation" and not by conquest and coercion. Russian historians Byzov and Lvov have described the Russian nation as an "Imperial nation" which is not the same as an imperialist nation.

Vernadski was in a way pleading for Russo-Muslim cultural cooperation and coexistence, which was also suggested by the Tatar educationist and leading Jadidist modernist reformer Ismail Gesprinsky. Russian policy in Central Asia was in general marked by a liberal spirit of non-interference in the national life of the region. No efforts were made to convert the local Muslim population. Interaction with democratic representatives of advanced Russian culture contributed to the development of democratic-socio-political thought in Central Asia, thus exercising a political influence in shaping the world outlook of many cultures and science. Calling Russia a "mediator" between the two worlds, Klyuchevsky aptly observed: "Culture has inseparably linked it with Europe but nature has left on it an imprint of the particularities and influences which have always drawn Russia to Asia or *vice versa*". "An empire does not die easily when it sits astride the geopolitical centre of the world's largest land mass", wrote Russian orientalist V. Belokristinski, and American scholars Ali Banuazizi and Myron Winer concurred with him. The exponents of the trans-Atlantic Anglo-American school of geopolitics represented by Halford Mackinder and Admiral Mahan were obsessed with the hypotheses of heartland and rimland. Mackinder pursued his objective by using his academic writings and also his practical activities as a member of the British Parliament and also during his brief tenure as British High Commissioner in south Russia where Admiral Denikin tried to unsuccessfully dislodge the Bolsheviks. Long before the appearance of Mackinder on the horizon of geopolitics, Filofei, a Russian monk from Pskov, had expounded another school of geopolitics that suited Russia's consolidation and defence. The vastness of Eurasian space called for a forward system of setting up a system of fortifications as a defence mechanism. The geostrategic compulsion was to meet the enemy at a distance. This defensive mechanism used by the state of Moscow Principality was deliberately projected as a harbinger of Russian empire's global ambition. But the fact remains that on the contrary it is the two stronger imperialist oceanic powers which have been using the natural efforts of heartland states on the Eurasian land mass to consolidate itself against expansionism of the states across the oceans posing a threat to it.

Recent years have witnessed a great revival of the Eurasian geopolitics which now has supporters ranging from extreme nationalists to the communists from V. Zhirinovski to G. Zyuganov. Publicists and scholars like Alexander Dugin[8] and Igor Podberezski are actively engaged in propagating ideas of Eurasianism. Igor Podberezski has gone to the extent of warning his countrymen against the grave consequences of turning their back upon Eurasianism. He wrote, "either Russia must realize its destiny as a Eurasian power, correct the mistakes made in the course of ill-advised reforms, adopt a workable plan for restoration of its economy and organize the post-Soviet space around Russia once again, or it will contract to the size of the Moscow's Tsardom before Ivan the Terrible". Parliamentarians V. Mitrafanov from the National Liberal Democratic Party and the leader of the Communist Party V. Zyuganov have been collaborating in the Geopolitical Committee of the state Duma supporting ideas of cooperation between Russia, China and India and formation of a new triangle of strategic cooperation between Germany, Russia and Japan.

Thus, given a revival of Russia as a great economic and military power, the reintegration process culminating in the incorporation of the Central Asian Republics (CARs) into a new Eurasian supra-ethnic state cannot be ruled out. Even otherwise, Russia has emerged as a big soft power in the Eurasian space and it has consolidated its position in the CIS countries through increased trade and aid. There is a large movement of population from the CARs to Russia as a labour force contributing sizably to the gross domestic product of these countries. In the military and defence sphere, Russia has strong ties with the CARs. The presence of ethnic Russians in the CARs in spite of a decline caused by migration still remains sizable. Similar is the case with the Russian language and Russian films and TV programmes, which are studied and watched by an increasing number of their citizens.

Russia, being a key state on the Eurasian land mass cannot drop out of this new "great game". It is a natural and compulsive player in it. The region is but a continuation of the Russian steppes, and both Russia and Central Asia have deep historical, cultural and economic ties going back to antiquity. To speak of a "civilisational divide" between them or to conceive Central Asia as a "buffer" between Russia in the north, and West and South Asia is nothing but a sheer mockery of facts. One has to be wary of messing up religion with civilisation and misrepresentation of geographic continuum which joins and does not divide as a "buffer".

Over the years, Russian interest in Eurasia has been on the increase. It seems to have gained an upper hand in present-day Russian politics. The National Security Concept adopted through a special presidential decree of 1997 refers to Russia as a "European-Asian Power" and emphasises its unique strategic location as a determining factor of its internal and foreign policy. However, a holistic Eurasian strategy remains to be worked out. One can witness "inexplicable twists, turns and sudden improvisations". The Russian leadership remains torn between westernisers and Eurasianists. It turns to the eastern direction in search of compensation for disappointments in the western direction. It was so with the former President Yeltsin and if the tilt toward the West is any guide, his successor president Putin also occasionally seems to follow in his footsteps though somewhat hesitantly.

President Putin continued further deepening the *Derzhavnic* or nationalist line of Primakov who followed a middle course between the "extremes of Soviet anti-Westernism" and Kozyrev's "pro-Western romantic" approach. The new concept of the Russian foreign policy of July 2000 stressed the role of foreign policy in assisting an effective solution of internal problems. It committed Russia to work for stable, fair and democratic world order based on international law and goals and principles of the UN charter and gave priority to the development of multilateral and bilateral cooperation with the member states of CIS. It declared relations with the European states a traditional priority direction of Russia's foreign policy and also listed development of friendly relations with leading Asian states, in the first place, strengthening the bonds of friendship with China and India as the most important direction of Russian foreign policy. It also recognised the importance of cooperation with the NATO and the scope for constructive interaction. While expressing willingness to forge a cooperating relationship with the United States on a mutually beneficial basis, Moscow under Putin made it clear that it was no longer willing to compromise with its national interests and had started looking for allies willing to work for a multi-polar world. It resumed weapon sales to Iran and defied the US-imposed no-fly zone by resuming humanitarian aid flights to Baghdad. Moscow opened talks with Libya for military contracts, and Putin paid a state visit to Cuba in December 2000. Under Putin, Russia also elevated its relations with China and India to the level of strategic partnership and developed a consensus with them to work for a multi-polar just and equitable world order.

But, a new twist in the Russian foreign policy course became noticeable in October 2001, when President Putin after his meeting with the EU and NATO Secretary General George Robertson stated that Russia was ready "to qualitatively change relations with NATO and to pull efforts with it for European system of security". Russian newspaper *Komsomolskaya Pravda* commenting on Putin's Brussels visit wrote, "it looks like Russia's support is becoming more ardent than that of certain NATO members". Putin was reported to have backed in Brussels the UN resolution to punish the terrorists of 9/11 and welcomed Tajikistan's and Uzbekistan's decision to support Americans. Putin supported the grant of bases by Uzbekistan and Tajikistan against the opposite view held by his Defence Minister Sergei Ivanov.

It can, however, be said in defence of Putin's position that the Russian president was taking a soft stand against the background of promises held out by US Commerce Secretary Donald Evans during his visit to Moscow in October 2001, reaffirming the US support for Russia's membership of the World Trade Organization (WTO) and recognition of Russia as a country with a market economy, thus paving the way for abolishing anti-dumping tariff against Russian exports. Russia also hoped to get its Paris Club debts rescheduled and partly written off.

The climax of cordiality in Russo-American relations was reached with the signing of Moscow Declaration on Strategic Partnership and Agreement on the Reduction of Strategic Arms between Russia and the United States on 24 May 2004 during the visit of President Bush to Russia in 2004. Particularly pleasing for the Americans was the Russian nod for presence of US troops in Central Asia. As an American analyst, McFaul observed, "The presence of American troops in Central Asia was as if Russian troops came into Mexico". By supporting President Bush, Putin totally revised his previous geopolitical orientation. To the question posed to him by the US press during his visit about territorial competition between Russia and the United States over Central Asia and where he "draws the line" in terms of Russia's strategic interests, Putin remarked that "what was important in the former frame of reference is becoming largely irrelevant at present". If Russia becomes a full-fledged member of the international community, it need not and will not be afraid of its neighbours developing relations with other states, including the development of relations between the Central Asian states and the United States. Putin added that Russian and US policy should not be guided by their former fear, rather there were real geo-economic benefits to be had from cooperation and deal-making in the region. Putin's stress on geo-economics and geo-strategy was the result of a sharp debate within the Ministries of External

Affairs and Defence, in which arguments of individuals favouring cooperation with the United States got an upper hand over the supporters of the traditional territorial line. It was reflected in Putin's state of the nation address of April 2002. Creation of a new general system of security through a permanent dialogue with the United States and working to change the quality of Russia's relationship with the NATO were listed as vital goals of foreign policy aimed at ensuring strategic stability in the world. The Asian aspect was not addressed in Putin's address, though cooperation with the CIS found a place in foreign policy priority. Again, in his speech in a conference of Russian diplomats in July 2002 President Putin dwelt on strategic stability through "confident partnership" with the United States as one of Russia's clear-cut priority.

Yet much need not be read in President Putin's remark signifying marginalisation of traditional thinking of influence in favour of geo-economic considerations. Even at his Camp David meeting with George W. Bush, Putin did not shy away from expressing disapproval over the US unilateral action in Iraq circumventing the UN. Russia did not miss an opportunity to take maximum advantage of the impending shifts in the global geopolitical landscape with international attention fixed on crisis in the Gulf. Moscow lost no time in exploiting the opportunity for promoting its interest in the former Soviet space. As the chairman of state Duma committee of CIS affairs Andrey Kokoshin stated during a discussion at the Council for Defence Policy in Moscow, "The world is now at the threshold of re-division that in many respects resembles the beginning of the 20th century. Each country seeks to create its own security sphere of interest in the post-Soviet space". Another political analyst V. Tretyakov wrote in *Literaturnaya Gazeta* weekly, "taking into account that the global restructuring has already begun, our country has to do its utmost to restore at least on the confederative basis, the greater Russia comprising Ukraine, Belarus, Kazakhstan and Russian Federation". Kokoshin also referred to the so-called Putin doctrine based on a highly integrated core of key states surrounded by a loose grouping of other CIS members. The components are the Union of Russia and Belarus, the Collective Security Treaty (CST), the Eurasian Economic Community and CIS Anti-Terrorist Centre.

US President George W. Bush, in his speech in Brussels on 21 February 2005, categorically asserted his belief that "Russia's future lies within the family of Europe and the Trans-Atlantic Community". Recognising that "reforms will not happen overnight, Bush also stated that the Russian government "must renew a commitment to democracy and rule of law". President Putin appears to have responded favourably to this advice, at least for some time. In his 2005 state of the nation address, Putin firmly declared that "Russia was an European power with a civilising mission in Eurasia". It looks as if Russia was trying to find a new *modus vivendi* between Russia and the United States in the manner of Russia-China cooperation in Central Asia. Some progress has been made in finding the desired *modus vivendi* in at least the field of energy, by an agreement on the Caspian Pipeline Consortium to carry oil from Kazakhstan's Tengiz oil field to Russia's Black Sea port of Novorossiysk. This has at least temporarily diffused the crisis created in US-Russia relations causing concern to the energy-rich Caspian states of Azerbaijan, Kazakhstan and Turkmenistan. The late American scholar Alvin Z. Rubinstein was reported to have held the view that "Putin's Russia is not bent on restoring the empire, much less seeking domination over the Eurasian heartland for which it lacks the capability, the resources and the ideological impetus".

Yet the dilemma continues as Russia just cannot leave the Eurasian land mass and pack up and go. Its stakes in this region remain high. There is a large number of Russians in Central Asia accounting for 11.7 percent of the sixty-five million Central Asian population in 2001, apart from the Russian-oriented ethnic communities living in the region. The area remains a relatively important source of labour for Russia in view of its large demographic deficit. There are many sites in Kyrgyzstan and Tajikistan which are of great military-strategic importance for Russia. The Baikanor space centre in Kazakhstan is the launching site for 70 percent of Russia's rockets. Tajikistan is also equally important for Russia in this sphere. It has given permission to Russia to set up a cosmos surveillance base besides a regular military base. In April 2003 Russian Defence Minister Sergei Ivanov stated that Russia would start recruiting from citizens of CIS to serve in its army who would be allowed to obtain Russian citizenship after three years of service. As already mentioned, there is a large number of Central Asians residing in Russia as seasonal workers. Their remittances back home are larger than the US assistance to some of these Republics.

Russia's long-term interests in the region as against the temporary interest of United States are mostly acknowledged by knowledgeable experts of the international studies. As Nikolai Zlobin, director of Russian and Central Asian Programmes at the Centre for Defence Information at Washington has observed, "America wouldn't be there forever but Russia will be there forever". To resolve the Afghan problem which has baffled the entire world community and caused great alarm over the situation after the withdrawal of American troops from Afghanistan in 2014, it is imperative that Russia takes over the firefighting on the border of the Eurasian land mass to douse the Taliban fire in Afghanistan, which threatens to engulf the neighbouring regions of Pakistan and India. All this increases the strategic significance of the Eurasian space for peace and stability in the region with which India has millennia-old ties of cultural, economic, and political interaction.

Summing up, the vast Eurasian land mass is both a great challenge and opportunity not only for the people inhabiting it – the Russians, the Kazakhs, Uzbeks, Tajiks, Kyrgyzs and Turkmens and the Caucasian peoples as also a multitude of other peoples belonging to hundreds of different smaller ethnic communities but also those living in its neighbourhood, peoples of China, Pakistan, India, Afghanistan and Iran. The developments on this vast land mass known in geopolitical terminology as the heartland are equally fraught with serious consequences for the rest of the world as well. The fires of conflict and conflagration in this vast region are likely to destroy the entire world as it is perceived as a chessboard by the distant oceanic powers.

On the other hand, if the forces committed to peace, tranquillity and development gain an upper hand in this region with the help of social policies conducive to the common good of humanity, it is bound to have global repercussions. The entire area will then be converted from a chessboard of new geopolitical game of exploiting the rich natural resources into a new field for geo-cultural and geo-economic cooperation dumping aside the dirty geopolitical predatory ideas. What the Eurasian heartland is harking for is the need to pool all the resources in the region for development of a mega-infrastructure by planning gigantic projects for development of high-speed railroads, ports, power houses, water management and irrigation dams and channels, giant environment protection projects to revive the drying-up Caspian and the Aral Seas, hydro, thermal and nuclear power houses and joint projects to develop alternate sources of non-polluting energies, thus relying less on the depleting hydrocarbon resources and also developing the latest technology to exploit the cosmos for peaceful purposes. The vastness of Eurasia suits high-tech mega-projects of infrastructure development. Its natural resources can only be exploited by increasing connectivity through a crash programme of building high-speed railroad projects. The completion of such mega projects would certainly help the world to overcome its present economic crisis. An intensified cooperation among the Eurasian powers and their neighbours India, China and Iran also has the potentiality to undo the adverse effects of unjust and inequitable unipolar world order. The world has already started moving towards a non-polar world order. The completion of the construction of a Eurasian land-bridge extending from the Atlantic to the Pacific and down to the Indian Ocean, the linking of Alaska with the Eurasian land mass through undersea tunnel by railroad will integrate nearly all the major continents of the world leaving nothing for geo-politicians to fight for. The missing links in the road connecting Asia with Europe must also be urgently completed. These mega-projects of the main global hub in Eurasia can be financed by putting aside the neo-monetarist policies which brought about the global economic collapse beginning in 2008. The current international financial system needs to be replaced by a new system based on national credit, for which there is need to convene a new Bretton Woods Agreement. The vast Eurasian land mass can serve as a laboratory of these innovative ideas based on the school of physical or real economy. It is worthwhile mentioning that Eurasia is the land that gave many physical or real economy school thinkers such as Mendeleyev and Vernadski who were inspired by Alexander Hamilton and Friedrich List. The prospects for this Eurasian dream to be realised are, however, not very promising. Infrastructure development in Eurasia is not moving ahead. The Russian leader wants to build roads in the scarcely populated Siberian region on a basis of a toll highway system. He complains of no takers for these projects for lack of quick returns, so the route of funding from the reserve is the only option. Only one road has been built in the western and eastern parts of Russia and just one survey work has been done on the high-speed rail route of Kazan. Equally dismal is the situation in Kazakhstan, a country larger than Western Europe. Kazakh President Nursultan Nazarbayev has created a National Fund of about 50 billion dollars, which has been accumulated from surplus oil resources. This fund can be used for infrastructure development and for other social security measures as building houses and hospitals. This fund is mainly meant for future generations to be used partly by the state as stabiliser of the economy in periods of downturn. The Kazakhstan president has set up a combined Samruk-Kazyna holding company which has been estimated to be worth 25 billion dollars. It comprises the big five industries which were until now under the control of the government – the railways, the post office, the national grid, telecommunications and the oil and gas companies. Kazakhstan needs to watch out for the neo-monetarist ideas and draw lessons from the recent global economic crises.

The leadership of Russia and Kazakhstan have moved forward in realising their dreams of reintegrating the Eurasian land by creating a single economic space combining Russia, Belarus and Kazakhstan which will ultimately lead to a European Economic Union with a common currency based on a Customs Union and a common market with other CIS republics. One would also wish India to be connected with the Eurasian region through a route once in use, linking the Ladakh region of the Indian state of Jammu and Kashmir with Central Asia through Xinjiang. Opening up of an overland route from India to Central Asia through the Xinjiang region of China will give yet another option for reaching Central Asia besides the already optional Bandar Abbas sea and railroad route through Iran and the still problematic route through Afghanistan. India has to join the Tibet-Xinjiang Road built by the Chinese through the disputed Aksai Chin territory of Ladakh in their possession. Tajikistan, Kyrgyzstan and Kazakhstan are taking keen interest in using the Chinese-built Karakoram Highway to gain access to the Pakistani port of Gwadar near Karachi. Tajikistan is seeking to link its city of Kharog in the Pamir region with the Karakoram Highway. The distance from Kharog to Karachi via Islamabad is 3,200 km. From Kharog to the Indian port of Kandla through Ladakh and Himachal Pradesh, it works out to about 3,800 km. This route through Aksai Chin in Ladakh has a definite advantage over the Karakoram route because of its lower height and better climatic conditions. It was for this reason that the British trader R.B. Shaw and British Commissioner of Jullundur Sir Douglas Forsyth had preferred it over the latter. This route was called the Chang Chenmo route and was quite popular with the Indian traders engaged in trade with Central Asia. There is an urgent need of engaging China, which is way ahead in the field of economic, military, scientific and technological fields, keeping aside the differences with this power. Cooperation not confrontation is the only sensible way to deal with China, which is surely a competitor. A few years ago, the chairman of the Xinjiang region of China, Ismail Tiliwandi, during his visit to India, proposed the construction of a direct pipeline from China to India. He also supported the export of hydroelectric power from Kyrgyzstan to India through this route. India's former petroleum minister, M.S. Aiyar, proposed the extension of the Iran-Pakistan-India gas pipeline across northern India and Assam to the Chinese province of Yunnan. Central Asia and India as well as China stand to gain by the fruition of these projects for overland transit of energy because of proximity between one of the world's biggest oil producing regions and one of the biggest energy markets. If these projects materialise, it will be a testimony to the success of multilateral cooperation between India, China, Russia and the Central Asian Republics. Atasu in northwest Kazakhstan (the starting point of the pipeline to China's Alashankou in Xinjiang), if joined by Russia's Omsk-Chardzhou pipeline, passing through this place, will also open up the possibility of Russian and Kazakh oil reaching India through Xinjiang region of China. The countries of the Eurasian region must carry forward their cooperation into the energy security to India and China. Let geo-economics prevail over the geopolitics of exclusion.

Notes

1 Bal Gangadhar Tilak, *The Arctic Home in the Vedas*. Poona, Tilak Bros., 1903.
2 A. Asov, *Russkie Vedy: Zvezdnaia Kniga Koliady*. 1996. (In Russian).
3 Yulia and Yuriy Mizyn, *Rus Vedicheskaya* (Vedic Russia). Moscow, 2004. (In Russian).
4 See note 1.
5 Rahul Sankrityayan, *Madhya Asia ka Itihas* (*History of Central Asia*). 2 vols. Patna, Rashtra Bhasha Parishad, 1956. (In Hindi).
6 Ibid.
7 Halford Mackinder, "The Geographical Pivot of History". *Geographical Journal* Vol. 23, No. 4, April 1904, pp. 421–37.
8 Alexander Dugin, *Eurasian Mission: An Introduction to Neo-Eurasianism*. Arktos Media, 2014.

2 Historical and cultural role of Indian Mitra and Maitreya cults in the uniting process of Eurasia

Sergey Lepekhov

According to ancient Indian geography, Mount Meru is situated in the Altai Mountains. The mystic Shambhala country was, according to the Kalachakra teaching, the source of the propagation of Buddhism in the world and was also associated with approximately the same region.[1] The national epic *Gesar* tells the story of a hero who recovers his rightful kingdom in horse races, after which he eliminates all the demons in his country. Later Gesar was identified with the future king of Shambhala. The myth of Shambhala comes back to the Hindu myth of Kalki. According to the Hindu mythology, Vishnu was born as Kalki in a village named Shambhala. There are many parallels between the epic of *Gesar* and the myth of Kalki. Both heroes have a miraculous steed symbolizing the power that enables both Kalki and the king of Shambhala to overcome the forces of evil. However, the connections of the concept of Shambhala, that is of ancient Mongolian mythology with that of India and Iran, are more profound and complicated than they may seem. It is possible to suppose that the formation of the ancient Mongolian mythology and religion was influenced by the Indian and Iranian cults, particularly the cult of Mitra that can be traced back to antiquity. The Avestian Mithra as well as the Vedic Mitra are the deities who personify the idea of agreement, of contractual relations, in a broader sense. Later the same functions, from the point of view of etymology, came over to the Buddhist Bodhisattva Maitreya. The idea of agreement was expressed in the oath of this Bodhisattva to save all good beings when, in the future, he comes to this world. According to Prof. Lokesh Chandra,

> Maitreya is a patronymic of Maitra and the form Maitraka is actually found on Roman coins. Mitra to Maitra to Maitreya are normal grammatical formations. Maitreya reflects the Iranian Mithra who was adored in the north western regions of India and the adjacent Parthian areas. The light cults of the Iranians inspired re-mythologisation from internal Buddhist premises.... The cult of saviour Maitreya has unmistakable parallels in Iranian beliefs. The very idea of a divine saviour in future is alien to the early teachings of Buddhism, and is from Iranian pantheon. The Sanskrit name of Maitreya is derived from Mithra.[2]

The principle of keeping an agreement is acknowledged to be the most important part of the system of values and regulations in the ancient Mongolian social relations. It is difficult to state that it was due to the influence of Mitraism, though there is no doubt that the Mitra cult had been known to the nomadic tribes of Central Asia. Besides, one can even speak of the double influence of the Mitraist ideas – the direct and the indirect one, through the Buddhist cult of Maitreya. This cult obtained the greatest influence and propagation in Central Asia and it was not at all by chance.[3] Maitreya's images in the Tibetan and Mongolian temples are often of enormous size. The size actually symbolizes the period (number of years) spent by the Bodhisattva in the Tushita Heaven. Consequently, the size of the Maitreya statue is suggestive of the period left till the future Buddha comes. That is, the greater the statue the sooner this time comes. The ritual of "Rotating Maitreya" held annually in the Mongolian and Buryat monasteries is designed to bring this time closer. Prof. Lokesh Chandra described his conversation with Buryat Hambo Lama:

> The sitting posture of Maitreya was interpreted to the author in 1967 by the late Bandido Hambo Lama of Buryatia Venerable Jambaldorje as follows: Maitreya has put down his legs and is about to descend on the earth to bring the golden age. Maitreya sits in a throne supported by lions, with legs pendent in European fashion. True to north west Indian origins, his sitting posture is derived from royalty, and is known as *bhadrāsana*. *Bhadrāsana* can refer to the mode of sitting prevalent in Bhadra or Bactria.[4]

Thus, the ancient Bactrian eschatological ideas in Buddhism found their institutional expression in the Central Asian region, in Mongolia in the first place. It is necessary to mention that the *Maidary Book* plays the role of a Destiny Book in the Central Asian epic.

Some personages of the Mongolian history, including Genghis Khan first of all, can be treated from the point of view of the myth of Shambhala. The destiny of the Yuan dynasty in the Buddhist mythological historiography has always been associated with this myth. The Yuan empire spread its influence over a vast territory, which contributed to certain unification of the basic Buddhist cultural patterns. Historically, Mongolians were the integrating force during the period of the Yuan empire – the force that united Tibet, China and Mongolia into a culturally integral whole. Culturally, the significance of this union for the further development of the civilization in Asia is comparable to that of Ashoka's empire in India. In *Debter-onbo* and *Pagsam-jonsan* the Tibetan dynasty Yatse is mentioned; one of the kings of this dynasty, Asode, "redeemed the image of forty four cities that had been given to Vajrasana as a gift and that was in *Mongolian possession* at the time. In honor of this acquisition he made a long sermon with offerings" (italics are of the author).[5] It is important to mention that in this case the image of the forty-four cities is a symbol of *vijaya* – "accession-conquest" – because by "constructing cities" the king is "creating" his kingdom. The construction of stupas and monasteries symbolizes "dharma-vijaya". The image of the cities presented by Ashoka is to be interpreted here as a symbol of power and a mandate for government.[6]

Thus, Sumba-khanbo's mention in *Pagsam-jonsan* (concerning the image of the forty-four cities presented by Ashoka that had been in Mongolian possession and afterwards got to Tibet) is to be interpreted as the way of the expansion of the Buddhist civilization, the image of the forty-four cities being its sacred symbol. It is noteworthy that it was Mongolia that Tibetans considered to be the initial point.

R. Ye. Pubayev mentions that

> the Tibetan King Srongtzangampo (620–649 AD) and the Yuan Emperor Kublai Khan (1280–1295 AD) devoted special attention to Ashoka because in the period of his rule in ancient India a concept of the political unity of the royal power (*rgyal srid*) and the religious power (*chos srid*) was formulated. It was based on two principles (*lus gnyis*) – "the law of the teaching" (*chos lugs*) and "the secular law" (*jigs rten lugs*).[7]

The integration of the secular power principle (the concept of *Chakravartin*) with the absolute spiritual authority of *Dharma* (that actually was first carried out, actively and consciously, by Ashoka in India) made it possible for Mahayana Buddhism to quickly occupy the leading position in a number of South Asian countries because it harmonized with the Devaraja cult that was widespread in many countries of this region. Genghis Khan's conquests were considered by Buddhist historiographers from this viewpoint.

In the history of the penetration of Buddhism into Mongolia and its obtaining the status of the state religion, the meeting of the Sakya monastery abbot Pagba Lama with Kublai Khan in 1253 in Shan-du was of great significance. During this meeting and the consequent diplomatic negotiations, the problem of the vassal subordination of Tibet to the Mongolian empire was solved. Besides, the famous "two principles" of the Mongolian khagan were first formulated and written down in two documents: the *Pearl Deed* and the *Tibetan Deed*. The essence of these two principles, as it comes out of these documents, consisted in the following: the state power was to be supported by the two basics – the secular (*Khaganat*) and the spiritual (*Dharma*) and those were to mutually support each other. The *Pearl Deed* was in fact Kublai's decree.

The revival of these principles in the period of the feudal disintegration and the decay of Buddhism in Mongolia were directed at regaining the ideological and political basis for consolidating the country and concentrating power in the hands of a single ruler. It was this aim that Altan-khagan kept in mind when he was proclaiming his adherence to the Gelugpa tradition and accepted the title of the "King Chakravartin Rotating a Thousand Wheels" from the Third Dalai Lama Sodnom-Jamtso. Among the Buddhist texts that served as an ideological and sacred support of Altan-khagan's power, *Suvarnaprabhasottama Raja-sutra* (*Mong. Qutuytu deged altan gerel-tü sudur-nuydun gayan neretü yeke kölgen sudur*) must be mentioned in the first place; this title may be translated as "The All-Conquering Royal Mahayana Sutra", called "The Golden Shine".

The "Golden Shine" *sutra* or the *Altan gerel-tü* was translated three years after the meeting of Altan-khagan and the Dalai Lama. Its popularity in all countries where Mahayana Buddhism had spread can be accounted for by the fact that it was considered to be a special teaching for the secular rulers. Otherwise it is called "teaching designed for kings", *raja-shastra*. *Altan gerel-tü* is, to a certain degree, a compendium of the Mahayana teaching. Its main ideas enter the framework of the general Mahayana doctrines – philosophy and soteriology. In this sense, the *Altan gerel-tü* does not differ much from other texts of the Mahayana sutras. Altan-khagan preferred this *sutra* mostly due to the fact that its title coincided with khagan's own name – it suggested the sacred and charismatic character of his personality, justified his special right for being the consolidator of Mongolia and for subordinating the other khans to his influence.

The two laws, or the two principles of the political rule proved to be the social philosophical interpretation of the theory of *the two truths* developed by *Madhyamika* philosophers. Some characteristic features of the Mongolian view of Buddhism were reflected in the work *Blos gar gyi bstan bcos yang dag lam du bkril pa'i rol rtsed ces bya ba* ("Play-šāstra Leading to the True Path"); its author was the twenty-first abbot of the Lavran monastery, Guntan Konchog Donbi Donme (Gung thang Dkon mchog Bstan pa'i Sgron me; 1762–1923). One of the personages in this play, Mongol Bilig, speaking of the values of different philosophic schools, states that one should study *Madhyamika* within the Gelugpa tradition, though when it comes to "preventing accidents, accumulating wealth, using power, shaking the horn *tunra* (*thun rva*)" – in cases of the kind *Nyingma* is indispensable. Why not take something from the *Nyingma* teaching "since such an easy remedy exists"? Another personage of the play, Tibetan Sheirab (Shesrab), mocking at the inconsistency of his opponent, mentions the saying: "To the Jewel (*dkon nchog*; ratna, i.e. Buddha, Dharma, Sangha) later, now – to Pekhar". Pekhar (*pe dgar, dpe har*) is an ancient Tibetan deity, "the God of the White Heaven", the master of the thirty-three heavens, actually the same Old Iranian Mitra (Persian Mikhr).

We can see that the pre-Buddhist roots of the Mongolian culture proved to be very enduring. Buddhist culture might be regarded as certain continuity of interacting symbolic structures generated in the process of activity of the adherents of various Buddhist religious and philosophic schools. Each of these structures is characterized by an invariant set of initial symbols common to all Buddhist schools as well as by openness allowing for their interaction with other structures including those of non-Buddhist origin.

The meaning which those structures appeal to is denoted as *Dharma*, which is not quite Buddhist in the strict sense of the word because, as it is explained in Buddhist canonic texts, Buddha's sermon is in fact merely a part of that ultimate *Dharma*. The Buddhist civilization evolved just as a result of development of such open symbolic ties. If Buddhism had isolated itself in its philosophic and soteriological concepts, values and rituals, it would forever have been merely one of those many religious Indian schools.

The Buddhist civilization as well as other "axial" civilizations are characterized by the break into the so-called big and small traditions, there being at any rate two "big" traditions, that is *Theravada* and *Mahayana*, and other local "minor" ones having nevertheless something in common. Within the kernel of the symbolic structure of the Buddhist civilization, one can single out a set of invariant religious symbols, notions, categories, values, ethical and aesthetic principles, texts arranged in one collection, pictorial images, architectural plans, historical schemes and so forth. One should add the system of knowledge included in the common educational system also possessing invariant features.

Among the basic elements of Buddhist civilization, one should mention *dharma*, *karma*, four noble truths, eightfold way, *pratitsamutpada* (dependent beginnings), *shunyata* (emptiness), *prajna* (intuition, wisdom), *vidjnyana* (consciousness), *alaya-vidjnyana* (consciousness – treasury), *trikaya* (Buddha's three bodies), and so forth. From among numerous Buddhist symbols, one should mention *dharmachakra* (the wheel of the doctrine – symbol of the first Buddha's sermon), *triratna* (three jewels symbolizing Buddha, Dharma and Sangha), *vadjra* (ritual rod, earlier denoting the weapon symbolizing invariable inviolable basis, meaning a method together with a bell), *gkhanta* (a bell symbolizing *pradjnya* – wisdom), *pradjnyakhadha* (sword of wisdom symbolizing the highest Buddhist knowledge cutting the fetters of ignorance), the lotus flower symbolizing purity, *shrivatsa* (an endless knot), *pustaka* (a book, symbolizing "Buddha's word"), *suvarna matsya* (a pair of golden fish) – the symbol of happiness, and so forth. From among the architectural Buddhist symbols the first is the stupa (relic), which in the Far East and South Asia took the form of a pagoda, symbolizing along with Dharmakaya (Doctrine's body) Buddha's thought as well.

Buddhist civilization is characterized by a multi-layer structure containing sense fields belonging to different social and historical substrata. The necessity to combine different variants of culture within a common historical whole required elaboration of a certain civilized highest principle. Such a principle enables differentiating the notion of Buddhist civilization from the notion of Buddhist cultural heritage in general, from which individuals or social groups are free to take what they in their opinion need at the moment. The need to combine various cultural layers within the common sense field brings about the demand in existence of civilization. Civilizations evolve in the process of interaction of cultures.

A number of crucial principles of Buddhist civilization formed throughout the millennium appear to correspond to the model of open society. The principles of universal humanism and compassion as the staple of the world; the principle of universal responsibility for forming social institutes and organizations aimed to solve problems common to all people; the principle of tolerance and common ethical direction of all world religions can be attributed to such principles.

Buddhism represents a system of spiritual-ecological values as an alternative to the ideology of the modern consumer society. Instead of the idea of man's rule over nature and paradigm of man's exceptionality, Buddhism brings forward the idea of the absence of personal "Self", inner self-sufficiency of every living being; instead of the necessity to conquer nature – the *ahimsa* principle – that is abstaining from doing harm to all living things; instead of the ideology of political violence – the concept of a natural non-violent way of development; instead of alienated values – genuine happiness (*nirvana*).

The social ideal of Buddhism is a harmonious society with spiritual and ecological priorities established. The humanistic ideal of Buddhism is a person satisfied with life in society and living in harmony with nature. Buddhism encourages self-restriction and social solidarity, justice and equality, pure thoughts and deeds. This is a powerful spiritual tool liberating us from human egoism and consumerist ideology.

The economic ideal of Buddhism is small energy (and material consumption) with results satisfying man. The Buddhist lifestyle would seem incredible to an economist due to its unbelievable rationality. Relations among people in Buddhist civilization controlled mostly by Buddhist values and ideals cause a specific, as a Western researcher may see it, economic activity within which there takes place distribution of religious merits involving not only people but all living beings as well. As M. Spiro has noted, the mechanism of such distribution involving both spiritual and material values (30–40 percent of the whole gross product) becomes an integrating factor of social life.[8] This fact has also attracted attention of Trevor Ling, who considers negative assessment of Buddhism by Max Weber wrong, because the Buddhist economic model cannot be judged from the viewpoint of Protestant individualism and Buddhism cannot be described as a "religion of individual salvation".[9] The implementation of an optimum consumption model is the main condition for sustainable development of man.

From the Buddhist viewpoint, economic development should promote the development of human qualities rather than material wealth. Today it is absolutely clear that economic growth by itself will not lead to sustainable development of the world. There is a need in global changes based on a new spiritual paradigm. According to Buddhism, spiritual evolution of the individual is a basis of society's sustainable development. When we have a spiritual harmony within us, we can live in peace with society. Moreover, the spiritual influence can involve the whole environment. In short, the world originates within each of us.

Buddhist civilization emerged as an alloy of the elements of numerous preceding cultures and civilizations, the experience of many generations of various ethnic groups. The peculiarity of Buddhist civilization's development lies in the fact that to a considerable extent such experience was selected quite purposefully, and the further development was greatly influenced by philosophic reflection. Even in those cases when logic was deliberately limited or even denied, the integrity of Buddhist culture, Buddhist knowledge, deliberate and responsible attitude to reality was not broken. Buddhist civilization lies "in between" because in most cases it acts a close-to-perfect mediator among other cultures and civilizations, various ethnic groups and peoples.

The historical experience of Buddhist civilization is of interest as mankind tries to understand its problems and find an optimal way of development. At present the major part of civilized mankind finds itself approaching a crisis. If the present-day trends of mankind's development remain for this quarter of the century, a sharp economic decline, depletion of natural resources, overpopulation and a global ecological catastrophe are predicted. Besides, there is a prediction of intensified struggle between the world's leading ideologies, aggravation of religious and ethnic conflicts and a clash of civilizations in perspective. Twenty-five centuries of Buddhist civilization's existence vividly prove that it is possible to live in equilibrium with the natural environment, in peace with the surrounding cultures, scientific progress, to retain stable moral values and norms and maintain high educational standards. Buddhism's tolerance of the cultural and religious values of others, its readiness to assimilate the best from the world culture, would let it gain the status of a global universalistic civilization spreading beyond the state, national and confessional borders. Buddhism lies beyond the presupposed struggle between the other major civilizations because it does not strive to control shrinking natural resources or to politically or ideologically rule the world. If the directions and ideals of mankind's development model for the twenty-first century, recommended by the present-day experts of global issues, are compared to the basic economic, ecological, cultural and spiritual parameters of Buddhist civilization, then it will appear that many of these ideals have already been put into practice by many generations of Indians, Chinese, Japanese, Koreans, Tibetans, Mongols, Buryats, Kalmyks, Vietnamese, Khmers, Thais, Singhalese, Burmese, and so forth. Buddhism does not claim to be exceptional and is wide open to philosophical dialogue, and this makes it still more appealing to the intellectual elite as a neutral ideological field opening possibilities for various contacts at all levels. Fairly strict moral norms of Buddhism presume a possibility and necessity to carry out that which are called inalienable rights of the individual and responsible social conduct. To some extent they correspond to the ideals of the Western democracy, but unlike the latter they remain the collectivist ideological trends and condemn individualism.

By the dialogue between civilizations we imply such interaction of various social-cultural worlds when each of them understands the need to reconsider its basis and prospects for the future in the presence of the other world and to treat the latter as a further extension of its own practice. The dialogue of civilizations implies equality of peoples and their positive cooperation. The dialogue is only possible when each of its participants respects others and treats them as equal. The definite forms of globalization during future evolution depend on the degree of development of the strategic partnership among various countries, social powers and local civilizations. Here various interests and values are compared. And they can be united by an idea common to all mankind. Such an idea, as we see it, can be one of sustainable and balanced development, that is an idea of long-term (eternal in perspective) existence of the human civilization in harmony with nature, the natural environment and cosmos.

Thus, the Mongolian culture and its bearers, the Mongolians, have long been viewed by the Buddhist world as the historically predestined embodiment of the idea of the expansion of the Buddhist civilization, based on the ancient Mitraist principle of agreement of the secular and the spiritual power, functioning in inseparable integrity. The Buddhist civilization played, in Eurasia, the role of the mediator and integrator. It united the regions of Central and Eastern Asia into a cultural and civilizational integrity and presented a universal model of interaction of the secular and spiritual power that often had different ethnic and cultural roots. It realized, by way of the Maitreya cult and the concept of Shambhala, the model of the sacred time and space directed into the future.

Notes

1 E. Bernbaum, *The Way to Shambhala*. New York, Anchor Books, 1980. p. 33.
2 Lokesh Chandra, *Transcendental Art of Tibet*. New Delhi, International Academy of Indian Culture and Aditya Prakashan, 1996. p. 12.
3 See: S. Levi, *Maitreya le consolateur Etudes d'orientalisme publiee par le Musee Guimet a la memorie de Raymonde Linossier*. Paris, E. Leroux, 1932. 357f. (In French).
4 Chandra, *Transcendental Art of Tibet*, p. 13. (History and Chronology of Tibet).
5 Pagsam-Jonsan, *Istoriya i chronologiya Tibeta*. Novosibirsk, 1990. p. 16. (In Russian).
6 See: N. V. Samozvantseva, *Buddhisty-palomniki: Religiya drevnego Vostoka* (*Buddhist Pilgrims: Religion of Ancient East*). Moscow, 1995. pp. 152–68. (In Russian).
7 R. Ye. Pubayev, *Pagsam-Jonsan – pamyatnik tibetskoi istoriographiyi XVIII veka*. Novosibirsk, 1981. 165 pp. (In Russian).
8 M. E. Spiro, *Buddhism and Society: A Great Tradition and its Burmese Vicissitudes*. London, George Allen & Unwin, 1971.
9 T. O. Ling, "Buddhist Values and the Burmese Economy". In: *Buddhist Studies in Honour of I. B. Horner*. Dordrecht, 1974. pp. 105–18.

3 The Vedic constants of historical and cultural kinship of the peoples of Siberia and India

I. A. Zhernosenko

The territory of Siberia, despite harsh weather conditions, has been developed by man since ancient times. And the geographic location of the Gorny Altai (Mountainous Altai) at the crossroads of Great Belt of the Eurasian steppes and open spaces of Central Asia, situated just on the way of the ancient Aryans, and then of huge masses of nomads during the Great Migration, played the role of a capacitor of Eurasian cultural diversity. It is no coincidence that the great Russian artist, scientist and traveler Nicholas Roerich pointed out: "Altai and Himalayas are two poles, two magnets" of the Eurasian cultural genesis.[1] Altai and Siberia keep ample evidence of existence on these territories of highly developed culture of the ancient Aryans, who built cities, temples, observatories and altars, where they worshipped the Sun and the Fire. This knowledge was inherited by two great nations – Russians and Indians – who have preserved it in the sacred texts: the *Vedas*. And the native peoples of Siberia and those who lived here in the later periods of history absorbed these pearls of wisdom, preserved them with reverence and built their own system of knowledge about the world on their basis.

The system of ancient sacred knowledge of different people who perceive a higher transcendent reality and the universal laws of the world order came to our time in the form of special rituals and sacred texts. In a broad sense – it is the Vedic knowledge, the knowledge of higher cosmic principles. All the world's religions have subsequently crystallized from the Vedic system of knowledge.

This chapter seeks to identify the Vedic origins of the sacred knowledge of Siberian peoples as in ancient times, and today, on the basis of a common semantic complex of the Fire cult, in its earthly and heavenly manifestations (worship of elements of Fire, worship of the Sun), as well as manifestations of Fire as vital energy. Methodologically the study is based on the comparative approach, which allows not only to define a common language environment of Vedic constants (Indian and Russian) related to the Fire cult, but also to identify the semantic meaning of rituals and attributes of this cult in Siberia.

Slavic mythology, constituting the most ancient stratum of Vedic doctrine of the Indo-Aryan super-ethnos, contains the ancient archetypes of the most Eurasian mythological systems. A complete set of Slavic folk songs, epics, religious verses and tales contains the Initial Vedas lost by the Aryans, which came from the north to India and Iran. Thus, many mythological subjects, summarized in the *Puranas*, in the Russian tradition give the song or tale, familiar to the people and almost not distorted by time. Many ancient Vedic texts and sacred hymns are preserved in the collections of Russian spiritual verses: *Book of Doves*, *Animal Book* and *The Secret Book*.

The *Veda of the Slavs*, published in the nineteenth century in St. Petersburg and Belgrade, includes ritual songs and prayers to Slavic gods, preserved in the South Slavic tradition. A. Asov asserts that "it is not less important for the Slavs than the *Rigveda* for the Hindus".[2] But besides the folk tradition, Russian Vedic literature is also represented by the ancient texts. The most important of them are *The Word about Igor's Regiment, Boyan's Anthem* and *Book of Veles*.

The Word about Igor's Regiment is the famous monument of the literature of Kievan Rus. The plot tells about unsuccessful campaign of the Russian Novgorod-Seversky Prince Igor Svyatoslavich in 1185 against the Polovtsians. *The Word* was written in the late twelfth century, soon after the events. One of the peculiarities of *The Word* is an appeal to Slavic Vedic (pre-Christian) mythology (Christianity was adopted in Russia in 988). The author of *The Word* glorified the Hors – "the Great" Sun God; names of Russian princes as Dazhdbog grandchildren, prophetic narrator Boyan – grandson of Veles, and the winds – grandsons of Stribog; mentions the mythological creature Div who calls at the top of the tree; Karna and Zhelya, personifying Fate and the Sorrow.

Boyan's Anthem is one of the monuments of Slavic runic letters, a copy of the sixteenth to eighteenth centuries of an earlier medieval written document. The text is named in honor of Bojan, referred to therein. It was first published in translation by Russian poet of the eighteenth century G. R. Derzhavin in the book *Reading in the Colloquy of Lovers of the Russian Word* in St. Petersburg in 1812. In the late nineteenth century, Derzhavin's archive was transferred to the public library in St. Petersburg. The copy of *Boyan's Anthem*, made by Derzhavin, has been preserved to our days. It was discovered in 1994 by Vladimir Goryachev in the papers of Derzhavin's archive. The document (61 lines) was published in the journal *Science and Religion* in 1995. The study of the newfound text showed that the runic text, saved thanks to Derzhavin, is not fake, as was believed for many years, but a unique document of *pre-Cyrillic letters*. This reinforces the attention to ancient and early medieval written monuments on the lands of Russia and deserves attention as the runic interpretation of ancient history. The style of the *Anthem* is reminiscent of *The Word about Igor's Regiment*. This text mentions epic *Sloven, Scif* and *Arius*, the real kings of the ancient Slavic tribes of the fourth century: of the ants king Bus and the Scythian king Germanarikh. (*Svarog* is the Supreme God of the Slavs).

The *Book of Veles* is a kind of scripture of the ancient Slavs, which was carved on birch tablets by Novgorod magi (priests of god Veles). Texts of the *Book of Veles*, like the ancient Indian Vedas, Avestan literature and biblical tales contain priestly hymns and descriptions of ritual practices, and also describe the history of the Proto-Slavs and many other peoples of Eurasia from the time of the progenitors (twentieth century BC and up to the ninth century BC).

Figure 3.1 Birch plank of the *Book of Veles*

The Book of Veles is complex and a voluminous source of ancient knowledge. This text proves that the ancient Slavs were not pagans (polytheists), but possessed a developed system of Vedic worldview. In particular, they worshipped One Supreme Transcendental Divine Essence: Rod. There is a mysterious and tragic story of finding *The Book of Veles*. During the civil war in Russia, an officer of the White Army, Izenbekov, found in the ruined estate of the princes Zadonskie small boards with old Slavic runic inscriptions. He took them abroad for safety. Then a Russian émigré writer Yuriy Mirolyubov copied and transcribed these records for fifteen years in Brussels. He rewrote 75 percent of the text. During the Second World War, after Izenbekov's death, his entire archive was gone, probably burnt. Only the manuscript of Mirolyubov and photos of several boards remained. There is a version that the archive of Izenbekov was withdrawn after his death by Anenerbe officers.

Perhaps the most important role in the Vedic doctrine is devoted to the concept of the Sun as the celestial incarnation of the Fire cult. The Sun, as a divine element, appears in the Indian pantheon in various capacities, in many guises: *Surya, Indra, Savitri, Agni*. The Slavs demonstrate a similar picture: *Khors, Kolyada, Yarylo, Dazhdbog*. Comparative historical analysis of etymons generated by the concept of "the Sun, the Fire", reveals an enormous amount of related words in Sanskrit, Hindi and Russian, demonstrating the diversity and presence of many levels in the mentioned concept.

Khors, the god of the Sun, is identified with the solar disk. Its symbol is a circle or a cross in a circle. When traits of fire dominate in the guise of Khors, it becomes *Semargl*, similar to the Indian *Agni*. The name of the *Khors* has a moral meaning: absolute blessing, good.[3] Etymologically, the name *Khors* carries the semantics of the circle, which, in turn, is the most harmonious figure who embodies the meaning of "well" (*khorosho*). These meanings are read in different Indo-Aryan languages: *Khors* (solar disk) – *khursid* (Persian. "the Sun"; *khvar* – shine; *khvarna* – divine energy, creative principle) – *khoros* (Greek. "circle", "a movement in a circle") – *khoro* (Bulgarian circle dance) – *khora* (round-trip around the Buddhist stupa) – *khor* (harmonious), good (*khoroshee*) singing, often standing round) – *khorovod* (to drive circles and to sing in chorus (*khorom*) – *khoroshulj* (round ritual chicken pie) – *khorosho* (Russian "well") – *khvars* (Ossetian. "well").

The word *khoro* linguistically corresponds to the word *kolo*, it also means "a circle", "a wheel", "a circle dance", "mundane gathering", "rim", "hoop", and so forth.[4] The meaning of the wheel gives life to a number of etymologically related concepts: *kolesnitza* (the chariot) – *kolimaga* (rattletrap) – *koleso* (the wheel). This is not only a technical device, but the main symbol of the sun. The same principle of linguistic correspondence builds unified etymological and semantic range: *Khors* – *Kolo* – Sun (*Solntse*). *Kolo* – one of the names of the sun, represents its infant subsistence (the nascent sun at the beginning of the New Year). It is in honor of this cosmic event that *Koljada* holiday is celebrated.

Koljada holiday is turning, after winter turns for summer, the day becomes longer, it is called *Kolovorot* (*Solntsevorot*). At that time, people bake *kolachi* (kalaches) and *kolobki* (balls). They move down lit wheels from the mountains, which symbolize the sun, which trundles across the sky. They also untwisted two torches, the related crosswise, set on fire at both ends, by the course of the sun or against. Some researchers believe that from this custom there has occurred a *Swastika*. The Sanskrit etymological source of *Swastika* emphasizes common values of Slavic and Indian Vedic words related to the concept of the Sun.

Svarga (*svar-ga* – Sanskrit. heavenly, leading to heaven) – heavenly, divine peace, shining, sunny – is called identically by the Slavs and the Indians. Demiurge, the creator of all that exists among the Slavs – *Svarog*. It is also called *Svabog* (shining, the God of heaven, compared with the Sanskrit *svar* – nebo, sky, sunny, shining a light), as well as *Tvastihrj* (one of the names of *Svarog*, emphasizing his demiurgic, creative principle (*tvorchestvo*), similar to the Hindu *Tvashtar* and Sanskrit *sattva* – meaning a living entity, creature (*tvarj*). *Svarog svarganil* (*sotvoril* – created) world. Hence it follows: *varitj* (to cook) – *tvoritj* (to create) – *svarka* (welding – modern technical term, that contains both senses: the shining and joining (is creative)).

Bird Lady *Swa* (women's hypostasis higher creative force that generates the Slavic pantheon of gods – *Lada*) generates its own set of meanings: *Swasti* (in Sanskrit, health, pleasure), *svasti!* (*Svaast'i* – in Sanskrit blessing, happiness, good!), *svakha!* (*svaha* – Sanskrit, magic spell), which is cited while making offerings to the fire. The same word is the name of the goddess of *Svakha*, the wife of the Hindu God of fire, Agni – it is likely that all the Russian bridal terminology comes out from this: *svadjba* – the wedding (*svayam-vara* – Sanskrit. choice of spouse, a form of marriage), *svakha* – the matchmaker, *svoyj* – own (*sva* – Sanskrit. own, personal), *svoyak* – legal relative, *svat* – kinsman- matchmaker, *sestra* – sister (*svasar* – Sanskrit.). In Siberia, the Vedic fire cult remained in the visible forms of architectural and sculptural works of its ancient inhabitants and it continues to live in the traditions and rituals of modern descendants of indigenous peoples of Siberia.[5]

The discovery by Bal Gangadhar Tilak, an Indian scholar of *Rigveda* and *Avesta*, of the ancestral homeland of the Aryans, which existed in the Arctic region (northern part of the modern Siberia), is well-known. Tilak has shown that these sacred texts reproduce historical, astronomical and geophysical realities specific to the Arctic. He came to the conclusion that the Vedas were created not in the territory of modern India but in the Arctic, by the ancient Aryans, the core of which during thousands of years, as a result of gradual cold snap, migrated through Siberia, still comfortably warm then, to India.[6] The same thing was pointed out even in early eleventh century by Al Beruni, the outstanding scholar and lexicographer of Khorezm.[7] Evidence of the great migration of the Aryans from the Arctic ancestral home is provided by "the Country of towns", situated in the south of the Urals, which attained international fame due to its unique city-temple Arkaim. The archaeologists have discovered in this "Country of towns" and other areas in Siberia more than fifty proto-cities. The length of the occupied territory of the ancient Aryans was 350–400 km north to south and 120–150 km west to east. The distance between the fortified settlements existing at the time was 50–70 km.

The etymology again lifts the veil of secret meanings. The Sanskrit root *arc*, which means "to shine, to radiate, to honor, to chant", is the basis of the names of ancient homeland of the Aryans – sun-worshipers – the Arctic, shining its snows, and their sacred center of the city, built in the form of a *Swastika* – an *Arkaim*. Scientists argue about the etymology: V. N. Demin bases it on the Greek word *arktos* – "bear".[8] Bears are associated with the north for the Greeks, hence

Figure 3.2 Model of Arkaim

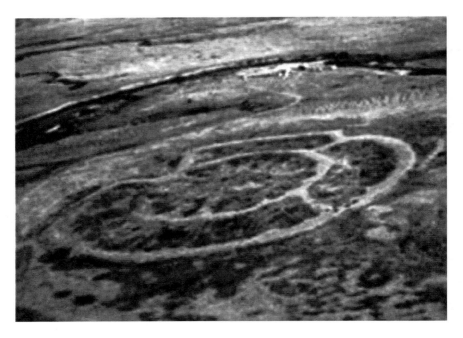

Figure 3.3 Arkaim

a different Greek word – *artikos* ("northern"). *Arka* is a Sanskrit word meaning "solar". Comparing these two words, Demin came to the conclusion that in times of early dismemberment of Indo-European linguistic and cultural community, the concept of the "north" and "solar" were identical.

E.A. Mironova, the researcher of comparative philology is considering another semantic layer of the root base *Ark*: "cryptic", "mysterious", "stored in secret" based on the Latin words *arcanum* – "secret, mystery", *arcanus* – "surreptitious, undercover", "hidden, latent" (let's remember the title of Tarot cards: *Arcana*). She brings an impressive list of toponyms, hydronyms and oronyms containing robust combination -*Ark* – (not only in Europe and Asia, but also in North America), as well as archaeological monuments, found near the geographical objects, containing the title of the syllable -*Ark*. The author comes to the conclusion that this whole layer of place names indicates the great antiquity of a stable combination of sounds in a syllable -*Ark*, as well as the connection of the syllable with the most ancient cult of the bear, widespread in Eurasia and North America since the Paleolithic period.[9] The cult of the bear is the forerunner of all temples, altars and related with them are mysterious ceremonies and rituals which arise in various religions of the world. Thus, only one syllable was able to build a semantic range of "northern – shining – solar – mystery – undercover". All this substantiates the sacredness of the town-temple of Arkaim and its importance in the development of Indo-Aryan community, which mastered the spaces of Eurasia.

There is another version of the origin of the name *Arkaim* of the Bashkir word *arka* – a back, a ridge. And then the mountain range, which stretches from the north to the south, as if indicating the direction of movement of the Aryan tribes, probably, not coincidentally has the name of the *Urals*.

The Sanskrit root *ra* – "helping, contributing" – contains the same solar, luminous sense:

> *ravi* – sun; *ratha* – chariot (in Indo-Aryan myths of the Sun personified the four horses harnessed to the chariot (*kolesnica* – Russian), wheels (*kolyosa* – Russian) which also represented the Sun – *Kolo*); *raajan* – king (viceregent of the Sun on the ground).

And, in practice, the following words are cognates:

> *rakta* (Sanskrit) – red (*krasnihyj* in Russian),
> *racita* (Sanskrit) – beautiful (*krasivihyj* in Russian),
> *ram* (Sanskrit) – to rejoice (*radovatjsya* in Russian),
> *raadh* (Sanskrit) – grow, prosper (*rasti* in Russian)

The city-temple Arkaim was at the same time an astronomical observatory. It had the form of a circle, with an outer diameter of about 160 m. In the outer massive wall four entrances were marked. The biggest of them was the south-western one, while the other three were smaller in size. The city had a single circular street with the width of about 5 m, which separated two rings of walls with the houses adjacent to them.

To come up to the small entrance of the inner ring, it was necessary to go along the entire length of the circular street. It pursued not only the defensive purpose, but also had a sacred meaning: the need to follow the same route that the Sun passes. The figure formed by four entrances in the outer wall of Arkaim is a *Swastika* following the movement of the Sun. In the very center was a square area in which rituals were conducted, according to the remains of a fireplace located in a certain order. Thus, the structure of Arkaim is a *Mandala* – a square inscribed in a circle. Builders of Arkaim recreated the model of the universe in their own land.

During the excavations in Sintasht, neighboring town of Arkaim, the remains of the magnificent building of the Temple of Fire – a nine-step pyramid – were found. Radiocarbon dating indicates the date of its construction was the twenty-first to twenty-seventh centuries BC. Such structures are also found in the earlier Siberian proto-cities, dating back to the third millennium BC, such as in the village of Tashkovo II, which had its own temples of Fire, personifying the Sun and Moon deities, while the inhabitants of the central house "were the keepers of the sacred fire".[10]

Probably the earliest proto-cities, fortresses, ritual and funeral structures remained in the south of Western Siberia from the Indo-European tribes who were moving towards Iran and India. In Syria, Anatolia, and the Balkans similar structures are found: circular cities with trapezoidal dwellings radiating to the center with their butt ends adjacent to the circular defensive wall. This fact indicates the direct contacts between the proto-cities of Western Siberia and Western Asia, as well as a high level of social and technological development of Siberia in the Bronze Age.[11]

L.R. Kyzlasov, the researcher of the Siberian proto-cities, based on archaeological evidence, comes to this conclusion: the founder and prophet of the ancient religion of fire worshipers, Zoroaster (Zarathustra), lived and acted in the area between the rivers Ural and Tobol, which flowed in different directions to the south and north along the Siberian facade of the Ural Mountains. In support of his argument, he refers to the statements of M. Boyce that "actually he (Zoroaster) lived in the Asian steppes east of the Volga, among proto-Iranians of Northern Kazakhstan and was a priest".[12] It confirms that the origins of Zoroastrianism, as well as the beliefs of the Indo-Aryans, occurred at the beginning of the second millennium BC, that is, at the time of existence of the Siberian proto-cities.

And its testimonies can still be found in Siberia: the city of Omsk stands on the river Om. Two hundred and fifty kilometers north of Omsk there is a powerful energy center, Okunevo, which geophysicists say is the area of exit of positive energy having a beneficial effect on the people. The Okunevskaya zone is located on the river Tara. This hydronym cannot be translated into any language of the Siberian peoples, and in Sanskrit it means "Lady Savior".

In 1928 in Khakassia in southern Siberia, in the area called Okunev ulus (the so-called Khakassko-Minusinskaya trough – KMT), archaeologist S.A. Teploukhov was the first to excavate the burial ground of an ancient culture, named by the region, Okunevskaya. Experts date this culture to the first half of the second millennium BC (Bronze Age). But much earlier, in the third and second millennia BC, in this place appeared an ancient sacred center, formed by huge stone steles (up to 4.68 m in height), which depict three-eyed faces. D.A. Machinsky, an archaeologist from the Hermitage in St. Petersburg, believes that the ancient inhabitants of the area (the period of the Afanasiev-Okunevskaya culture) had a developed system of knowledge about the relationship of man with the Supreme Principle, which is implemented through a system of special psychosomatic practices that enabled the ancient inhabitants of KMT to carry on this relationship.[13]

Steles located in the open steppe Khakassko-Minusinskaya trough represent a unique sacred center, signifying that during the Bronze Age in Siberia there lived a community of people who had a high level of spiritual development, had knowledge of the common nature and energy structure of the macro- and microcosmos, which would later be presented and preserved in the sacred texts of the Indo-Tibetan tradition. Analyzing the typological features of the ancient statues of KMT, D.A. Machinsky indicates the kinship of cultures in the Khakassko-Minusinskaya trough and India:

- The faces, bulging relief and ovoid, are placed on a high stele in the middle part of the narrow side and are turned to the east, which is typical for all solar cults.
- There are three eyes on the faces (the third eye in the middle of the forehead), which corresponds to the body of clairvoyance in the Indo-Tibetan esoteric

tradition – *Ajna chakra*; two nostrils, wide enough for a deep breath, may indicate the practice of *pranayama*; and mouth with corners curved up conveys the state of bliss and enlightenment.
- The central part of the skull above the third eye had one or more lines (straight or curved) climb upward; sometimes this is supplemented by small images of faces.
- On most steles *chakras* marked in the form of a circle with four petals, arranged on a central axis under the face, and sometimes at the sides and back. The scientist noticed an interesting pattern: on the steles are marked only the upper *chakras* (four to seven), which may be explained by the presence of the cult of the virgin-goddess.
- Exaggerated ovoid faces, and the location near some of stone steles of "eggs" with faces, as well as archaeological finds in the KMT of egg-shaped vessels, dating from the third millennium BC – all this testifies to the presence and distribution in Siberia of universal myth of the World Egg as a primary form of cosmic energy potential.

According to D.A. Machinsky, the described images represent the type of enlightened person who realized the practices of spiritual ascent and descent, of internal struggles and enlightenment.[14]

It is a striking fact that the secret, esoteric knowledge, which in ancient times was available only to the initiated in the ritual center of the Minusinskaya trough, was open to a wide range of audiences or pilgrims. Most people in this area seem to have understood the symbols, which in a simplified way showed the system of "energy channels" and *chakras*, including *Ajna chakra*, the "third eye".[15] They erected huge and labor-consuming images, accessible for the public view. Here one sees the manifestation of the third feature of the Fire cult – the life energy that runs through the macrocosm and its model, man.

A.D. Machinsky proves that *Aryanam Vaejah* (scope of the Aryans) is located in Siberia, stretching from the South Urals to Khakassia. He bases his argument on a meticulous analysis of the texts of the *Avesta* and the *Mahabharata*, on a linguistic analysis of names and geographical descriptions. The author refutes the existing versions of the localization of the ancestral homeland of the Aryans:

> The Iranians carried this archetype (the sacred homeland) in all areas of their resettlement and projected it on suitable natural sites. Hara Berezajti has embodied at Alburs of Hindukush mountain range, in the Ehljburs south of the Caspian Sea and in Mount Elbrus in the Caucasus. Echoes of the epithet *Vakhvi* can be seen in the name of one of the sources of the Amu-Darya river Vakhsha, which allows us to identify the Amu-Darya with Daitjya, and sometimes for other reasons – with Ardvi. Salt water and desert are considered by the Zoroastrians, the creature of Evil Spirit, and therefore neither the Caspian nor Aral may be considered a primary Vourukasha, located at the foot of Khukarjya, receiving water of Ardvi and giving the beginning for other "waters". This flows through freshwater lake near the mountains in the north of the steppe zone.

It is important to name *Khukarjya* (gold). Subject of gold at all times is connected with Altai (*Altay, Kinshan* – gold). "The name 'High Hara' says about the high mountains, and the measure of height for a resident of Iran – Central Asia was only the presence of snow-capped peaks, so there is no identity with the Urals."[16]

Years of research led the scientists to the following conclusions:

1. Primary Hara Berezajti – is an Altai mountain system, extending from northwest to south-east;
2. "Gold" *Khukarjya* – this mountain Tabyn-Bogda Ola (five sacred peaks) and its main peak Khuyjtehn/Kuyjtun, at a height of 4,356 m. This peak is the center of the largest snow-ice array of Altai, located on the border of Russia, Mongolia, China and Kazakhstan, from which diverge ridges, separating the basins of the Ob and Irtysh rivers and Khobdo. "This array is just asking for the role of 'World Mountain' from its location and natural features".[17]
3. River Ardvi – the Black Irtysh, the origins of which are in the Altai Mountains, and one of them, Burchum, flows from the snowy Khuyjtehn.
4. Vourukasha – the Lake Zaysan, into which empties the Black Irtysh (Kara Irtsis) and out of which flows the White Irtysh (Ak-Irtsis – now Irtysh).

The author compares the sacred center of the Minusinskaya trough with the Vedic tradition of ideas about "the country of blessed", located to the north of the World Mountain Meru. Indian Vedic texts also testify that the Aryans revered the Axis of the Universe – the sacred Mount Meru, connecting the Earth with infinite space. They determined the position of Meru in the north. Indian scholar Padmashri V. R. Rishi finds original homeland of the Aryans in the Altai. He argues that the

> homeland of the Aryans is Mount Meru or Sumeru Parbata, as it is mentioned in some of the *Puranas* and *Mahabharata* . . . that Meru in the *Puranas* is nothing else than the Altai Mountains in Central Asia . . . that the main seat of the God-Creator, Brahma, was at the Meru itself.[18]

And in the notes of N. Roerich we find the confirmation: "The legendary Mount Meru of the *Mahabharata*, and the legendary to the same extent peak Shambhala of the Buddhist teachings – both were on the north".[19]

In the hymns of *Avesta* it is said that the Creator of the Universe Ahura Mazda built a palace for the great god Mithras, and for the god Sraosh built a thousand-pillared house in the mountains of the North. Around this sacred abode of deities, the Aryan heroes and kings of the earth made sacrifices. This is the "center of the earth".[20]

The great artist and traveler Nicholas Roerich, during his trans-Himalayan expedition, wrote in his travel diary:

> At the center between the four oceans exists Northern Mountains – Sumyr, Subur, Sumbyr, Siberia – Sumeru. All the same are at the center from the four

oceans. In the Altai, on the right bank of the river Katun, there is a mountain, its value equals the World Mount Sumeru.[21]

Roerich believed that Sumeru in Altai is the pinnacle of Belukha, which by its geographical parameters corresponds to the mythological World Mountain. The Buddhists say that the World Mountain Meru is made of pure gold and it is located in the north, and at the foot of it there is Milky Lake. The old Russian legends spoke about the blessed land *Belovodye* (White Water). In the difficult years of religious and political persecution, from the heavy yoke of serfdom the Russian people fled deep into the country, to Siberia, in inaccessible and abundant places, where the "rivers of milk and honey flow", where people live happily, and where the secret of peace is kept. Such a promised land for the Old Believers was the Uimon valley and the valley of the river Ak-Kem, which flows from the lake of the same name from the foot of Belukha mount. Ak-Kem in Turkic means "white water". Indeed, the water in the river is milky white, opaque from the vast amount of mineral slurry flows from thousands of rivulets and streams coming down from the top of Belukha. The valley of the river Ak-Kem is famous for abundant herbs, "honey", on the bank of the milky river. During a trip to Altai, Nicholas Roerich wrote in his travel notes: "In the area of Ak-Kem there are traces of radioactivity. The water in the Ak-Keme is milky white. Real Belovodye".[22] Roerich saw in the legends of the local Old Believer population about *Belovodye* a similar Himalayan legend about Shambhala, of a mysterious country, that opens only by the righteous and enlightened.

Figure 3.4 Belovodye White Water River Ak-Kem

Figure 3.5 Karakolsky culture

But, when Roerich searched the legendary peak in Altai, he did not know that the indigenous population of the Altai designates the same name to another peak, situated in the heart of the Altai mountains, considering her the navel of the planet. In the Karakol valley, located at the foot of this peak, a sacred complex was formed during thousands of years, inherited by one nationality from the other, replacing each other in this area. Scholars here number more than five thousand archaeological sites of Afanasiev, Scythian and Turkic cultures. Just recently, in 1985, the archaeologist V.D. Kubarev discovered a new archaeological culture, called "Karakol culture", dating back to the late third to the beginning of the second millennium BC.

On the inner surface of the stone sarcophagi were depicted humanoid creatures in masks with crowns of feathers resembling the sun and painted red, black and white. Apparently, five thousand years ago in this land shamanic mysteries were played out depicting the sun-headed deities with black hand-wings. These petroglyphs surprisingly coincided exactly with the costumes of the Apache (Native American) who worship the Great Spirit and its incarnation the Sun during their rituals, perform ritual dances, depicting birds. In their hands they hold the fan from black feathers, and their headdresses of colored feathers resemble the solar crown. The Aryan tribes were living at the Bronze Age in this territory (*Karakoi*), in whose language *Kolo* means "the sun".

New discoveries of the archaeologists increasingly convince many researchers that Western Siberia can be considered as one of the probable centers, where at the very threshold of the Bronze Age a highly developed culture of ancient Aryans flourished, which gave rise to the formation of the majority of the Indo-Aryan peoples of Eurasia. Here the innumerable artifacts, toponyms and hydronyms preserve the evidence of ancient Vedic faith, which later achieved its highest development in the culture of the Indian people, and is maintained with reverence by their descendants living in Siberia.

Notes

1. N. Roerich, *Russia – India: Diary sheets*. 3 Vols. Moscow, MCR, Master Bank, 1996. 688 pp.
2. A. Asov, *Slavic Gods and the Birth of Russia*. Moscow, Veche, 2000. 544 pp. (In Russian).
3. B. I. Kuznetsov, *Bon and Mazdaizm*. St. Petersburg, Evraziia, 2001. 224 pp. (In Russian).
4. B. A. Rybakov, *The Paganism of the Ancient Slavs*. Moscow, Nauka, 1994. 608 pp. (In Russian).
5. I. A. Zhernosenko, *Russian Veda – "The Secret Doctrine" of the Ancient Slavs*. Barnaul, 2003. 58 pp. (In Russian).
6. V. N. Demin, *Secrets of the Russian People*. Moscow, Veche, 2006. 352 pp. (In Russian); Abu Rayjkhan Biruni, *Selected Works. Volume 2. Indiya*. Tashkent, FAN UzSSR, 1963. 727 pp. (In Russian).
7. Biruni, *Selected Works*.
8. E. A. Mironova, *The Syllable 'ARK' Proto-Language in Modern Geographical Names of the World* (Electronic resource). www.organizmica.org/archive/605/ark.shtml (In Russian).
9. L. R. Kyzlasov, "Proto-towns in Ancient Siberia (in the Bronze and Early Iron Ages)". *Vestnik*. Moskowskogo un-ta. Series 8. Istoriya. No. 3. 1999. (In Russian).
10. Ibid.
11. M. Boyce, *Zoroastrians: Their Religious Beliefs and Practices*. London, Routledge, 2000.
12. D. A. Machinskyi, "Land of the Arimaspi in the Ancient Tradition and 'Expanse of the Aryans' in Avesta". In: *Priesthood and Shamanism in the Scythian Epoch: Materials of International Conference*. St. Petersburg, 1996. pp. 3–15. (In Russian).
13. D. A. Machinskiyj, *Minusinsk "Three-Eyed" Images and their Place in the Esoteric Tradition*. St. Petersburg, SPbGU, IIMK, The Museum of Anthropology and Ethnography, the State Hermitage Museum, 1995 (In Russian); D. A. Machinskyi, *Unique Sacral Centre III – ser. I Millennia BC in the Khakass-Minusinsk Basin*. St. Petersburg, Petro-RIF, 1997. 290 pp. (In Russian).
14. Machinskyi, "Land of the Arimaspi".
15. Ibid.
16. V. R. Rishi, *India i Rossiya: Altay – Gimalai*. Novosibirsk, Conference materials. 1992. 225 pp.
17. P. F. Belikov and V. P. Knyazeva, *N. K. Rerikh*. Samara, Agni, 1996. 200 pp. (In Russian).
18. Kyzlasov, "Proto-towns in Ancient Siberia".
19. N. K. Roerich, *Altayj – Gimalai; Travel Diary*. Riga, 1992. 336 pp. (In Russian).
20. Ibid.
21. Ibid.
22. N. K. Roerich, *Flowers of Moria: Way of Blessing; Heart of Asia*. Riga, 1992. 261 pp.

4 Eurasia and India
Historical-cultural linkages

K. Warikoo

India and Eurasia have had close social and cultural linkages, as Buddhism spread from India to Central Asia, Mongolia, Buryatia and far wide. Buddhism provides a direct link between India and the peoples of Siberia (Buryatia, Chita, Irkutsk, Tuva, Altai, the Urals, etc.) who have distinctive historical-cultural similarities with the Indian Himalayas, particularly due to common traditions and Buddhist culture. Revival of Buddhism in Siberia is of great importance to India in terms of restoring and reinvigorating the lost linkages. The Eurasianism of Russia, which is a Eurasian country due to its geographical situation, brings it closer to India in historical-cultural, political and economic terms. This chapter reflects upon this author's experiences of travels in Buryatia, Khakassia, Altai and Tuva Republics of the Russian Federation, bringing to light certain commonalities of traditions and beliefs still prevalent in this Siberian region and India.

There is wide scope for developing economic and cultural interaction between Eurasia and India, as the two regions maintained cultural contacts since ancient times. An Indian fire temple existed at the Caspian coast near Baku, which used to be visited by Indian pilgrims even as late as in the nineteenth century. The *Lotus Sutra* was transmitted to China and Japan and became a dominant underpinning of their political and religious culture. Archaeological evidence supports the concept of unity of the Eurasian region and the links of Russia and Central Asian states with India into a complex of cross-cultural bindings. Indian Vedas, Shamanism and Tengrism of Eurasia have so many commonalities. In the eighteenth century Buddhism penetrated to Altai, where Buddhist rituals were assimilated with the traditional Shamanist practices. One can find traces of ancient Vedic doctrines in the traditional rituals and practices of the Siberian people even today.

Buryatia

Covering an area of 351,000 km^2 and situated in the southern part of East Siberia to the southeast of Lake Baikal, the Republic of Buryatia borders Mongolia in the south, the Republic of Tuva in the southwest, the Irkutsk Oblast in the northwest and Chita Oblast in the east. The major part (about 60 percent of coastline) of Lake Baikal, 636 km long and the deepest freshwater lake in the world, falls within the territory of Buryatia. The capital city of Ulan-Ude is the administrative, political, economic and cultural centre of the Republic of Buryatia. It is one of the oldest and large cities of Siberia. Ulan-Ude is small, compact and well-organised. On the main Arbat Street, there is a symbol of Ulan-Ude – the *Swayambo* placed above two dragons, which reminds of strong Indian cultural influence. On a visit to the Rimpoche Baksha Temple in Ulan-Ude on 27 September 2007, this author met a Buddhist Lama from Ladakh (India), who was spending over three months in this monastery. On the outskirts of Ulan-Ude, there is a traditional Buryat restaurant, Yurt, where one can have the ethnic Buryat cuisine and national music and dance. They make a circular dance around the fireplace in the centre of the restaurant. That *Ogun*, the Sanskrit term for fire, is still in vogue here only testifies to the continuing Indian connection with Buryatia.

Selenga, which is a major river at over 1,200 km and flowing through Russia, Mongolia and Buryatia, flows into Lake Baikal. The Selenga River has a strong flow of water and depth. It is like the Ganges of India and is an integral part of Buryat culture. So many national Buryat songs have been written about the Selenga. Well-known Buryat artist Anna Subonova has composed and sung several songs eulogising the grandeur and essence of Selenga for Buryatia. the Selenga River flows along the road to Lake Baikal, and the clouds of vapour over the course of the Selenga river present an extraordinary sight.

Buddhist lamas from Buryatia who had access to the rulers of Russia from the time of Empress Elizabeth (1741–1762) became influential at the Tsarist Russian courts of Alexander III and Nicholas II through the efforts of Peter Alexandrovich Badmaev (1851–1919), a Buryat physician and practitioner of Tibetan medicine at the court.[1] Well-known Buryat Lama Agvan Dordji (Dordjiev) had gained substantial influence with the Dalai Lama in the early twentieth century. When he was received by Nicholas II in October 1900 and in July 1901, Dordji proposed to the Tsar that "Russia should proclaim herself the champion of Asia and the defender of Buddhism".[2]

In 1741, the Empress Elizabeth Petrovna issued an imperial decree "recognising Buddhism in Buryatia and 11 *datsans* which existed at that time were confirmed with 150 lamas in them".[3] In 1764, the Russian government appointed the Buryat lama Damba-darja Zayayev as the Chief Bandida Hambo Lama of all Buddhists living to the south of Lake Baikal. He became the supreme official head of the Buddhist order in Buryatia as the first Bandida Hambo Lama (1766–1777).[4] This tradition has continued till modern times. In 1811 the foremost Aginsky monastery was set up, with separate departments of philosophy, tantras and medicine. Its degrees were recognised. In 1853 Russia issued a decree on "the Status of the Lamaist Clergy in Eastern Siberia" which regulated the administrative and economic status of *datsans* and lamas until the 1917 Revolution. By 1917, there were forty-seven Buddhist monasteries (*datsans*) in Buryatia, each a spiritual and cultural centre.

After the October Revolution of 1917, the Buryat-Mongol Autonomous Soviet Socialist Republic was established in the year 1923. All Soviet and administrative personnel in Buryat Republic were initially recruited from lamas, ex-lamas and students of lamaist monasteries. These lamaist modernists projected Buddhism as atheistic and Buddha as a predecessor of Lenin. The leading Buryat historian Zhamtsarano stressed that "Gautam Buddha had given the world an accomplished system of Communism". Though lamaism was crushed during Stalin's period, a new generation of Buryat intellectuals who had grown up in the 1950s started writing in Russian and Mongolian languages about Mongolia and the Mongols. Several Buryat poets such as Dondok, Dashi Dambaev, Lopsan Taphkaev and Bayar Dugarov played key roles in the reawakening of Buryat Mongol consciousness. One Buddhist monastery became the centre of Buddhist preaching and practice, and several Buryat lamas even represented the former Soviet Union at international peace conferences.

Gorbachev's policies of *glasnost* and *perestroika* facilitated the revival of Buryat culture and traditions. In 1989 Bayar Dugarov led a successful campaign for the celebration of the ancient Buryat holiday *Sagaalgan* (New Year). In 1990 Dugarov and other Buryat cultural personalities initiated the five-year celebrations of *Geser*, thus reviving the local heritage. In fact, the campaign to promote *Geser* as figure of national unity assumed an official character, following a decision to this effect by the Supreme Soviet of the Buryat Republic at its meeting on 15 November 1990. This decision led to the organisation of festivals dedicated to the *Geser* epic for which a special Geser directorate was created by the government of Buryatia. On 27 March 1991, the republic was named as the Republic of Buryatia of the Russian Federation. The first All-Buryat Congress was held on 22 February 1991 to discuss issues of the revival of the Buryat language, culture and history. This was followed by the establishment of the All-Buryat Cultural Association with the objective of promoting the Buryat language, culture and contacts between Buryat Mongol areas. Buryatia is also witnessing the revival of Shamanism and Buddhism.

Despite having a long, chequered history, Buryats have always demonstrated benevolence and respect to their neighbours, who arrived in the Baikal region at different periods of time. Notwithstanding their Russian education and training, Buryat intellectuals played key roles in retaining the Buryat traditions and culture while modernising themselves. In this process of syncretisation, as a result of application of Russian science, technology, language, literature and culture in the traditional nomadic society of Buryatia, the indigenous Buryats retained their local traditions and ethos, adjusting themselves to the new wave of dominant Russian and later Soviet cultural and political influence. Even though the use of the Russian language became widespread among the Buryats, they retained indigenous Mongolian characteristics, a nomadic lifestyle, Buddhist and Shamanist religion and traditions, Tibetan language, and Buryat history and folklore. The majority of Buryats, though following Buddhism, remain attached to the Shamanist practices. The rites of birth, marriage, death, seasonal festivals and others have Shamanist characteristics, notwithstanding the participation by lamas and their recitation of sacred Buddhist texts. Today cultural, religious and social traditions of different peoples in Buryatia are closely interwoven, forming a unique pattern of peaceful coexistence. Buryats have maintained their Shamanist and mythical traditions and practices. Buddhism and Buddhist traditions, which were brought to Buryatia from India, Tibet and Mongolia, form the main base of its culture. The Buddhist philosophy, Tibetan system of medicine, astrology, language and printing of literature have not only survived but even developed in Buryatia.

Harsh climatic conditions, a nomadic lifestyle, dependence on natural resources (forests, mountains, lakes etc.), sparsely populated remote settlements and other environmental factors played a role in the development of various rituals, traditions and culture of the Buryats. Thus we see the Buryats revering the elements of nature – earth, sun, moon, fire and water. Similarly collectivism, mutual help and hospitality are accorded importance in their day-to-day life. It is considered sinful to defile fire and water. Also one must not break trees, instead one should give them gifts by hanging coloured pieces of cloth on their branches. This practice is quite prevalent in Buryatia as in most parts of India. On both sides of the highway from Ulan-Ude to Lake Baikal, the birch and pine trees are in abundance. Golden yellow leaves of birch trees provide a beautiful sight in autumn. On the way to Lake Baikal, visitors stop and bow before the birch trees offering tea, bread, coins and so forth. Moving closer to Lake Baikal, they pay obeisance to *Usan Lopsan* – the god of Baikal, offering coins to its wooden statue. They make three rounds from the left clockwise around the statue like the one we have in the Hindu tradition. Buryats attach great importance to colours, certain numerals and so forth. White (*saagan*) is considered to be the colour of sanctity and well-being. Black symbolises danger, grief or death. Red is revered as it is related to fire, light and warmth, and it is believed to bring power, joy and well-being. So we find *Ulaan* (red) in the words Ulaan-Baatar, Ulaan-Ude, Ulaan-Hongor and so forth. Yellow is associated with the Sun and gold, and is given prominence in the palette of colours in Buddhism. Blue denotes the eternal sky and water. Green symbolises the earth, vegetation and growth.

Today there are eighteen Buddhist *datsans* (monasteries), twelve Buddhist communities, seventeen Orthodox temples and parish churches, seven ancient Russian Orthodox communities, and over twenty religious denominations and movements of various kinds in Buryatia. A temple complex called Jarun Khashor, which unites different Buddhist sects, was opened in Kizhinga. The past several years have witnessed the revival of old traditions in Buryatia. Old *datsans* are being restored and new temples are being constructed. In July 1991, a jubilee was celebrated in Buryatia to mark 250 years of the official recognition of Buddhism in Russia, and the Dalai Lama was invited to Buryatia on this occasion, which made the event extraordinary and historic. People in Buryatia and Chita Oblast braved heavy rains and stood waiting to see the Dalai Lama. Buddhists of Mongolia and the Russian Federation, particularly the Republics of Buryatia, Kalmykia and Tuva, look to the Dalai Lama as their spiritual leader. In early November 2007, about 400 Buddhists from Mongolia and the Russian Federation visited India and organised a week-long cultural festival in Dharmshala, the seat of the Dalai Lama and Tibetan government in exile. They held an exhibition showcasing Buddhist culture and traditions in the Russian Republics, besides having concerts and performances by visiting cultural groups. This was a major organised effort by the Buddhists of Buryatia and Tuva to revive their ancient historical

38 K. Warikoo

Figure 4.1 Offerings made at birch trees (Buryatia)

and spiritual ties with the homeland of Buddha. Notwithstanding their limited means, hundreds of Buddhists from the region travel to India every year to make their pilgrimage to Bodh Gaya and also to visit other Buddhist centres in Sarnath, Dharmshala to fulfill their spiritual quest.

After 1990, several monasteries were renovated and new ones constructed at Tsugol, Gusinoozersk, Kyrensk, Atzagat, Egituevsk, Murochinsk, Gegetui, Anninsk, Sanaginsk and Ust-Ordynsk.[5] A school for higher Buddhist studies was opened in 1991 at Ivolginsk *datsan*, with a few students having enrolled there.

The combination of the influences of Buddhism, Shamanism of indigenous peoples, and *Staroobryadchestvo* (Old Russian Orthodox Christianity) has enriched the spiritual sphere of the society in Buryatia. The most ancient traditional religion of Buryats and Evenks has been Shamanism since ancient times. Both the Indo-Buddhist, Mongolian and Russian-European cultures and Shamanism, Buddhism and Christianity have played a role in the formation and development of Buryat culture through history. Due to its unique geographical location (situated on the borders of Russia, Mongolia and China) and historical-cultural development, Buryatia presents a unique synthesis of both culture of the East through Buddhism and Mongolian language and culture and that of the West through the medium of Russian language and culture. The three main value systems of the Buryats – Buddhism, Shamanism and epic-heroism (*Geser*) have become important for the preservation and promotion of Buryat ethno-cultural identity. The reopening of Buddhist monasteries, the forging of close contacts with Mongolia and the Dalai Lama, the renewal of shamanist practices and claims, and the promotion of heroic figure of *Geser* signify Buryats' assertion of their distinct and indigenous identity.

This author, along with a group of five Indian musicians, participated in the International Festival on *Sounds of Eurasia* from 25 September to 1 October 2007. The festival was organised by the East Siberian Academy of Culture and Arts and the Ministry of Culture and Mass Communications, Buryatia Republic of the Russian Federation at Ulan Ude. It was a major event in renewing the age-old cultural contacts between Buryatia and India. The only foreign participants in this festival were the group of Indian musicians representing the Himalayan Research and Cultural Foundation, New Delhi (Mrs. Savita Bakshi, sitar; Mr. R. K. Majumdar, santoor; Mr. Anil Kaul, tabla; Mr. Rakesh Anand, flute/bansuri; Mr. Ravinder Kaul, comperer) which was led by this author. It was for the first time that any Indian cultural group visited Buryatia/East Siberia during the past several decades.

In his inaugural message, Mr. V. V. Nagovicin, president-chairman of the government of Buryatia, expressed his happiness at this occasion as it provided "an opportunity to the people of the Republic to learn traditional instrumental music of Russia and India". Mr. G. A. Aidaev, mayor of Ulan-Ude, while speaking on the occasion of the Inauguration of the festival on 25 September 2007, stated that "participation of our Indian friends in the Festival once again emphasises our kind fraternal ties". Prof. R. I. Pschenichnikova, rector of East Siberian State Academy of Culture and Arts, described the traditional music as a bridge between the past, present and future. This author described this festival as another link in the long chain of historical-cultural contacts. He added,

> And we are thus seeing history being enacted, as this composite cultural programme, academic presentations, artistic performances by well known and

experienced artists from Buryatia, Khakasia, Krasnoyarsk, Chita and India symbolise common cultural traditions, values and aspirations of the people in this entire region.

The festival concluded on Saturday, 29 September 2007. In the evening, a formal ceremony was held at the main hall of Ulan-Ude Musical College, where a gala concert of all the participants from India, Buryatia, Chita, Krasnoyarsk, Khakassia and other parts of Siberia was held. All these artists and musicians from different cultural/ethnic backgrounds presented a fantastic musical programme which demonstrated both harmony and symphony between different musical traditions. Indian classical music of santoor, sitar and flute accompanied the Russian balalaika, Buryat chanz and yatagan, and other instruments. The gala concert of all these artists and musicians spellbound the audience with their musical performances.

Altai

Altai has been variously described as "Gate to Shambhala", "Pearl of Asia", "Siberia's Switzerland", "The Golden Mountains" and so on. The Golden Mountains are revered by the Altaians, Buddhists and Burkhanists. In 1988 UNESCO declared the Golden Mountains and Mount Belukha a World Heritage site. The name Altai comes from Mongolian *Altan*, which means golden. The Altai region spans over vast area at the junction of Russia, Kazakhstan, Mongolia and China. Altai is full of natural bounties – rivers and lakes, the splendour of snowy peaks, luxuriant taiga, steppes, and rich flora and fauna. Amazing natural landscapes, historical antiquity, rich mineral resources, agriculture and tourist attractions lend Altai a unique character. Bordered by Novosibirsk, Kemerovo Oblast and the Khakassia and Tuva Republics of Russia, the Bayan-Olgii province of Mongolia, Kazakhstan and Altai Prefecture in the Xinjiang region of China, Altai is situated in the centre of Eurasia. The area has witnessed criss-crossing of different ethnic and linguistic groups through history. The region has been ruled by the Mongolian Xianbei state (AD 93–234), the Rouren Khaganate (330–555), the Mongol Empire (1240–1502) and the Zunghar Khanate (1634–1758), following which the area was incorporated in the Russian empire. During the nineteenth and twentieth centuries the region developed with the discovery of rich mineral deposits in the Altai mountains and also due to good agricultural land.

After the October revolution in Russia, the Oyrot Autonomous Oblast was established on 1 June 1922, as a recognition of distinctness of the Altai people. On 7 January 1948 the oblast was renamed as Gorno-Altai Autonomous Oblast. And soon after the disintegration of the former Soviet Union, Gorno Altai Autonomous Oblast was reorganized in 1992 and split into two administrative units, Altai Krai and Altai Republic. Whereas Altai Krai is dominated by the flat farmland and big industries, Altai Republic mainly consists of mountains and forests inhabited by the indigenous Altaian people. Barnaul is the administrative centre of Altai Krai, which is a part of the Siberian Federal *Okrug* (District). The discovery of rich reserves of jasper, porphyries, marble and granite in the Krai promoted the development of stone-cutting industry. World-famous masterpieces of stone-cutting art have been created here. By the end of nineteenth and early twentieth centuries, flour and grain mills, distillery works, skin works and so forth were established here. Agriculture became the mainstay of Altai's economy. Later metal processing industries were set up, turning the region into an agro-industrial complex. Covering an area of about 169,000 km^2, Altai Krai has (as per 2010 census) a total population of over 240,000, with Russians constituting over 90 percent of the population, followed by Germans, Altaians and others.

Altai Republic is largely mountainous and covers an area of 92,600 km^2. Having a population of about 200,000, Altaians constitute over 34 percent, Russians being about 56 percent and Kazakhs about 6 percent. Gorno Altaisk is the administrative centre of Altai Republic, which is part of Siberian Federal District. Nicholas Roerich described Altai as the centre of Eurasia being situated at "an equal distance from the four oceans". And in the centre of the Altai is the northern point of the Central Asian mountain range, and the highest peak of Siberia: Belukha (4,506 m). To Roerich, Mount Belukha symbolized Shambhala. Roerich painted Belukha several times. He "viewed Belukha as a local counterpart to Mount Kailas",[6] the holy peak in Tibet. To Roerich "Belukha and Kailas were geographic and metaphysical twins".[7] During his Central Asian expedition (1925–28), Roerich studied antiquities, traditions, customs, medicinal herbs and the history of migrations of peoples. Roerich wrote: "The Katun is affable. The blue mountains are clear. The Belukha mountain is white. The flowers are bright and the green herbs and ciders are soothing". The region is blessed with rivers, lakes, hot springs, forests and significant mineral reserves. The main rivers are Biya and Katun, which originate in the mountains and flow northwards. The Katun River is central to the spirituality and culture of the Altaians, who like in India conduct several rituals in reverence of the river. The junction of the two rivers forms the Ob River, one of the longest rivers in Siberia which flows northward to the Arctic Ocean. The river has about 20,000 tributaries sprawling throughout the Altai territory covering over 60,000 km. There are about 7,000 lakes, the biggest lakes being Teletskoye, Kulundinskoye, Kuchukskoye and Mikhaelovskoye.

This author visited Altai in June 2014 and also in June 2015. Notwithstanding the preponderance of the Russian population, an aura of Asianness pervades in this part of Russia. The ethnic Russians here strongly identify with the Altaians and are keen to protect the local environment, nature and culture. The Russians here are quite friendly, straightforward and nourish deep affection and ideological/civilisational affinity with India. The concept of "Altai-Himalayas" – the close geocultural and spiritual affinity between the two great mountain systems and cultures – is a common issue brought in for academic discussion between Indian and Altai specialists. A local painter, Ms. Larisa Pastushkova, has done a lot of paintings devoted to India, Tibet, Nepal and Mongolia. One could see that the people here have some sort of deep cultural and spiritual affinity with India.

Altai academics stress the need to strengthen the historical-cultural heritage of Eurasia to save the region from the adverse effects of Western social and political influences. They look forward to Russia to take into account the historical-cultural background of its Asiatic space. This author gave a call for reviving the civilisational links between India and Eurasia. He stated that Buddhism provides a direct link between India and the peoples of Siberia (Buryatia, Tuva, Altai, etc.), who have distinct historical-cultural similarities with the Indian Himalayas particularly due to common traditions and Buddhist culture. He stressed the need to have collaborative research to study in depth various aspects of ancient history, race movements and archaeological remains in India and Siberia, common sources and roots of Indic and Siberian culture. Prof. M.A. Shishin described India as a core part of the Eurasian concept. He believed that the power of spirituality will integrate Eurasia.

It takes about twelve hours to drive from Barnaul, the capital city of Altai Krai, to Ongudai, the capital of Gorno Altai. One crosses the Ob River and passes through lush green grassfields, pine and birch trees lining the road, and wheat and mustard fields on the way. The area is sparsely populated and the highway is well maintained. The Katun and Biya Rivers join at Biysk, about 200 km from Barnaul, to form the Ob River.

The Karakol valley is home to several villages, many ancient burials and the sacred mountain of Uch Enmek (Sumeru). The valley is the heart of the Uch Enmek Nature Park, managed by Danil Mamyev. A geologist by training with over thirty years' experience in environmental field and indigenous issues, Mamyev is the initiator and moving spirit behind the development and functioning of the Karakol ethno-national park. He has been an ardent promoter of traditional culture, customs and beliefs of the indigenous Altai people, at the same time being very committed to the preservation of local environment. Several yurts and a modern guest house have been erected here for the tourists. An aura of sacredness prevails here. A fireplace is marked by a tripod in the kitchen dining hall and is considered to be the sacred space.

Pilgrimage to Mount Sumeru

Mount Meru is a sacred mountain in Hindu, Jain and Buddhist cosmology and is considered to be the center of all the physical, metaphysical and spiritual universes. Meru is also called Sumeru in Sanskrit. Roerich believed

> Belukha and Kailash to be earthly manifestations of Mount Meru (Sumeru), the sacred mountain, which through a process of syncretism, can be found in a number of Siberian and Central Asian shamanic traditions. Roerich saw Belukha-Kailas-Meru as a reflection of what he felt was a universal tendency of all faiths to create central cosmological structures that were vertical in nature – be they mountains, trees or built structures. Whatever its physical form, any such *axis mundi* around which the universe revolved, linked the earthly world with heaven above, and also with whatever underground realm existed below.[8]

According to Puranas, Meru is the home or seat of the gods. A fourth-century Sanskrit dictionary *Amarkosha* (1.49) describes Meru/Sumeru as "Golden

Mountains", the mountain of jewels and the abode of gods (*Meru: Sumeru hemadri-Ratansanuh Suralayah*).[9] According to *Itihasik Sthanwali* (a historical dictionary of place names), north Meru is situated near Siberia.[10] In his book *The Arctic Home in the Vedas*, Bal Gangadhar Tilak concludes that "the ancestors of the Vedic Rishis lived in an Arctic home in inter-Glacial times".[11] According to Tilak, "Mount Meru is the terrestrial North Pole of our astronomers".[12] The *Surya-Siddhanta* states that Mount Meru lies in "the middle of the Earth". *Narpatijayacharya*, a ninth-century text, mentions Sumeru to be in the middle of the Earth. Varahmihira in his *Panch-siddhantika* states Mount Meru to be at the North Pole. This description in the ancient Indian text tallies with the belief firmly held by the indigenous Altaians even today. The Puranas and Hindu epics, often state that Surya, that is the sun-god, along with its planets and stars together as one unit, circumambulate Mount Meru every day. According to Tilak, Mount Meru is described in the Vedic literature as the seat of seven *Adityas* in the *Taittiriya Aranyaka*, while the eighth *Aditya* namely Kashyapa is said never to leave the great Meru or Mahameru.[13] Kashyapa is further described as communicating light to the seven *Adityas*, and himself perpetually illumining the great mountain.[14]

Prof. K. S. Valdiya, professor of geodynamics at Jawaharlal Nehru Centre for Advanced Scientific Research, Bangalore, has interpreted the historical data provided by ancient Indian *Puranas* and epics to identify and pinpoint the ancient geography of India. While pointing to the position of *Bharatvarsh* (India), Valdiya cites *Kurma Puran* (43) and *Vishnu Puran* (Part 2, 2) as stating that "in the middle of *Jambudweep* is situated the many-splendoured Meru, the focal point of the world of the Puran people".[15] And "*Bharatvarsh* lay south of the Meru massif, across the arch-shaped Himalaya mountain belt".[16] Valdiya also cites *Markandeya Puran, Varah Puran, Matsya Puran, Devi Puran, Kurma Puran* and *Mahabharat* to pinpoint the northern neighbours of *Bharatvarsh*. He writes, "Northwest of *Bharatvarsh*, across the Himalaya, was a country known a *Ilavritvarsha* following a bow-shaped terrain around the Meru massif of great height and tremendous splendor".[17] And the "countries neighbouring *Ilavritvarsh* are *Bhadrashwavarsh* in the east, *Hiranyavarsh* in the northeast, *Kimpurushvarsh* in the southeast, *Bharatvarsh* in the south, *Harivarsh* in the southwest, *Ketumalavarsh* in the west, *Ramyakvarsh* in the northwest and *Kuruvarsh* in the north".[18] According to Valdiya, this configuration places "Meru at the centre of *Jambudweep* in the Pamir massif in Central Asia".[19] He identifies the countries described as *Ilavritvarsh, Ketumalavarsh, Harivarsh, Bhadrashwavarsh, Hiranyavarsh, Ramyakvarsh* and *Kuruvarsh* as the Central Asian countries of Tajikistan, Turkmenistan, Afghanistan, Xinjiang, Uzbekistan, Kyrgyzstan and Kazakhstan.[20]

On the basis of the Puranic description of the northern neighbouring territories of India, Professor Valdiya's interpretation and this author's extensive field visits in Central Asia, Siberia and the Altai – the Sumeru Parvat – can easily be identified to be in *Hiranyavarsh* of the Puranas and not near the Pamir massif (*Ilavritvarsh*). Quite interestingly, a publication of Dandi Swami Shri Jaybodh Ashram titled *Avichal Prabhat Granth* (published in Delhi, India) describes the approximate geographical situation of Kalap Gram, which is stated to be bounded by mountains of which Sumeru is one gate. It further states that Kalap Gram is full of small and big trees, flowers, pure cold water and natural beauty.[21] This publication describes the place as a divine abode of gods, where great sages including Narayan Markanday, Ved Vyas, Diptiman, Galav, Ashwathama, Kripacharya, Parshuram and so forth come from the sky to meet and meditate.[22] This only testifies to the general belief among the Hindus of India about the sacredness of Sumeru and it being the abode of gods. That this belief is also prevalent even today among the Altaians in Altai territory – the actual place of Sumeru – bears ample testimony to the existence of the sacred space of Sumeru in Altai and its spiritual importance for Hindus, Buddhists and the indigenous people of Altai.

On the way from Karakol Park to Sumeru, one sees the remains of Scythian Kurgan burial complexes, which were earlier excavated by the Soviet archaeologists. Their finds are preserved in the Hermitage Museum at St. Petersburg. It takes about four to five days riding on horses to reach Sumeru and return to Karakol Park, depending upon the weather conditions. The horse is intelligent enough to walk on the right path astride dense forests, streams, sharp edged stones and wet land. On reaching the forest, we dismount and perform a ritual by tying white bands to the pine trees seeking nature's blessings for our onward strenuous trek to Sumeru Parvat. Strong winds and heavy rains accompanied by lightning continued through the night, reminding of the difficulty of reaching the destination. While moving towards the mountains in a zigzag fashion, several mounts have to be covered one after another. While reaching the base of Sumeru, the tradition and practice is to go to Sumeru from this point on foot as a mark of reverence to the holy place. The path is laden with sharp-edged stones and difficult terrain.

We stop at the altar place before moving towards Sumeru. Danil (the leader and master of ritual ceremonies) performs the traditional rituals, tying white bands to the altar, and making a fire to which *sampa* (barley flour), ghee, herbs and so forth are offered. Milk is also fed to the fire by each one of us. The flame of the fire was good, indicating the approval of the spirits for our pilgrimage to Sumeru. We also do *parikrama*, making rounds of the altar and fire. This tradition closely resembles to that of a *yagna* by Hindus in India. Danil offers milk to sky and earth and around to the spirits. He stated that good wind has blown after his ritual, which was a positive signal of the acceptance of our offerings by the spirits. The Altaians also have the tradition of reciting the name of the person, his family, clan, age and so forth while performing the fire ritual, which is similar to the practice among Hindus in India.

Sumeru and its surrounding territory have been considered sacred by the Altaian people since ancient times. Altai people have powerful emotional connection with this sacred territory and have kept this place secluded from public exposure. Even photographs of Sumeru have not been popularized, which is not the case with Belukha. When Nicholas Roerich climbed Belukha, he mistook it as Sumeru. Later on he wished to get to Sumeru, but he did not receive the Soviet visa in time. And when his visa reportedly arrived, Roerich had passed away in Kulu (India) two weeks earlier. Altai people believe that Sumeru, locally called Uch Enmek, is the abode of holy *chakras*, which regulate this earth. My experience at Sumeru testifies to this belief.

Sumeru (about 2,600 m high) is barren, devoid of any trees and so forth. On the top, there are three peaks connected with each other. Altaians call these peaks the three antennae connecting the earth with the cosmos, and imparting energy to this world. There are several lakes around Sumeru and several freshwater streams originating from the mountains. The Altai people do not have any scriptural tradition. Their rituals and traditions are in oral form, having been passed on from generation to generation by word of mouth. According to Danil, knowledge of these rituals and traditions comes to the chosen few from the spirits of the land, from earth and sky. Fire and wind are considered to be sacred. Danil is the only chosen Altaian master who can lead pilgrims to Sumeru. Churla, the horseman, is his junior follower and is still learning the Altaian rituals. After spending few hours at the foot of Sumeru and on the banks of the lake, we move back to our camp and retire in our tents after having tea and dinner.

On our return to the Karakol Valley, we see ancient objects. Danil has developed the park in a manner that the main Altaian symbols and objects like the traditional Altai home *Ail*, fireplace, wooden poles having several knots denoting the three words – sky, earth and below the earth – are preserved and showcased here. We tie white bands to the tree. Different ethnic groups. Mongois, Tuvans, Altaians and others have their separate fireplaces to make their fire rituals. Later on, the ashes are brought and put together at a central fireplace. A triangle made of three poles standing in a corner of the park denotes a smaller Mongolian mountain. On the road one can see ancient petroglyphs having marks of deer and some runic script on the rocks believed to be about 4,000 years old, lying in the open alongside the roads. There is a site where two *kurgans* were excavated by the Soviet archaeologists who had found a dead body covered with ice and a dead horse lying alongside in the grave. Several huge stelae (rocks) are embedded in the vast grassland, not straight but at a particular angle. Altai people believe in spirits, fire, wind and sky. They attach great value to the horse, and as a mark of respect they do not throw the bones of a dead horse on the ground, but keep them on the trees. Moving further on, we reach a hill with dense forest, where a *Chortan* in chiseled stone has been erected over the ashes of a Buddhist lama who had come back to Altai preaching Buddhism and died at the age of 108 years. However, the Altai people believe more in Burkhanism – a mix of Shamanism and Buddhism.

Verkhniy Uymon is an old Altai settlement of Old Believers. During his Central Asian Expedition (1925–28), Nicholas Roerich had stayed at an Old Believer Vakhramey Atemanov's house in Verkhniy Oymon. On the completion of his Central Asian Expedition, Roerich planned to come back to Altai and settle in Verkhniy Uymon. Nicholas Roerich had told to Uymon dwellers, "Golden is this locality, in five years I'll be here". Roerich believed Altai to be the centre of Eurasia, stating it to be at "an equal distance from the four oceans". The northernmost point of the Central Asian mountain range – the highest peak of Siberia – Belukha is here in the centre of Altai. Quite nearby there is a small old house which has been turned into a museum about Old Believers, who migrated to Siberia in the eighteenth century to escape persecution during the reforms in Russia carried out by the Orthodox Church. This house is about 150 years old and belongs to an old

Figure 4.2 Danil Mamyev, Altaian Shamanka and Prof. K. Warikoo performing fire ritual at Karakol Park, Gorno Altai

Figure 4.3 Swastika symbols spun in handwoven cloth in Altai

lady. Various artefacts, spun cloth items, bands and so forth, traditionally used by the Old Believers, are preserved here. The lady in charge explained passionately for over an hour about the lifestyle, culture and beliefs of Old Believers, in poetic fashion. It was interesting to note *Swastika* symbols spun in the clothing and embroidered items of the Old Believers, which leads one to believe the prevalence of ancient Vedic customs and traditions in this part of Russia.

Historical-cultural linkages 47

On our way back to Ongudai we saw few caves in the hills, where in old times some people are believed to have meditated. It may be relevant to point out here that a popular myth associated with Kalaroos caves located in Kupwara district, some 90 km from the summer capital Srinagar, Kashmir, is that these caves are secret tunnels to Russia. There is a mammoth stone called Satbaran, meaning "seven doors". Local belief is that it was the temple built by Pandavas. Though few persons have ventured to go some distance inside the cave, nobody has dared to go till the end. Any possible connection between the caves in Altai and the Kalaroos cave is a subject of further investigation by the scientists and archaeologists.

About 100 km away from the Karakol Park there is Kol Baktash *kurgan* near Inya village. There are many petroglyphs of deer, the sun, ancient big-horned cows (stated to have existed about 30,000 years ago), shamans performing their rituals and so forth. A group of visitors from Yakutia, Kazakhstan, Kyrgyzstan and Turkey were also there to see their ancient heritage. They speak and understand each other's languages (in Turki dialect). On the way to Kol Baktash there is a big rock along the banks of the Katun River believed to be the abode of local spirits. Moving further near the Yelman stream, we climb a hill on foot to see the ruins of an ancient sun temple, believed to have existed over 10,000 years ago. There are two layers of stone walls with an entrance marked by two vertical stones. The Altai sacred bush *Archin* is sufficiently found here on the rocks. Local Altaian people first make their ritual prayers and then pluck *Archin* for use in their ceremonies, including the fire rituals.

Figure 4.4 On the way to Sumeru Mount (shown in circle)

Figure 4.5 Stone gate at the ruins of ancient temple near Yelman Stream, Gorno Altai

We move on to stop at a place where the Chui River, which comes from the direction of Mongolia, joins the Katun River, which originates from Belukha. This point, being the meeting place of two rivers, is held sacred by the Altaians. They tie white and blue ribbons to bushes nearby. A group of Kyrgyz tourists was also doing the same here. This tradition is quite similar to the Hindu tradition of holding the *Sangam* of rivers as holy, as we witness in Allahabad where the rivers Yamuna, Ganges and Saraswati meet, or at Shadipur (also called Prayag) in Kashmir where the Jhelum and Indus Rivers meet.

Moving on, we reach a site where three big ancient stones are preserved. Two stones which somewhat resemble a Shiv linga, have distinct marks of two lines making three subdivisions – sky, earth and below the earth. The Altaians believe in three-world cosmology (upper, middle and underworld), pray to many spirits and hold mountains, lakes, trees and fire as sacred. This is in many ways similar to Vedic and Hindu beliefs prevalent in India even today.

In the evening we return to our guest house in the Karakol Park. A local Altai folk singer (*Kaichi*) treats us with his folk songs playing local instruments – flute, two-stringed instrument and so forth. He recites *Om Mani Padme Hum* and also an ode to the holy Sumeru. Around 10 pm, after dinner, Danil performs the closing ceremony/thanks-giving fire ritual in an *Ail*, in the park. He lights fire, performs traditional rituals and offers milk, vodka and ghee to the fire. Each one of us does the same. The fire was very good, smokeless, with full flame rising to the top of the *Ail*, thereby signalling the auspicious culmination of our pilgrimage to Sumeru.

Figure 4.6 Ancient stones, Gorno Altai

Tuva

Covering an area of 170,500 km² and bordered by Mongolia in the south, Altai to the west, and the Khakassia, Krasnoyarsk, Irkutsk and Buryatia Republics of Russian Federation in the north, Tuva is recognised as the geographical center of Asia. Notwithstanding the domination of Mongolia over Tuva from the thirteenth to early eighteenth centuries and subsequent Chinese sovereignty over Tuva till 1911, Tuva and its people retained their indigenous traditions, culture and religion. Over 80 percent of the total population (300,000) are Buddhists. Despite being adherents of Mahayana Buddhism, Tuvans continue to believe in native shamanism. Tuvans often go to shamans for healing their ailments and to seek remedies to their problems. And shamans do visit Buddhist monasteries to offer prayers. Both beliefs coexist here following the basic principles of respect for and harmony with nature.

Tuva was incorporated in the former Soviet Union in 1944, after overcoming Chinese claims over it. As per official data, in 1929 there were twenty-five Buddhist monasteries (*khuree*), 4,813 lamas and 487 shamans in Tuva.[23] During the Soviet period, religion remained suppressed and Buddhist monasteries were closed and destroyed. In 1937, there were only five monasteries, sixty-seven lamas and thirty shamans in Tuva, the practice of religion and beliefs being confined to individual homes. The lamas and shamans suffered due to the Soviet anti-religious policy. However, both managed to continue their religious activities underground.

After the disintegration of former USSR, there has been unprecedented resurgence of indigenous language, culture, beliefs and Buddhism in Tuva. About twenty Buddhist prayer houses (*dugan*) and fifteen Buddhist monasteries (*khuree*) have been built in Tuva. The visit of Dalai Lama to Tuva in 1992 gave big impetus to the revival of Buddhist practices, publication of Buddhist texts, construction of monasteries and so on. The people of Tuva came in huge numbers to have a glimpse of the Dalai Lama. During this visit the Dalai Lama offered prayers at Hayirakan Mountain about 105 km from Kyzyl, and suggested a spot for building a replica of the ancient Buddhist shrine along with the carving of ancient Buddha rock engraving, so that the ancient shrine is recreated. Work has already begun on this site and is expected to be completed by the end of 2017. This site is located up in the mountains where water cannot reach and flood the new rock-cut Buddhist shrine. Tuvans hold this mountain as sacred and there are many mystic legends associated with Hayirakan. Tuvans come to this place offering prayers to Buddha and take back with them fistfuls of the sacred land's earth.

Overlooking the capital Kyzyl and located on the right bank of the Yenisie river, stands the 1,002 m mountain, Dogee. Tuvans consider this mountain sacred and offer prayers. There are numerous pyramids built of stone with a pole in the center, hung *chalama* (band of cloth), *kadako* (silk scarves) as well as the remains of fire on this mountain. In the year 2006, the Buddhist mantra *Om Mani Padme Hum* was built of stones on the hill Dogee. The 120 m long sacred mantra was painted with 500 kg of white colour and sanctified.

Construction of a new central Buddhist monastery in Kyzyl began in 2014 at a spot identified by the Dalai Lama. Dr. Kaadyrool Bichildey, former minister of education and science of Tuva and a Buddhist himself, has been leading the movement for restoring the historical, cultural, linguistic and Buddhist heritage of Tuva. Many Tuvan Buddhists make their donations to raise funds for these projects, which also get support from the government of Tuva. The federal government of Russia is tolerant of this process, and many Tuvans feel free today to practice their religion and culture. A festival of music and culture, *Ustuu Hurae*, was held beginning in 1999, when reconstruction of the ruins of an ancient Buddhist temple in Chadan began. The festival, usually held in August, showcases the simplicity of life in tents, natural atmosphere, music, tolerance and kindness in Tuva.

Tuvan shamans have also become popular now, with many tourists visiting them from abroad. Shamans' hymns and *algyshes* (wishful songs) have been translated into German and English. Shamans also perform their ritual ceremonies. The cult of *ovaa* (spirit guardians of a place) and *eeren* (protectors of the family), both being shamanist traditions, have been adopted by Tuvan Buddhists. Shamanism is flourishing alongside Buddhism. There is a central shamanist organisation in Kyzyl with local branches in different parts of Tuva. In 1993 first Tuvan-American conference of Shamanism was held in Tuva with participants from the United States, Canada and Finland besides Tuvan academics and members of shaman society *Dungur* (drum). The Tuvan government has also set up a research centre for the study of shamanism, providing land and buildings for the shamanist organisation.

In the Chaa-Hol district, about 100 km from Kyzyl, there is an ancient image of Buddha (thirteenth century AD) in a carved rock niche. After the Sayano-Shushensk hydro power station became operational, the rock niche became submerged in the dam water. However, the niche, with a bas-relief image of Buddha and his two pupils, has been recreated on the hill, 99 m above the sea to protect it from any flood waters. This has been possible due to Bicheledey's efforts. He has also spearheaded the campaign for the preservation and promotion of Tuvan language, history and culture. The 1st of November is now celebrated as the Day of Tuvan language. A symbol of Tuvan letter has been erected at Beldir Keji, near Shaganar about 100 km from Kyzyl. A Buddhist monastery, a symbol of Tengrism and an image of Buddha have been built here. A huge cultural complex is being built at this place, which is expected to be completed by the year 2017. In short, Tuva is experiencing an organised revival of its indigenous language, culture, traditions and beliefs of Buddhism and shamanism.

Figure 4.7 Burgan Daa Buddhist Shrine, Chaa-Hol, Tuva

Khakassia

Covering an area of 61,900 km² in the eastern part of Siberia, the Republic of Khakassia of the Russian Federation is situated in the valleys of the Abakan and Yenisie Rivers. Besides occupying the Minusinsk Basin, it also occupies part of the Chulym-Yenisie valley. Khakassia borders Krasnoyarsk Territory in the north and east, the Republics of Tuva and Altai in the south and southwest, and Kemerovskya Oblast in the west. Khakassia is known as an "archaeological Mecca" because it is a repository of archaeological sites and a rich historical and cultural heritage. From ancient times, Khakassia has maintained trade and cultural relations with Russia, Mongolia, China, Tibet and Central Asia.

Khakas people revere mountains, lakes, *beruza* (birch) and pine trees. On the outskirts of Abakan, a small museum housed in a *yurt* has a large ancient stone locally known as Old Mother Stone, which has marks of a third eye and a trident. This stone is venerated by Khakas people, particularly the women who come to seek its blessings for bearing children. Dolls, milk and other items are offered by the visitors to the stone. Believed to be over 2,000 years old, the stone has three segments denoting the three worlds – sky, earth and below the earth. About 30 to 40 percent of Khakas people still follow/practice Shamanism. This author witnessed the performance of a Shamanist ritual in Abakan in August 2009. Khakas shamans (both male and female) were dressed for that occasion in flowing robes laced with threads and bird feathers; they danced and proceeded around a fire citing verses and softly beating their drums. Some Khakas participants even put some flour in the fire. Small bands of cloth (red, blue and white) were tied to a big *beruza* tree. *Beruza* is held sacred in Siberia in the same way as is done in India. Smoke of incense burnt in a bowl is waved/touched by the people, a practice common in India.

On the way to the Kazanovka village open air museum are so many rock carvings. Victorina, director of this museum, pointed to a hilltop near the bank of the Askis River, which about a century ago had a big stone. People used to visit this place in large numbers believing that this stone had healing powers. There was a cave under the stone having two small stones. This stone was stated to have been destroyed during Khrushchev's time, as idol worship was anathema to the Soviet communist ideology. It is believed that the Magnashev family, whose family deity was this hilltop stone, killed themselves after the destruction of this stone. In Khakassia, as in parts of the Indian Himalayas, each clan has its own family/clan deity/stone, which they revere. Victorina also took us to one semi-white stone lying in a big steppe land which is believed to have healing powers. This author saw a number of men and women coming in their cars to seek blessings of the stone. They removed their shoes and went around three times and hugged this stone offering money at its feet. Victorina explained that the stone, believed to be over 2,000 years old, has three eyes which have become somewhat invisible due to vagaries of nature over a long period of time. All these practices still prevalent among the Khakas people are a clear reflection of Indian influence since ancient times.

Figure 4.8 Mother Stone near Abakan, Khakassia

54 K. Warikoo

Figure 4.9 People pay reverence at the stone near Abakan, Khakassia, Russia

Nicholas Roerich: the bridge between Eurasia and the Himalayas

Nicholas Konstantinovich Roerich, who was born in St. Petersburg, Russia, on 9 October 1874, became a world-renowned painter, philosopher, historian, archeologist, writer, traveler and founder of an international movement for the preservation and promotion of cultural heritage. Even during his student years at the Petersburg Academy of Arts, Roerich became involved in various archeological expeditions in various regions of Russia. He was a prolific artist, having created thousands of paintings. His paintings are known for a distinct style, with deep historical and philosophical content, colour purity and simplicity of expression. Roerich's quest for an understanding of philosophy, universal values of humanism and ethics led him to also study philosophy of the East and the works of great Indian thinkers and writers – Ramakrishna, Vivekananda and Rabindra Nath Tagore. Roerich became interested in the study of common roots and values of Russian and Indian cultures, seeking to correlate their history, mythology, folklore and traditions.

In this pursuit, Roerich and his family travelled to India in 1923, taking their abode in Kullu valley in the lap of the Himalayas. From here Roerich began his famous expedition (1923–28) to Central Asia, traversing high mountains and unexplored paths through Sikkim, Kashmir, Ladakh, Xinjiang (China), Russia, Siberia, Altai, Mongolia, Tibet and so forth. The Roerich expedition is not only known as one of the major expeditions in Central Asia and the trans-Himalayas, but it also contributed immensely to the development of Russian Oriental studies, with a particular focus on Central Asia. Roerich's books – *Heart of Asia* (Southbury, 1929), *Altai Himalayas* (Moscow, 1974) and *Himalayas: Abode of Light* (Bombay, 1947) – are outstanding works in this field. Roerich also made a distinct contribution to the understanding of Himalayan culture and spiritualism through his painting series *Himalayas, Maytreya, Sikkim's Path* and others. Nicholas Roerich conducted another expedition in the years 1934–35 in Inner Mongolia, Manchuria and China, with the objective of collecting seeds of plants which prevent the destruction of soil. This mission showed his great concern for the denuding of forests and vegetation.

Nicholas Roerich broadened the view of culture which includes the cosmic evolution of mankind, ethics and spiritual experiences of man, beauty, knowledge, science, art, education, history and traditions. He propagated peace through culture, which encompassed art, science and religion. The creative artist in him prepared the Banner of Peace which became the symbol of the unity of mankind and its cultures. The Banner represented three spheres within a circle, in amaranth colour on a white background, the spheres meaning the past, present and future achievements of humanity surrounded by the circle of Infinite. In his words, "What the Red Cross flag is for the preservation of physical health, our Banner of Peace is the protector of spiritual health of humanity".

Nicholas Roerich passed away in Kullu valley in India on 13 December 1947, where he was cremated. The Institute of Himalayan Studies, *Urusvati* in the Kullu valley, which he founded, is a living monument bearing testimony to his multi-faceted contribution. He promoted international peace and understanding through culture, cross-country exchanges and knowledge.

Conclusion

In view of the foregoing, there is need for collaborative research to study in depth various aspects of ancient history, culture, race movements and archaeological remains in India and Eurasia, common sources and roots of Indic and Siberian cultures and civilisations. That the concept of three worlds, third eye and trident were embodied in ancient stones of over 2,000 years old and which were and continue to be revered both in Khakassia, Tuva and Altai, has direct resemblance to the tradition and cosmic philosophy prevalent in India even today. Similarly, the practice of treating lakes, springs, mountains and *beruza* trees sacred in Eurasia is quite similar to the Indian tradition and practice. The Altaian, Tuvinian and other indigenous peoples perform fire ceremonies and also haircuts of young children (*mundan*) in the same manner as the Hindus do in India. The Altaian people also believe in Seven Stars (*Sapt Rishi* in India) and Seven *Kans* in Altai. There is also a tradition of placing amulets at the time of laying a foundation stone of a house, in Burytia, Tuva and Altai. This practice is quite similar to that prevailing in India.

It, therefore, becomes necessary to identify common traditions, beliefs and practices among the peoples of Eurasia and India.

Resurgence of Buddhism in Buryatia, Tuva (in Siberia) and Kalmykia Republics of Russian Federation accompanied with the urge of Buddhist devotees in Russia to visit the Buddhist centers of pilgrimage in India, is bringing this otherwise peripheral region closer to India in civilisational and ideological terms. On an average about a thousand Buddhist devotees, mainly youth, from Russia (Kalmykia, Buryatia, Tuva, Moscow, St. Petersburg, etc.) visit India each year to make their pilgrimage to Bodh Gaya, Sarnath, Varanasi and other places or to attend the sermons by Dalai Lama at Dharamshala. The Kalachakra ceremony by the Dalai Lama attracts even more devotees. Many young students from Tuva and Kalmykia visit India to study Buddhism and the Tibetan language. Many people particularly in Tuva and Buryatia have Indian names like Rita, Sanjay, Sanjeev, Ramesh, Padma and Indira. This author found a young Russian in Altai named after the Indian sage Vasishta. Indian classics *Panchtantra* and famous stories of Birbal, the wise minister of the Mughal emperor Akbar, have left their imprint on the folklore of Tuva and the adjoining regions, mainly due to the penetration of Buddhism and Buddhist lamas from India. Currently, over fifty Buddhist lamas from India, mainly Tibetans trained in Karnataka, Dharmshala and so forth are staying and offering their services in various monasteries in Tuva and Buryatia. Revival of Buddhism in Siberia has direct relevance for India for restoring its lost linkages. India for its part needs to restore and turn its vast fund of ancient historical Buddhist sites into centres of international cultural tourism. This will attract tourists as well as pilgrims from our neighbours in Eurasia. Siberia is a corridor through which cultural and civilisational interaction can be reinforced to form a cultural axis between India and Russia.

Notes

1. Emanuel Sarkisyanz, "Communism and Lamaist Utopianism in Central Asia". *Review of Politics* Vol. 20, No. 4, October 1958, p. 627.
2. Ibid., p. 628.
3. Ibid., p. 629.
4. Lokesh Chandra, "Life of Damba Darja Jaya Yin". In: *Cultural Horizons of India*. Vol. 7, New Delhi, Aditya Prakkashan, 1998. pp. 265–6.
5. Ibid.
6. John McCannon, "By the Shores of White Waters: The Altai and Its Place in the Spiritual Geopolitics of Nicholas Roerich". *Sibirica*. Vol. 2, No. 2, 2002. p. 174.
7. Ibid.
8. Ibid., p. 175.
9. *Amarkosa of Amarasimha*, Edited by Pt. Haragovinda Sastri Varanasi, Chowkhamb Sanskrit Series Office, 1998. p. 17.
10. *Itihasik Sthanwali*. Jaipur, Rajasthan Hindi Granth Academy. p. 758. (In Hindi).
11. Bal Gangadhar Tilak, *The Arctic Home in the Vedas*. Poona, Tilak Bros., 1903.
12. Ibid., p. 62.
13. Ibid., p. 65.
14. Ibid.
15. K. S. Valdiya, *Geography, Peoples and Geodyanamics of India in Puranas and Epics*. New Delhi, Aryan Books, 2012. p. 33.

16 Ibid.
17 Ibid., p. 36.
18 Ibid., p. 37.
19 Ibid., p. 38.
20 Ibid.
21 *Avichal Prabhat Granth*. New Delhi, n.d. p. 118. (In Hindi).
22 Ibid.
23 Cited by Kara-ool, Chairman of the Government of Tuva in his welcome speech at the International Conference on Buddhism (7–9 September 2016) held in Tuva.

5 Fine arts and music
The cultural links of Southern Siberia and India

M. V. Dorina

The territory of Southern Siberia – the present Republics of Khakassia, Gorny Altai and Tuva – are united in a common historical-cultural region of the Sayan-Altaisk upland. The Republic of Khakassia (area 62,000 km^2) is situated in the center of the Sayan-Altaisk upland, within the boundaries of the western part of Minusinsk basin, the Sayan and Kuznetsk Alatau foothills. In the south, Khakassia borders on the Republic of Tuva (area 168,600 km^2), in the south-west – on the Republic of Gorny Altai (area 92,600 km^2). The landscape, flora and fauna of each republic are marked by richness, peculiarity, beauty of colors and unique character. The region is dominated by open steppe space, picturesque meadows, river valleys, lakes, thick forests and taiga and a high mountain mass covered with never thawing snow. Since the Paleolithic Age man has been developing this land, adapting to its climate, interacting with nature, using its rich resources, accumulating knowledge and ideas about the world, creating his culture, traditions, ceremonies and rites and reflecting them in stone, metal, wood and other materials. For example, one can mention a ceramic reed-pipe of the Paleolithic Age (34,000 years ago) made so skillfully that scientists can not consider it as the most ancient instrument, and a unique anthropomorphous statuette made of glazed clay about 13,000 years ago (the sites of Malaya Syia and Maininsk, the Republic of Khakassia).[1]

One of the oldest monuments of culture and art of the Bronze Age (Tazminsk, early third millennium BC; Okunevsk, late third millennium to early second millennium BC) in the territory of Khakassia are sculptures presenting pillar, cigar and saber-like boulders 3–4 m high as well as small egg-like boulders and flat stone slabs with the drawings of ancient deities and mythical images. Scientists have classified them into three groups according to their complexity and technique of composition.

L.R. Kyzlasov proved that the sculptures had been used as idols at ancient sanctuaries. They were set facing the sunrise, and scientists associate them with the Sun or a sun-faced deity. According to other versions, those were the symbols uniting all parts of the world and natural phenomena, or images and plots of ancient myths, the result of cosmological ideas of the ancient world outlook. The sculpture of a symbol of a world mountain presented a model of the universe divided into three parts. There is another, a bit different interpretation of a cosmological model: a three-tiered face is interpreted as an anthropomorphic first being of the type of Vedic *Purush*. According to still another point of view, the sculpture is interpreted as the world pillar in a number of cases personified in a cosmic snake-like dragon. All other personages presented on him are his outcome and the face is divided into two parts: the upper part symbolizing a male origin, the lower part symbolizing a female origin. Together they are associated with the image of a world egg – the beginning of every real thing in the universe.[2]

Some shells of kauri[3] were also found together with various pieces of adornment (stone beads, spiral rings of copper wire, finger rings, bronze pendants, convex pendants with a loop, and so forth, tools with a top part in the form of a ram head and wild animals) in the burial mounds of Karasuksk epoch (the end of the second millennium to the beginning of the first millennium BC – the prime of the Bronze Age). Till the end of nineteenth century such shells were highly valued by both the Khakas, Altai and Tuvinian people, and were considered a piece of protection and sewn onto clothes together with other pieces of adornment (Khakas woman's outer garment's upper part adornment *pogo*), the festive decoration for a horse – horse-cloth, a Khakas, Altai, Tuvinian shaman ritual costume.

The beginning of the first millennium BC is known as the time of formation of the most interesting and rich art, first of all by its unique works made of copper, bronze, gold and silver as well as wood, leather, thick felt, and silk of Scythe-Siberian culture in the steppes of Eurasia. In Khakassia this period is associated with the mound burial of the Tagarsk epoch (the eighth century BC to the early first millennium AD). The most famous of them are the so-called Tsar burial vaults – Big Salbykh burial mound and burial mound Barsuchiy Log, which were aimed at burying either one person who must have been the chief or Tsar of a great union of Tagarsk tribes or a representative of social elite. These are monumental constructions, with areas of 2,500–4,900 m^2; the height of the ground embankment of about 9–10 m, fenced with stone slabs and vertically set steles of red grit stone, 3.5–6 m high and weighing 40–50 tons each. The peculiarity of the fence of Barsuchiy Log is a number of various interesting drawings on the stone slabs both of Scythian time and the earlier period.[4] A specific feature of the petroglyphs of Tagarsk "animalistic" style is the predominance of a stylized flying deer with branched horns and a mountain goat.[5] The whole settlements with houses, people and herds as well as the figures of skiers and archers, horsemen, boats with rowers and of course a lot of animals are imprinted on famous Boyarsk *pisanitsa*. The many-figured *pisanitsa* is the most complicated one presented both in Khakassia and the whole steppe world.

In the Republic of Gorny Altai this period is associated with Pazyryksk burial mounds (sixth to second centuries BC), and in Tuva with the burial in "The Valley of Tsars", Arzhaan-1 and Arzhaan-2 (seventh century BC). The objects of everyday life, implements, weapons, adornment and amulets were made in the Scythian animalistic style. The domestic and wild animals, birds and mythical creatures were presented with extraordinary refinement, beauty, subtlety and expression. Some musical instruments (small tambourines made of two bent horn plates and a stringed harp) were found together with well-preserved items of everyday life in some Pazyryksk burial mounds. The scientists consider that today the peoples of Tibet, Afghanistan and Iran play such tambourines and a harp resembling the instruments of the bas-relief of the palace of Sargone II in Khorsabad (eighth century BC).[6] Besides, some coriander seeds – one of the oldest cultivated plants used as a medicine and spice brought here from the shore of the far-away Indian Ocean – were found in one of the burial mounds.[7]

A bronze looking glass found in the excavations of the burial mound group Rogozikha – one in Altaisk territory in 1985 – also belongs to the fifth century BC. The engraving of the looking glass is made in the ancient Indian traditions of folk bast (*pata, patta, pattika*) used by traveling narrators of folk tales for illustrating fairy tales, epics and myths. According to Ya. V. Vasilkov, by the eleventh century such graphic traditions had been reflected in Jain book miniature in Western India. The drawing on the looking glass – a white elephant with a bird on its back in the company of several women in typical clothes and hairstyles – presents a plot of an old Indian fairy-tale (Gunadkhja's *The Great Tale* – first and second centuries AD, Somadeva's *An Ocean of Tales* – eleventh century). In V. Ya. Vasilkov's opinion, such a plot was popular in the centers of urban civilization in the ancient East. The noble Scythians who served in the Akhemenid garrisons of North-Western India in the sixth and fifth centuries BC might bring those looking glasses as items of wealth and recollection of a civilized life.[8]

The first century BC to the fifth century AD was an epoch of Hun conquest and the creation of new archeological (Tashtyksk) culture of the Iron Age. It was the time of intensive interracial marriages of European-looking men (*dinlin*) and the Turkic language–speaking Mongols (*guangun-kyrgyz)*, cattle breeding, farming, handicrafts and further formation of class relations. While the art of that period stuck to the old traditions, it became more realistic. One can mention small planks with carved drawings of a size of about 10 cm presenting battle scenes of the warriors on foot and on horseback, chase and hunting scenes, animal figures (those of stags, elks, bulls, bears, horses) and so on among the archeological finds of this period. Researchers consider that these are illustrations of historical and mythical works of folk art and their presence in the burial mounds demonstrates a high level of folklore of Tashtyksk tribes.[9]

Apart from it, the following items were found in the burial mound: plaster masks of the deceased, bronze statuettes of people and domestic animals covered with a thin layer of gold, and iron items incrusted with gold and silver. The same kind of material was used for making different adornments. The most widespread type of adornment was the amulet. The most frequently found in Khakassia is a solar sign in a circle form with a cross and a pair of horse heads looking in opposite directions. A horse was not considered a mere sacred animal in that period but a symbol of the Sun, a zoomorphic model of the Universe. Bronze amulets with such a symbol must have been obligatory attributes of warriors buried in the vault.[10]

One of the brightest and most dynamic pages of the history of Sayan-Altai peoples (sixth to twelfth centuries AD) was an epoch of old Turkic states (*kaganats*), an epoch of the prime of the state of the Yenisei Kyrgyz people closely connected with present Khakas people.[11] The art of that period was characterized by the creation of stone statues of noble warriors (*chaatas*),[12] runic manuscripts, fine original Kyrgyz vases made on a potter's wheel, an ornamental technique of silver and gold articles and pieces of adornment, horse harnesses, the prime of crafts, musical-poetic creation, town castle and church construction. In the Middle Ages long before the Mongol invasion, Buddhism began to be practiced in the Sayan-Altai territory. The scientists opine that it was practiced due to the efforts of the representatives of Kyrgyz nobility who studied in China and Tibet.[13] The Buddhist symbols were borrowed and interpreted by Kyrgyz master-jewelers and became apparent in the pieces of decorative-applied arts.[14] Apart from it, some Buddhist statuettes, the remnants of Buddhist temples and suburgans, were found in Khakassia. In the later periods of history of the peoples of the Sayan-Altai, Buddhism continued to influence their world outlook, though it was widely practiced only in Tuva.

But the cult and secular musical instruments of the Sayan-Altai Turks that have analogues in the culture of the peoples of Central, Middle and Southern Asia are preserved till today. One can draw some interesting conclusions if one compares, for example, the names and the construction of such musical instruments as metal hand bells and little bells used both in cattle breeding, hunting and shaman practices and in Buddhist cult: *khongyro* (in Khakas language) – *khonguraa* (Tuvinian) – *kongyrau* (Kazakh) – *ghungru* (Hindi). These names among the Khakass, Tuva and Altai people are known to have meant bronze, brass and iron bells of a trapezoidal shape as well as little bells (*sharkuntsy*, *botalo*) of a round form made of the same material. The latter could be 10–48 mm in diameter and consisted of two halves connected in the wide part. The lower part had a cross-like cutting with a hidden reed in it. When shaken, the tinkling of the bell was tuneful with "a shuffling note". Such bells were hung on the necks of cattle, used in hunting, sewn to shaman ritual clothes, tied to a diametrical shaman drum cross-beam and so forth. Today they are used in musical practice. A number of such small bells are sewn to a strip of cloth that is put on an Indian dancer's ankle, serving as an accompaniment to a dance.

In our opinion, there is some similarity in the name and structure of wind-instruments of a flute group: *choor* (Kyrgyz), *shoor* (Khakas, Altai, Tuvinian), *tsuur* (Mongolian), *sur* (Buryat), *bansuri* (Hindi). The name of a north Indian flute originates from two words: *bans* meaning "bamboo" and *sur* meaning "melody".[15] The Turkic names of a bamboo pipe like hollow angelica are *shoor* (*choor, tsoor, tsuur, sur*), which in our opinion goes back to a verb "shorla".[16] There is its derivative noun *sorlaas* (chorlas) in the Khakass language which means "a gutter made of angelica" for water flow, drinking water.[17] Besides, the words *choor* (*tsoor, tsuurai, kurai*) mean stuff for making a pipe "hollow angelica" as well as "echo". Thus, all these names are close in meaning and can be compared in a line – purling-echo, echo-melody – and can be applied to musical instruments of a group of longitudinal and diametrical flutes, one of the oldest shepherd musical instruments.

As for string instruments, some links can be drawn with dulcimer instruments: Khakas *chatkhan*, Tuvinian *chadagan*, Indian *santur*. Stringed bowed instruments are Khakas *yykh* (Altaian *ikili*, Tuvinian *ighil*) and Indian *sarangi*. Despite the difference in the outer structure of the body of the latter instruments, the number

Figure 5.1 An Altaian-Khakassian flute *shoor*

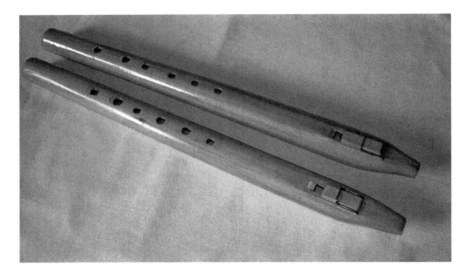

Figure 5.2 A Buryatian flute *sur*

Figure 5.3 An Indian flute *bansuri*

of strings, the stuff and technique of its making, the technique of playing them is remarkable. An *yykh* (*ikili, ighil*) performer and an Indian *sarangi* player changes the pitch of sounds touching the strings with a nail plate of his left hand while running a bow over the strings with his right hand. Such a technique of playing string-bow instruments, unlike pressing strings with the tips of the fingers, is typical of the musical culture of some Turkic peoples and the Mongol people.

Santur translated from Persian means "a hundred melodies".[18] A hundred steel strings are stretched on a trapezoidal resonator box made of mulberry tree or a nut-tree; sound is produced with two upturned wooden sticks. The instrument has a status of an Indian classical and Sufiana instrument. Similar instruments are played both in Europe and Asia. At present an Indian *santur* has more in common in construction and sound with a Tuvinian *chadagan* and Buryat *iochin*. A Khakass *chatkhan* can be compared with *santur* only partially. *Chatkhan* is inseparably connected with legends of heroic epics, where it is one of the attributes of a hero – *alyp* and a *chatkhan* player at the same time and is glorified by him as "a golden, sixty-stringed *chatkhan* with a resounding resonant voice"; its sounds cast a spell over all nature and help the hero in various epic situations.

The main genres of Khakas, Altai and Tuvinian folklore were created in the Middle Ages: myths, legends, clan, genealogical, historical stories, heroic epics, fairy tales about animals, songs, shaman incantation, children's folklore, proverbs, sayings and so forth. According to the research of Brontoy Bedyurov, a song is believed to have been brought to Altai from faraway India and people are believed to have been taught to sing by the goddess of song.[19] In old times people went to India and admired the art of Indian singers and musicians, wishing they had songs in their motherland. A goddess-patron of music and songs heard it and ordered a song to fly over the Himalayas to teach other peoples to compose a song and to play musical instruments. Thus having visited the Mongol people, a song flew to Tuva. It taught local people to play a resonant *topshur*, a violin – *ikili*, a reed pipe – *shoor*, a small lip vargan – *komus* and other instruments. Since that time the Tuvinian people have become famous as talented singers and musicians. The song visited the Tuvinian land and later it flew to the heart of Altai and was very glad to see the beauty of the local nature and the mountain peaks covered with glaciers looking like the Himalayas. It was greeted everywhere there with honor and respect. Wherever it flew, a lot of people gathered there to learn songs, to play musical instruments. Since then there are so many talented singers and musicians in an Altai village who are highly respected by the ordinary people. Ever since the Altai people and a song have become inseparable. Any kind of human activity: grazing cattle, riding a horse, working out hides, making hay is accompanied with a song. Everything one does to the accompaniment of a song turns out quite nice. They sing both the songs taught by the heavenly messenger from India and the ones they have composed themselves.[20] So this legend confirms the presence of common features both in the instrumental musical cultures and in vocal art of the Turkic people of the Sayan-Altai and India. In our opinion, it is especially clear in melodic ornamentals, timbre and texture way of woman folk singing of Altai and Tuvinian singing culture and in improvising and oral art forms that haven't lost their significance today.

The myths and legends about heroes-defenders of the Motherland, brave warriors who fought for the freedom and happiness of their fellow tribesmen are the basis of present theater performances in Khakassia. The acting is accompanied with singing and music, the sound of traditional musical instruments. Among such performances one can mention the performances of the Khakas Musical-Drama Theater *Chitigen*: *Abakhay Pakhta, Akhol, Forgotten Gods*; *Kharool and a small black horse, Khan-Mirgen, A wicked raven* of A. M. Topanov Khakas national theater. There are such forms of theater art in the dramaturgy of the peoples of India as well.

To sum it up, the culture and art of the population of Southern Siberia as well as Indian art is several millennia old. There was long fruitful trade and cultural cooperation among the peoples of Southern Siberia, Central Asia and India. As research shows, some cultural and aesthetic values are beneficial for being promoted, borrowed, thought over and kept on in art, amateur and folk creative work of the present reality. Unfortunately, only a few aspects of cultural cooperation that seem to us most obvious and accessible are highlighted in this article. Further research of these and other problems of culture and art may lead to more interesting results and promote discovering more valuable, still unknown facts.

Notes

1. V. Zubkov, "First Settlers in Khakassia". *Heritage of Generations: Popular Science Magazine*. Moscow, "Archeological Heritage" Archeological Monuments Protection Assistance Fund, 2009. No. 1. pp. 28–33.
2. V. Tarakanov, "What the 'Third Eye' Looks At". *Heritage of Generations: Popular Science Magazine*. Moscow, "Archeological Heritage" Archeological Monuments Protection Assistance Fund, 2009. No. 1. pp. 80–85.
3. *Khakassia: Guide Book*. Moscow, Avangard, 2003. p. 53.
4. A. Gotlib and A. Nagler, "Barsuchiy Log – 'Royal' Burial Monument of the Scythian Period in Southern Siberia". *Heritage of Generations: Popular Science Magazine*. Moscow, "Archeological Heritage" Archeological Monuments Protection Assistance Fund, 2009. No. 1. pp. 54–61; A. I. Gotlib and V. S. Zubkov, "Ancient Historical and Cultural Heritage of Khakassia". *Himalayan and Central Asian Studies* New Delhi, April–September 2009. pp. 29–41.
5. S. Taskarakov, "Sacred Petroglyphs of Khakassia". *Heritage of Generations: Popular Science Magazine*. Moscow, "Archeological Heritage" Archeological Monuments Protection Assistance Fund, 2009. No. 1. pp. 44–7.
6. Ancient Siberia: "Culture and Art of Ancient Population of Siberia. 7th Century B.C.–13th Century A.D." Exhibition Guide Book. Hermitage. Leningrad, Avrora, 1976. p. 24.
7. Ibid., p. 12.
8. Ya V. Vasilkov, Indian Story Identification on the Mirror from Rogozikha-1 Burial Mound, Altai (5th century B.C.). In: *Actual Issues of the History of Sayan-Altai and Adjacent Areas International Practical Research Conference*, October 6–12, 2001. Edited by L. V. Anzhiganova. Abakan, Khakas State University Publishing House, 2002. pp. 42–5.
9. I. Tashtandinov, "Tashtyk Plaquettes in the Funds of Khakas Natural History Museum". Heritage of Generations: Popular Science Magazine. Moscow, "Archeological Heritage" Archeological Monuments Protection Assistance Fund, 2009. No. 1. pp. 86–9.
10. P. I. Chebodaev, *History of Khakassia*. Abakan, Khakas Book Publishing House, 1992. 156 pp.

11 V. Ya Butanaev, *Khakas Ethnic Culture: Higher Educational Establishments History Students Manual*. Khakas State University Publishing House, 1998. 352 pp.
12 L.A. Evtyukhova, "Stone Sculptures of Siberia and Mongolia". MIA No. 24. *Siberian Archeological Research Materials*. Vol. 1. Moscow, 1952. pp. 72–120.
13 V. Ya Butanaev, *Burkhanism of Sayan-Altai Turks*. Abakan, Khakas State University Publishing House, 2003. p 11.
14 N.V. Leontjev, "About Buddhist Motifs in Medieval Toreutics of Khakassia. (On Materials of the Minusinsk Natural History Museum Collection)". In: *Historical, Cultural Links of the Peoples of Southern Siberia*. Abakan, "Khakassia" Aggregate Polygraph Enterprise, 1988. pp. 184–92.
15 R. Anand, "Indian Flute (Bansuri). From Traditions to the Present". In: Folk Music of Eurasia: Articles of the Scientific Conference of the II International Festival "Sounds of Eurasian Instruments". Edited by V.V. Kitov. Ulan-Ude, "Informpolis", 2007. pp. 54–9.
16 *Large Turkish-Russian Dictionary*: 200,000 Words and Word Combinations. Moscow, Russian Language, 1998. 958 pp.; *Khakas-Russian Dictionary*. Edited by N.A. Baskakov. Moscow, Foreign and National Dictionaries State Publishing House, 1953. 487 pp.; *Oirot-Russian Dictionary*. Compiled by N.A. Baskakov and T.M. Toshchakova. Moscow, Ogiz, 1947. 312 pp.; *Khakas-Russian Historic Ethnographic Dictionary: Russian-Turkic Republics Arts Teachers Manual*. By V. Ya. Butanaev. Abakan, "Khakassia" Aggregate Polygraph Enterprise, 1999. 240 pp.
17 Ibid.
18 R.K. Majumdar, "Santur – Indian Cimbalos". From Traditions to the Present – Folk Music of Eurasia: Articles of the Scientific Conference of the II International Festival "Sounds of Eurasian Instruments". Edited by V.V. Kitov. Ulan-Ude, "Informpolis", 2007. pp. 44–7.
19 B.A. Bedyurov, *Word About Altai*. Gorno-Altaisk, Altaisk Publishing House, 1990. 400 pp.
20 Ibid., pp. 162–3.

6 Heritage in Central Asia
The case of nomads

Baatr U. Kitinov

Central Asia has been under the influence of Indian culture since ancient times. Buddhism started to spread all over this vast region from the beginning of the new era. Its traces are found in the ruins of stupas, viharas and monuments, as well as in political actions of the past. Dealing with various forms of Buddhism in different parts of this huge continent, one should remember their Indian origin and main features. This article focusses on the Indian Buddhist heritage among nomads of Central Asia, who have contributed a lot to the propagation and spread of Buddha's teaching across this vast region.

Steps to North

The expansion of Buddhism in Asia was peaceful and occurred in several ways. Shakyamuni Buddha himself set the precedent. Being primarily a teacher and tutor, he traveled to nearby kingdoms to share his insights with those who were receptive and interested. Likewise, he instructed his monks to go forth in the world and expound upon his thoughts and teachings. He did not ask others to denounce and give up their own religion and convert to a new one, and he was not seeking to establish his own religion. He was merely trying to help others to overcome their unhappiness and suffering and improve their understanding of the world. Later generations of followers who were inspired by Buddha's example shared with others his methods that they found useful in their lives. This is how what is now called "Buddhism" spread far and wide.

Sometimes the process evolved organically. For example, when Buddhist merchants travelled to and settled in different lands, some members of the local populations naturally developed an interest in these foreigners' beliefs. Such process occurred with Buddhism in the oasis states along the Silk Route in Central Asia during the two centuries before the Christian era and later times.[1]

Often, however, the dissemination was due primarily to the influence of a powerful monarch who had adopted and supported Buddhism himself. In the mid-third century BC, for instance, Buddhism spread in Northern India as the result of personal endorsement by Mauryan King Ashoka. This great empire-builder did not force his subjects to adopt the Buddhist faith. But by posting edicts engraved on iron and stone pillars throughout his realm exhorting his people to lead an ethical life and by following these principles himself, he inspired others to adopt

Buddha's teachings. King Ashoka also actively proselytized outside his kingdom by sending missions to distant Eurasian lands: Greece, Egypt and the Middle East. Other Central Asian kings, such as Altan Khan, the sixteenth-century leader of the Eastern Mongols (Tumets), invited Tibetan Buddhist priests to their lands and proclaimed Buddhism as official creed of the nation in order to unite people and consolidate their rule.

If Buddha Shakyamuni told people not to follow his teaching out of blind faith, but to examine it carefully before accepting it, how less so should people accept Buddha's teachings out of coercion from zealous missionaries? Thus, for instance, when Neiji Toin, the well-known Oirat lama, in the early seventeenth century tried to bribe Eastern Mongol nomads by offering them livestock for each Buddhist verse they memorized, people complained to the highest authorities. At the end, this overbearing teacher was punished and exiled.

According to the prominent Indian scholar Prof. Lokesh Chandra, the first period of the spread of Buddhism in Central Asia was connected with the Uyghur, Khotanese and other Central Asian peoples.[2] Buddhism appeared in Afghanistan as early as the mid-third century BC. According to the Pali *Mahāvamsa* chronicle, Buddhist monks from the countries of Pallavabhogga and Alasandra arrived to take part in a Buddhist festival. Alasandra was probably Alexandria in the region of modern Kabul, while Pallavabhogga lay on the eastern frontier of Parthia – in Margiana or a Parthian subject state in Afghanistan.[3]

In the first century BC Buddhism was already known and widespread in Bactria, and later the teaching reached modern Xinjiang and continued moving eastward. An Shih-kao, the Buddhist priest from Margiana, reached China in AD 148, where he became known as a translator, who translated about ninety sutras.[4] Sogdiana, another known region of Central Asia, was also an important point of Buddhist civilization. According to the Chinese source *Gao Sen Chuan*, a renowned preacher, "KanSen-hui was of Sogdian origin". In AD 247, the tenth year of the reign of U dynasty, he came to Nanjing. "At that time the U lands had just been sprinkled by the Great Law (i.e. the Buddha's teachings) and were not yet soaked by its spirit". After some tests by the ruler Sun Quan, this monk founded a monastery Tszyanchusy ("Monastery, which laid the beginning"). "The surrounding lands were called as Village of Buddha. The Great Law gave shoots in the grounds of Tszyantszo".[5]

The Tokharians also played significant role in the spread of Buddhism. It should be noted, that Buddhism penetrated to Bactria-Tokharistan in early times – perhaps, it happened during the reign of Kanishka the First, the Kushan ruler. In the era of the highest power of the Kushan state (second to fourth centuries), Buddhists were able to spread their teaching up to the valley of the Surkhan Darya River. Even after the fall of the Kushans, when the Sassanid dynasty established its power in Persia, Buddhism was flourishing in the region, and the famous Buddha statues in the Bamiyan region of modern Afghanistan were erected.

During the Sassanid period, Buddhism penetrated further to Merv (the modern town of Mary in Turkmenistan), where the Buddhist monuments appeared (fourth to sixth centuries). The considerable dimension of the monuments allows one to assume that in the Kara-Kum Desert and near the Caspian Sea the Buddhist community enjoyed considerable influence. North of Bactria and the Merv region were the endpoints (at least to date) of the north-west spread of Buddhism at that time. In Termez, in Balkh (the capital of former Bactria-Tokharistan), where large Buddhist temples were erected, the local Buddhist communities were rich and influential. According to the testimony of XuanZang and Hui Chao, the famous Chinese pilgrims, the construction of the Buddhist monuments in Tokharistan was still continuing in the sixth century.

Tokharians have translated Buddhist sutras, such as *Ashtasahasrika Prajna-paramita Sutra*, *Vajraccheddika Prajna-paramita Sutra* and others, from Sanskrit into their own language. It was due to these translations that the Mongolian, Turkish and other peoples became acquainted with the Indian Buddhist culture. Of course, the local forms of Buddhism differed considerably from each other. China, where Buddhist teaching appeared around the first century AD, developed its own tradition of Buddhism, and later the Chinese form of *Mahayana* spread to Korea, Japan and North Vietnam. The Tibetan *Mahayana* tradition, founded by Guru Padmasambhava, Tilopa, Gampopa, Tsonkhapa and other prominent lamas, inherited the full historical development of Indian Buddhism, and spread throughout the Himalayan regions and to modern Mongolia, East Turkestan, Kyrgyzstan, Kazakhstan, northern Inner China, Manchuria and Siberia. It is well-known that many Buddhist texts, written in Sanskrit, had been translated into Tibetan, and Tibetan sacred buildings (temples, monasteries) were often decorated in Indian (Indo-Tibetan) style.

Close to the time of Mongolian invasions, the Uyghurs were able to create a vast collection of Buddhist literature, translating from Sanskrit, Tibetan, Chinese and other languages. The Buddhist treatises in Uyghur were known in Dunhuang (where some caves still keep the frescoes painted by Indian Buddhists), in the Tangut state and among West and East Mongolian tribes. Uyghurs were the first teachers of Buddhism to the Mongol nations, as it is pointed out in Tibetan and Mongolian sources and by the scholars.

Mongolian nations and Buddhism

Mongolian invasions completely changed the religious map of Central Asia and the whole of Eurasia. The Mongols were able to support Buddhism at the time of the great Khagans, for example Kublai and his brothers, especially Hulagu Ilkhan, who governed over Persia. Rashid-al-Din wrote in his chronicle that in China there were "many lamas... from Hindus and others"[6] at the end of Kublai's reign. Marco Polo agrees with him: "these witches are called Tibetans and Kashmiris; they are nations of idolaters... their monasteries and abbeys are large".[7]

The Ilkhanid Iran was covered by the Buddhist pagodas and temples. Many Buddhist teachers and priests were invited from Tibet, India, Kashmir and China. As it was pointed out by the Armenian historian Gandzaketi:

> [Hulagu] has built dwellings for giant idols, collecting for the purpose all kinds of craftsmen who worked with stone and wood and painters as well.

> These [Buddhist clerics] are wizards and magicians; they can use their magic skills to make horses and camels talk, as well as the dead people ... All of them are priests and shave their heads and beards, and wear yellow robes and worship everything, but most of all Shakmoni [i.e. Buddha Shakyamuni] and Madrid [i.e. Bodhisattva Maitreya].[8]

Another Armenian historian, Vardan the Great, also describes the religious predilections of Hulagu:

> He was deceived by astrologers and priests of some pictures, called Shakmunia, who, as they say, was a God living for 3,040 years and will be still living for another 37 *t'umans* (a *t'uman* equals 10,000 years). They say he will be succeeded by another (God) whose name is Mandrin. The priests, whom he believed and followed to decide whether to wage a war or not, were called Doins.[9]

The fate of this region began to change in 1242, when after the death of Ugedei (the son of Chinggis Khan) his widow Tureghen-khatun began to replace the old dignitaries, who were from the circle of Chinggis Khan. One of her first decisions was to send Argun-Aka from Oirats (Western Mongols) to Khorasan (Greater Persia) as governor. According to Rashid-al-Din, Argun-Aka's origin was not clear, but he was from Oirat tribes, and he grew up as member of Keshig. Later, being in Khorasan, he was able to develop the fruitful economic relations with nearby regions, for instance, with the north-western parts of India. Argun-Aka is well-known in history due to his achievements as a politician during the reign of the early Ilkhans. He was a faithful Buddhist. Perhaps, he was able to be in direct contact with Buddhist priests from the proper lands, for example, from Kashmir – Buddhist lamas from this part of India were known in different parts of the Mongolian empire, and in lands of Ilkhans.

According to various sources, Ghazan-Ilkhan (r. 1295–1304), who converted to Islam in the autumn of 1295, was constantly surrounded in his childhood by foreign Baksi-idolaters (i.e. Buddhist priests). Rashid-al-Din pointed out that Ghazan built up "the beautiful shrines" "and exposed himself to mortification and asceticism".[10] When Ghazan united the empire after the execution of his rival cousin Baidu, in his first royal decree he ordered to destroy all churches of any religion (except mosques), including the Buddhist temples, in Baghdad, Tabriz and all over the kingdom.[11] The Buddhists, including Mongols, had to accept Islam or leave Persia. Most of them accepted the new religion and remained under Ghazan's rule, while the rest fled eastward towards Central Asia (Tibet and Mongolia).

If in India Buddhism reckoned with the centuries-old culture of Vedas and Upanishads, in other parts of Central Asia and Eurasia it reached the popular layers of societies only after their local gods were introduced into the Buddhist pantheon. There was another important thing: Buddhism usually supported the ideological basis of the state. This very feature of Buddhism, which helped to sanctify the united state against factionalism, was an advantage in its early stage of establishment in India, where Buddhists were allies of the rulers of the ancient Indian states in their struggle against the clan autonomy.[12]

The spread and strength of Buddhism in the East (East Turkestan) and West (up to the Caspian Sea) parts of Central Asia was supported by various nationalities, among them the West Mongolian tribes of Oirats, or Kalmyks, playing a considerable role. Actually they are the only people who, being familiar with Buddhism from Chingghis Khan's time up to today follow this religion; also they are the single Mongolian-speaking population in Europe. Therefore, the author emphasizes the connections of Indian Buddhist culture with the Oirat Buddhist culture (way of life).

Oirats as the keepers of the Buddhist path

Being in Persia along with Hulagu and his descendants in the thirteenth century, and again arriving at the Caspian shores at the beginning of the seventeenth century, these nomads (Oirats) continued to follow Buddhism, despite the local negative trends and neighboring different faiths and cultures. Oirats, even being surrounded in Persia by Muslim culture, kept their traditions closely related with the Buddhist ones. For instance, the sources inform us about living Buddhist customs among them at the time of Arghun Il-khan (rul. 1284–1291):

> On the 7th day of the Safar month of the same year Tugluk Khatun, daughter of Tengiz-Turgay from (tribe of) Oirat, mother of Hitai-Ogul Prince, passed away. On the 7th day of Rabi al-Awwal month the messengers from ulus of Nokay came to Juy-i-nov river banks and delivered a *sharil*. The idolaters have such kind of (belief): when Shakyamuni Burhan has been burning, his *pishdil*, a bone transparent, like glass beads, did not burn. They opined that: if anyone, who has reached the highest position, like Shakyamuni-Burhan, will be burned, one's *sharil* will not burn. In short, when it (*sharil*) was carrying, Arghun-khan went out to meet, he was showered with flowers, (they) cheered and indulged in a few days of feasting and amusements.[13]

Those Oirats, who inhabited Central Asian region (East Turkestan) in the fifteenth and sixteenth centuries, seem to have had quite limited ties with India. Nevertheless, they were able not only to keep the Indian Buddhist heritage, but even to have the trade contacts with Indian merchants. There are, at least, two important evidences, which prove the information pointed out earlier. Kalmyks, perhaps, were the only Buddhists from Central Asia who have had their business in faraway Hurmuz (Ormuz), the biggest seaport in the Persian Gulf in the Middle Ages. The well-known Persian traveler Abd al-Razzaq al Samarkandi (1413–1482), who visited Ormuz in 1442, pointed out:

> Hurmuz . . . is a port without any similar one all over the world. Merchants from all seven climates – from Egypt, Syria, Asia Minor, Azerbaijan, Iraq

Arabic and Persian, provinces of Fars, Khorasan, Mava-ar-nahar, Turkestan, Kipchak steppe, from lands inhabited by Kalmyks, from Chinese provinces and Beijing – go to this port. Inhabitants of the ocean coasts come here from China, from Java, from Bengal, from Ceylon . . . In this city, people of all faiths, as well as idolaters are in a large number.[14]

One can assume that the merchants from Indian subcontinent also could be counted among the partners of Kalmyks. According to Marco Polo, to Ormuz

> merchants come from India with ships loaded with spices and precious stones, pearls, cloths of silk and gold, elephants' tusks, and other goods; they sell it to the merchants who in turn carry all over the world to dispose of again.[15]

As for keeping the Indian Buddhist heritage, there is an interesting page in the history of Buddhism among Kalmyks. It deals with the sandalwood statue of the Buddha, known as *Tsandan Jo wo*. As researched by scholars, the Tokharian monk named Dharmanandy wrote in AD 385 that one day Buddha Shakyamuni went to Tushita heaven to preach *Dharma* to his mother Mahamaya. At that time, Raja Prasenajit of Udayana, being sad, wished to see the Enlightened Lord. Then Maudgalyayana (Molon-toyin in the Mongolian language), one of the closest disciples of the Buddha, using the miraculous power, brought the art masters to Buddha so they could see him, and returning to Earth, they created a life-size statue of Buddha from sandalwood. Later this statue was kept in various parts of India. In the fourth century, a Kashmiri monk named Kumarayama brought the statue over the Himalayas to the town of Kucha in Xinjiang. The local ruler asked him to forsake his monastic vows and marry his sister Jivaka. Kumarajiva, their son (344–413), became known as a great Buddhist philosopher and translator. He studied *Hinayana* and *Mahayana* scriptures in Kashmir under the guidance of Bandhudatta, a famous Buddhist monk of his time. He became known as an outstanding Buddhist scholar all over Central Asia and in Northern India. In AD 384 Lu Guang, the general of former Qin (351–394), was sent to Kucha to bring Kumarajiva to Fu Jian, ruler of former Qin. Kumarajiva had to go to China, taking the sandalwood Buddha statue with him.

It was the beginning of long story of the statue's travels all over China, which lasted over fifteen centuries. Sarat Chandra Das noted that the sandalwood Buddha statue had been moved from Bodh Gaya to Bactria in the third century BC, and from there it was moved to China at the end of the first century AD. He also noted that the statue was stored in the temple Zandan-sy (Hunzhansy, built in 1665) in Beijing and was seen (by him) in 1885.[16] Actually, the statue, while being in Beijing, changed its location six times, moving from one temple to another. For Buddhists, the statue was an important object of worship; it was accepted as the main Buddhist shrine of Beijing. When Zandan-sy monastery was destroyed in 1900, during the Boxer Rebellion in China, the statue was taken to the Russian region of Transbaikalia by Buryat Cossaks, and is now kept in Egituidatsan.

It is obvious that the history of the statue has been little known until now due to the lack of specific references to the dynastic periods and the abbots of the temple.

72 Baatr U. Kitinov

Figure 6.1 Statue of Tsandan Jo wo in Egitui Datsan
Photo by author

There are some archival documents in the Kalmyk National Archive in Russia, which lead us to assume that the Kalmyk lamas, who lived in Beijing in the first half of the seventeenth century, were involved in the attempt of bringing this statue to Kalmyk lands in the Volga River region of Russia.[17] This author believes

Heritage in Central Asia 73

Figure 6.2 Egitui Datsan
Photo by author

that perhaps the Kalmyk spiritual leaders wished to build the same temple and keep the statue in the Kalmyk lands. The aim was to guarantee the prosperity of the Buddha's teachings among Kalmyks, who lived very far away from the religious centres of Buddhism. The new data allows to admit that they wanted to bring the statue itself to Kalmyks. Perhaps, when in 1730 the members of Kalmyk delegation to Lhasa and Beijing discussed the problem of "steppe way" (one of the problems in studies, dedicated to the exodus of Kalmyks to China in 1771), it could be not the way for the exodus of Kalmyks to China, as it is usually supposed by scholars, but the real way, or path to deliver the sandalwood statue to the Kalmyk lands. The fate of this statue has also been discussed in a recent publication by Prof. Lokesh Chandra.[18]

Other issue related to the discussion is the sutras; there are quite a lot of Indian sutras which have been translated into other languages and thus remained in the literature and folklore of many peoples. For instance, the well-known Golden Light Sutra (*Suvarnapramhosottama sutra*), an extremely important *Mahayana* sutra, was translated into Chinese, Tibetan and other languages (Khotanese, Old Turkic, Tangut, Tibetan, Mongolian, Manchu, Korean and Japanese). It became one of the most important sutras among many nations, including Kalmyks. The sutra also expounds upon the vows of the Hindu goddesses Saraswati and Lakshmi to protect any *bhikshu*, or monk, who will uphold and teach the sutra. The sutra discusses the necessity of defending the country and calls for patriotism. It was important to explain to the new followers of the teaching that it would be wrong to accept Buddhism as teaching, which cannot defend itself.

It should be noted that the founder of this religion – the Buddha – was born and grew up in a military environment. Belonging to the *varn* of Kshatriyas, that is, being born among the military caste, the future Buddha had proper military training. According to sources, from his childhood he was a winner in various kinds of military-sports competition, as it now would be called: in the javelin, archery, horseback riding and so forth. Scientists have already called attention to the military side of the Buddha's teachings.[19] For example, Robert Thurman wrote the article "Tibet and the Monastic Army of Peace", where he discusses the issues of interaction of war and peace, the Buddhist ethics and so forth.[20] Besides, Johannes de Groot has also drawn attention to the fact that "Sutra (*Brahmajalasutra* – B.K.) translated by Kumarajiva ... allows the violence (including the armed violence), if it is aimed at the salvation of the living beings".[21] Groot wrote that one should not be surprised by the presence in Chinese books of different passages about the participation of Buddhist monks in military expeditions.[22] Scientists believe that although historical research on Buddhist government is far to be completed, it seems likely that the tradition has defined the doctrine of just war; moreover, the Buddhist texts do permit, if the government is unfair, to organize the uprising and so forth.[23]

The Golden Light Sutra had played a very special role in the growth of nomadic states in Central Asia. Its text had been known to Oirats before their "official conversion" into the teaching of the Geluk Tibetan Buddhist school in the 1570s. Thus, when lama Sodnam Gyatso, the leader of the Geluk, visited East Mongol in 1578, one of the Oirat Khans came to worship him. In the *History of Tibet*, the Great Fifth Dalai Lama wrote: "Teacher Sonam Gyatso had an Oirat visitor who presented him with Sutra of Golden Light. When the Teacher asked him about the title of the sacred text, the Oirat answered that it was Altan Gerel".[24]

What is the specific character of the Sutra of Golden Light? It was one of the few sutras which, when read regularly, ensured not only "maintenance of the interaction" with the deities-patrons of the teaching, but also helped "to protect the country". Besides various formulas, philosophical arguments, lengthy description of Bodhisattvas and so forth, the sutra contained instructions on how to rule the people and state.

The idea of support of *sangha* by the local authorities was one of the core foundations for the spreading and flourishing of Buddha's teaching. Sometimes the local kings have been called *Chakravartins*, the leaders, who unite the spiritual and secular powers. This idea also had another appearance when the civil leader was able to appoint the Buddhist monk as his spiritual adviser or assistant. One of the most evident examples is the time of reign of the Mongol Yuan dynasty in China.

In 1260 Emperor Kublai issued a decree, where he granted title of the State Tutor *dishi* (ti-shih, Imperial Tutor) to Phagpa-lama from Sakya Tibetan Buddhist school. Thankful for such high estimation, the Sakya hierarchy identified Kublai with Bodhisattva Manjushri and granted him the title of *Chakravartin*.[25]

Later this concept of the "two powers", that is the unity of the secular and spiritual powers was developed in the book *A White History – Tsagan Tuuji* (*Arban buyantu nom-un cagan teuke*: *A White History of Ten Virtues*): the supreme lama had no right to interfere in secular affairs, and the emperor provides every support in religious sphere; the lama did become the religious tutor and teacher of the emperor; the emperor did become his pupil. Due to this theory, the interactions between Tibet and China developed into an alliance known as *yon mchod* – very special system of relationship between religious leader and secular ruler.[26]

The lama was recognized as the live Buddha while the emperor was *Chakravartin*. This special argument appeared in Sakya Pandit's letter citing Godan Khagan, who said that if he, Khagan, secures peace by means of the secular law (*mi chos*) and lamas do the same by means of the sacred law (*lha chos*), then the Shakyamuni teachings would go beyond the borders of the "outer ocean". Khagan asked to propagate the teachings in peace and tranquility of mind while he would provide Lama with everything necessary.[27] According to famous Mongolian scholar Sh. Bira, the concept of the "two principles of the state administration were first developed by this very lama (Pagba) on the Kublai Khagan's urgent request. Of course, Pagba relied both on the Buddhist ethical-moral teachings and on the old Indian and Tibetan traditions".[28]

Conclusion

Indian Buddhist heritage in Central Asia has long and interesting history. From the first century AD it became the principal trend of cultural, social, economic and other spheres of many nations, and its special characteristics were developed after its conjunction with the local customs and traditions. The nomads played a significant role in the maintenance and further evolution of Buddha's teaching, especially Mongol nations and particularly Oirats.

Nowadays it is obvious that Buddhist culture and civilization is still able to make a positive impact on regional interactions of peoples, cultures and civilizations. Indeed, the growing process of interaction (so-called globalization) causes the phenomenon of activation of Buddhist civilization. Revitalization is to be understood as a necessary process, carried out in social life, either to revive or for the protection of certain provisions of its culture.

In modern times, the Indian Buddhist heritage in Central Asia becomes more and more important. Many scholars and politicians consider the Buddhist tradition as the organic and necessary part of the greater Indian civilization. The Buddhist period of Indian civilization played a vital role in the life and fate of many nations in Central Asia. The Indian Buddhist heritage of this vast region, which consists of sacred monuments and statues, translated or written books, events and processes, is further developing in various nations of this huge continent, which played key roles in preservation, promotion and propagation of Buddha's teaching.

Remarks

[1] *Keshig* – or Turkhaout-Keshig (in Mong., Turk.) – the bodyguard from time of Chinggis-Khan.
[2] *Sharil* – from Sanskrit *sharira*, means "bone", "solid support". Usually defines the magical remains of the cremated body of saint person, and looks like little balls.
[3] *Hurmuz* (*Ormus*) – is modern seaport of Bandar Abbas in Southern Iran.

Notes

1. For more information about Buddhism's role on the Silk Road see: Elverskog Johan, *Buddhism and Islam on the Silk Road*. Philadelphia, University of Pennsylvania Press, 2010.
2. Lokesh Chandra, *Materials for a History of Tibetan Literature*. Delhi, SPS, 1967. Also see: Lokesh Chandra, *Buddhism across the Grasslands of Chinggis Khan*. New Delhi, Aditya Prakashan, 2013. p. 17.
3. B.A. Litvinskiy and T.I. Zeimal, *Buddiyskiymonastyr' Adzhina-tepa (Tajikistan): Raskopki. Arkhitektura. Iskusstvo* [*The Buddhist Monastery of AdzhinaTepa (Tajikistan). Excavations. Architecture. Art*]. St. Petersburg, Nestor-Istoriya, 2010. pp. 231–2. (In Russian).
4. M. Ye. Kravtsova, *Istoriya kul'tury Kitaya* [*The History of Chinese Culture*]. St. Petersburg, Lan, 1999. p. 263. (In Russian).
5. Khuey Tszyao, *Zhizneopisaniyadostoynykhmonakhov* (*Gaosenchzhuan'*) [Hui-Jiao, *The Lives of the Eminent Monks (GaoSenChuan)*]. Moscow, Nauka, 1991. pp. 110–12. (In Russian).
6. Rashīd al-Dīn Fadhlallāh Hamadānī, *Sbornik letopisey – Dzhami at-tavarikh* [*Compendium of Chronicles*]. www.vostlit.info/Texts/rus16/Rasidaddin_3/frametext8.html. (In Russian).
7. Dzhovannidel' Plano Karpini, *IstoriyaMongalov. Gil'om de Rubruk. Puteshestviye v vostochnyyestrany. Kniga Marko Polo* [Giovanny da Piandel Carpine, *History of the Mongols. Guillaume de Rubrouck. A Journey to the Eastern Countries. Marco Polo's Book*]. Moscow, Mysl', 1997. pp. 243–4 (In Russian).
8. Gandzaketi Kirakos, *Istoriya Armenii* [*History of Armenia*]. Moscow, 1976. p. 239. (In Russian).
9. Vardan the Great, *Vseobschaya istoriya* [*World History*]. www.vostlit.info/Texts/rus11/Vardan/frametext4.htm. (In Russian).
10. Rashīd al-Dīn Fadhlallāh Hamadānī, *Sbornik letopisey – Dzhami at-tavarikh*. [*Compendium of Chronicles*]. Tr. by A.K. Arends. Moscow-Leningrad, 1946. Vol. III. p. 162. (In Russian).
11. Ibid., p. 165.
12. G.M. Bongard-Levin, *IndiyaepokhiMaur'yev* [*India of the Mauryan Era*]. Moscow, Nauka, 1973. p. 235. (In Russian).
13. Rashīd al-Dīn Fadhlallāh Hamadānī, *Sbornik letopisey – Dzhami at-tavarikh*. pp. 117–18.
14. Ahmad ibn Majid, *Kniga pol'z ob osnovakh i pravilakh morskoy nauki* [*The Book of Prophets on the Basics and Rules of Marine Science*]. Moscow, Nauka, 1985. p. 125. (In Russian).
15. Dzhovannidel' Plano Karpini, *IstoriyaMongalov*. p. 215. (In Russian).
16. Sarat Chandra Das, *Tibetan-English Dictionary*. Calcutta, Bengal Secretariat Book Depot, 1903. p. 996.
17. Baatr Kitinov, "Shakur Lama: The Last Attempt to Build the Buddhist State". In: *Buddhism in Mongolian History, Culture, and Society*. Oxford: Oxford University Press, 2015. pp. 37–52.

18 Lokesh Chandra, *Buddhism across the Grasslands of Chinggis Khan*. p. 56.
19 *Buddhism and Violence*. Edited by M. Zimmermann with the assistance of Chiew Hui Ho and Philip Pierce. Nepal, Lumbini International Research Institute, 2006.
20 R.A.F. Thurman, "Tibet and the Monastic Army of Peace". In: *Inner Peace, World Peace: Essays on Buddhism and Nonviolence*. Edited by K. Kraft. Albany, State University of New York Press, 1992. pp. 77–90.
21 Khuey Tszyao, *Zhizneopisaniyadostoynykhmonakhov (Gaosenchzhuan')* Vol. 1, p. 17. (In Russian).
22 J.J.M. de Groot, "The Militant Spirit of the Buddhist Clergy in China". *T'oung Pao* Vol. 2, No. 1, 1891. p. 127.
23 *Buddhism and Politics in Twentieth-Century Asia*. Edited by Ian Harris. London and New York, Continuum, 1999. pp. 5, 7–9.
24 Ngag dbang blo bzang rgyam tsho, *Gangs can yul gyi sa la spyodpa'I mthoriskyir gyal blong tsobor brjod pa'i deb ther* [*History of Tibet*]. Delhi, 1967. p. 120. (In Tibetan).
25 M. Rossabi, *Khubilai Khan. His Life and Times*. Berkeley, University of California Press, 1988. pp. 144–5.
26 D.S. Ruegg, "Mchod yon, yon mchod and mchod gnas/yon gnas" ["On the Historiography and Semantics of a Tibetan Religio-social and Religio-political Concept"]. In: *The History of Tibet*. Edited by Alex McKay. London and New York, Routledge Curzon, 2003. Vol. 2. pp. 362–72.
27 G. Tucci, *Tibetan Painted Scrolls*. Vol. I. Roma, Libreria dello Stato, 1949. pp. 10–12.
28 Sh. Bira, *Mongol'skaja istoriografija (XIII-XVII vv.)* [*Mongolian Historiography (13th–17th Centuries)*]. Moscow, 1978. p. 87.

7 Nikolai Roerich and Eurasia
The ambivalent horizon line

Rashmi Doraiswamy

Nikolai Roerich (1874–1947) was a Russian painter who had travelled widely in Europe and America and settled down in India, in the mountains in the north. He was a painter, poet, writer, ethnographer, archeologist, collector, set designer and an activist responsible for the Roerich Peace Pact and the Banner of Peace. He, more than any other Russian artist of his time, stayed creatively with the Eurasian vision till the end of his life, outliving the Bolshevik Revolution, two world wars, the partition of India and India's independence from the British. This chapter examines the ideological horizon (as Pavel Medvedev/Mikhail Bakhtin would call it) that shaped his worldview, a view that he more or less remained committed to all his life.

Eurasianism

The ideological horizon of Roerich included the myriad tendencies of the Silver Age (symbolism, modernism, neorealism, occultism, mysticism) and the ideology of Eurasianism. Eurasianism was a philosophy propounded by a group of émigré thinkers in the 1920s: P. N. Savitsky, Nikolai Trubetskoi, D. S. Mirsky, P. Supovchinsky, S. Efron, K. Cheidze and P. Arapov. The Eurasians believed that Russia is neither Asia nor Europe, but a mixture of both. Like the Slavophiles they believed that Russia should look towards Asia rather than towards Europe, for that was where her roots are to be found. According to Madhavan Palat,

> The Eurasian doctrine argues that Eurasia ... is unique in itself as a civilization, distinct from Europe and Asia, and as such comparable to Europe, China and India but not to the nation-states like France, Germany, England and others. This civilization, therefore, must not commit the cardinal sin of attempting to integrate with Europe.... It has evolved as a civilization over the past 700 years since the Mongol conquest of Russia in the thirteenth century; its most significant cultural constituents are Orthodox Christianity, Buddhism and Islam, all combined into the "symphonic personality of Eurasia".[1]

The Eurasianists thus had some meeting ground with Soviet ideology in that they supported the USSR's turn towards the East. They differed from them in their belief that the origin of the Russian state lay not in Kievan Rus but in the Mongol empire.

> The Eurasianist authors acknowledged their debt to the Russian Slavophile tradition, yet rejected their predecessors' populism, their idealization of the peasant community's collectivism, and their identification with Slavic ethnicity. The Eurasianists recognized the importance of creative individuals and praised Russia as a multi-ethnic empire, where non-Russian nationalities were in close contact with the Russian people as active participants in the building of Russian culture, based on an "affinity of souls" and mutual economic interests. The Eurasianists rejected communism, yet interpreted the Russian Revolution as an elemental act of resistance against forced Europeanisation.[2]

These "roots", however, were not envisaged in any sense of purity, but were seen as being severely in-mixed.

> To the Eurasians, Russians are neither Slavs nor Turanians. They had formed as a people over a long process in the course of which various ethnic groupings, inhabiting Eurasia from time immemorial, mixed, joined together, and mutually influenced one another. The Greater Russian element played a significant part in this process; this nationality became the "centre" of cultural and ethnic synthesis, incorporating the culture of other groups and conveying their own to them.[3]

The look towards Asia found its echo in the aesthetic philosophies of the time. They were not all celebratory and had the hint of fear, but nonetheless, realized the importance of this large continent in Russia's sense of identity. Apocalypse and eschatology were reflected in major works by eminent writers of the period: *Panmongolism* (1894) and *A Short Tale of the Anti-Christ* (1899) by Vladimir Soloviev, Valerii Briusov's *The Coming Huns* (1904–1905) and *The Scythians* by Aleksander Blok (1918). According to Judith Kornblatt,

> Soloviev speaks *to* the Russians *about* an eastern, swarming, unaccountable threat; Briusov speaks instead directly *to* the eastern threat, this time *about* Russian false "wise men and poets", and ends on a hymn for the Huns. Blok for his part speaks in the other geographical and metaphysical direction, *to* the Europeans, with the voice of the Russians who have now become like the eastern threat itself.[4]

The geographical divisions of the Eurasian continent were important for the Eurasianists.

> The Eurasian "continent-ocean" is composed of four latitudinal strips from north to south – the tundra, the forest zone, the steppe, and finally, broken and

> undulating, the mountains. The steppe extends from the Pacific to the Danube, the Hungarian plains, the historic limits of the great nomadic expansions from Eurasia, most famously the Huns under Atilla and the Mongols under Chingis Khan. These are then divided longitudinally by the river systems of European Russia and Siberia – the Dneister, the Dneiper, the Don, the Volga, the Ob, the Enisei, the Lena, and others so famous in Russian and Eurasian history. Riverine states have been limited to their respective basins; only the control of the latitudinal sweep, of the steppe and the forest, could burst those bonds and erect large empires and states . . . The Mongol empire of Chingis Khan was unconstrained because it controlled first the steppe and then the forest, through the conquest of Russia. The Muscovite empire repeated that performance in reverse by controlling the forest and then the steppe. . . . The origin of the Russian empire therefore lay in the Mongol empire, not in the Kievan principality.[5]

Savitsky goes further and contrasts the "flag-like" scape of Eurasia as against Europe's "chequered" one.

> Eurasia in the sense given to the word by Savitsky and Trubetskoy (who have described the term respectively from the geographical and ethnographical points of view), is *neither* Europe nor Asia. It is a "continent" by itself, situated east of Europe, and north of Asia, roughly contiguous with the old Russian Empire, and even more closely with the present USSR. . . . The characteristics common to the whole of Eurasia are so numerous that there are many ways of defining it, and the boundaries arrived at will necessarily vary somewhat in detail according to what feature is taken as the *principium divisionis*.[6]

Climatic and surface features are the most characteristic. Savitsky defines Eurasia as that part of the main continental block of the Old World, where the normal succession of North to South of climatic zones is least disturbed by latitudinal factors (seas or mountains). This regularity in the succession of zones stands in sharp contrast to the chequered "regional" structure of Europe. Savitsky calls the

> structure of Eurasia "flaglike": the zones of the tundra, forest, steppe and desert follow each other from top to bottom of the map like the stripes of a flag. . . . Each of the zones is subdivided with equal regularity into subzones. . . . Each zone and subzone has its characteristic complex of plants and its characteristic soil. Each extends unbrokenly from West to East over scores of degrees of longitude. Such latitudinal regularity of zones is not to be found anywhere else in the world (except perhaps in West Africa).[7]

The expeditions

The Silver Age and the philosophy of Eurasianism were inextricably woven into Nikolai Roerich's own vision. Nikolai and Helena Roerich's spiritual quests, their belief in Agni Yoga and the lure of Buddhism brought them to India. From India they undertook arduous expeditions into the heart of Asia. These expeditions into Eurasia from India were very important from the point of view of anthropology, folklore, ethnography, archaeology and art.

Roerich's first expedition to Central Asia from 1924 to 1928 spanned a large territory from Sikkim to Srinagar, Leh, Ladakh, Karakoram, Chinese Turkestan, the north-western Taklamakan Desert, the Tienshan Mountains, Central Asia, Moscow, Siberia, Altai, Mongolia, the Gobi Desert, Tibet and Darjeeling. It covered over 25,000 km and thirty-five mountain passes, and many of them were marked on a map for the first time. Paintings such as *Mountain Pass* thus are representations that document as well as show the arduous treks through the mountains. Henry Wallace, head of the US Department of Agriculture (and later US vice president) who was an admirer of Roerich, funded his expedition in 1934–1935 to Inner Mongolia, Manchuria and China. Roerich was accompanied by James Stephens and H. G. Macmillan of the US Department of Agriculture, and they collected herbs, seeds and several hundred species of xerophytes. Roerich also did his archeological and ethnographic research and found ancient manuscripts. Suchandana Chatterjee writes:

> What is significant about Roerich is his uncanny ability to extrapolate these options. . . . There were contestations of power among imperial and regional authorities, provincial rivalries in Chinese Turkestan and the end of prosperity of the Turkish Begs of Yarkand, Khotan and Kashgar, tenuousness of Mongolian borders, the new prospects of Mongolia as a Soviet protégé, the new age thinking about a messianic upheaval and an urge for spiritual brotherhood in the Himalayas that would challenge the imperial ambitions of the British Indian empire. It is intriguing how and why, as an émigré from Soviet Russia, he tried to represent himself as a supporter of Soviet development-oriented programmes in Tibet and Central Asia. So, his art-based expedition also had other tags and there are implications that Roerich was a political player in the highlands of Asia who moved in and out of Soviet-dominated Mongolia (Outer Mongolia), Chinese-dominated Mongolia (Inner Mongolia) and British-influenced Tibet.[8]

Although the countries covered in the expeditions differed in the economic, political and cultural systems they espoused, Roerich saw in them what was preserved of the past and what would serve as the basis of a bright spiritual future.

Religions of Eurasia

An important link with Eurasian thinking in Roerich's paintings is the equal valency given to all religions born on Eurasian soil: the Prophet Mohamet (two paintings made in 1925); Zoroaster (1931); Christ (*Descent into Hell* / 1933), in which a Christ-like figure is shown against the background of a rocky/mountainous formation, descending into a space with the strange, snake-like creatures of hell);

and Buddha (as in *Buddha, the Conqueror* / 1925–26). Of course, Buddhism and Christianity are represented more often, but the Eurasian space is seen as the crucible of all the major religions. What is of further interest is that Roerich places the figures of these religious leaders in compositions that have to do with mountains. Zoroaster, Mohamet and Moses are atop mountains. They are at a height and dealing with an element that plays an important part in the composition: in the case of Mohamet, it is smoke (from fire, presumably); in the case of Moses there is a huge canopy that seems to cover the mountain tops and which has formed a pattern, under the impact and energy of wind; in the case of Zoroaster, it is water, pouring forth from his hands, a motif repeated twice in the painting with a water body visible beyond the mountains. These leaders are not "particularised". They are depicted as extraordinary people, as abstractions (their faces are not distinct), standing alone in the landscape, who have the energy to summon the forces of nature, and who have reached metaphoric heights. Krishna, usually associated with the plains, is shown in Roerich's paintings in the mountains (1930, 1936, 1938), playing his flute, but surrounded by foliage. The mountains are depicted in different seasons, but even against the "winter" snow-capped mountains (1938), the mountain he is sitting on supports greenery. Buddha is shown in many avatars and legends. While Buddhism and Christianity remained close to Roerich, it is important that he chose to depict all the religious prophets of the Eurasian space. In his painting *Crossroad of Christ and Buddha* (1925), it is the Buddhist and Christian places of worship that are depicted, once again recognized by their abstract architectural form on the mountain slopes. The painting, despite its title, does not depict the subjects, but only the architectural forms on the mountains that were built for worship and meditation. The paintings of Roerich of habitats on the mountains also hold a special place in this Eurasian thinking, for the buildings are ensconced in mountain slopes, growing almost organically out of the mountainous earth as in *Sekhar Dzong* (1933).

This deliberate abstraction of features in the religious paintings, shorn of ethnographic details, is a significant feature of his work, a feature that does not lead to an Orientalist interpretation. The magnitude of nature, the scalar representation of the human figure that is proportionally smaller in this large scheme of things and the theme represented through broad generalisation rather than small detail. This is also true of his paintings on mythic or legendary figures from across the Eurasian space, like *Padma Sambhava* (1924), *Oirot – Messenger of the White Burkhan* (1925), *Milarepa – the One Who Harkened* (1925), *Gesar Khan* (1941) (along with *Host of Gesar* (1931) and *Abode of Gesar* (1947)), or *Confuscius, the Just One* (1925).

Spiritual geography

The distinguishing geographical features of the Eurasian continent were of great import in Roerich's thinking. He decided to focus on the mountains, more than on any of the other "flag-like" land formations, leading to innumerable paintings on mountain ranges and peaks. The last period of his works is usually characterised as the "Mountain Period". He in fact travelled across the expanse of Eurasia more through the mountains than the plains. It is this firsthand knowledge of the mountain heights that is the unique point of view he adopts in his paintings. For Roerich, the mountains were the link with the celestial, with the higher, mystical world. To depict this, he often employed dynamic cloud formations, sometimes as "messengers" in the sky, sometimes as a dividing line in the composition between the real and the ethereal. The mist and clouds "lift" the mountains into a non-geographic, at times atemporal space. *Confucius, the Just One* is one such painting, where the clouds split the composition into the upper and lower parts, with Confucius going gently along in a cart in the lower half.

Writing on the seventeen peaks of the Himalayas near Sikkim, Roerich says:

> It is a whole snowy realm, altering its outlines with every variation of light! Verily it is inexhaustible in impressions and unceasingly evocative.
>
> Nowhere else on earth are expressed two such entirely different worlds. Here is the earthly world, with its rich vegetation, brilliant butterflies, pheasants, leopards, panthers, monkeys, snakes, and the innumerable other animals that inhabit the ever-green jungles of Sikkim. And above the clouds, in unexpected heights, shines the snowy kingdom, which has nothing in common with the busy ant-hill of the jungles. It is an eternally moving ocean of clouds, with untold varieties of mist.
>
> Kanchenjunga has attracted the attention equally of Tibetans and Indians. Here was created the inspiring myth about Shiva, who drank the poison of the world for the sake of humanity. Here, from the churning of the clouds, rose the brilliant Lakshmi, for the joy of the world.[9]

In works such as *Voice of Mongolia* (1937), *Tsagan Kure Inner Mongolia* (1936), *Mongolia* (1936), *Mongolia Hills of Chahar* (1936), and *Batukhalkalka* (1936), Roerich paints landscapes that are on the plains or at lower heights.

The places he visited were also represented by mountainous or hilly landscape and a few buildings which evoked a sense of the dominant religion, the domes, the spires showing Islamic, Buddhist or Christian links. In *Pilgrim of a Radiant City* (1933), it is clear that the pilgrim is looking up to a Christian city. *Karakirghizes* (1932) and *Gobi Desert* (1928), on the other hand, reflect prehistorical, man-made artefacts (tents, stones as markers) that have lived through what Bakhtin calls the "big time", through history. It is this strange telescoping of time that is evident in *Karakirghizes*, a clearly ethnographic subject, shorn of its ethnicity by being placed in this big time. The gaze of the indistinct man on the camel at the tents is thus very interesting: Is he an "insider" or an "outsider"? Is he returning home, or has he come upon this settlement by chance? The camel looks elsewhere. The settlement is itself shorn of inhabitants outside the tent, adding to the feeling of time and timelessness in the painting. The wanderer, the pilgrim, the ascetic, the seeker are all alone but not lonely in the landscape, a landscape that in its vastness is their home. What Roerich culls from the landscape is that which will endure through time and transposes onto his canvas.

The Altai mountains were central to Roerich's vision. This was where the origin of human civilization lay. This was the land of the White Burkhan (another avatar of Buddha), the land of the mystical white waters (*belovodiye*). This was where Chud has gone underground. An underground network of tunnels, in Roerich's vision, connected the Altai with the Himalayas. The Altai was thus the heartland of the Eurasian space. Buddhism ruled, and in the mountain facades were carved the visages of Maitreya through the ages. All this prefigured the coming of the utopian age of Shambala. Thus it was that Eurasianism and the mysticism of the Silver Age of Russian culture came together in his vision, as did the occultism, inaugurated earlier by Madame Blavatskaya. It was in Eurasia that Indo-European civilizations and languages had arisen. At the height of the mountains are inscriptions on rocks in prototype Indo-European language in *Path to Kailas* (1932 and 1933). In the 1932 painting the word *agni* can be made out, referring to Agni Yoga, in which Roerich and his wife, Helena, believed.

Treasure in the mountains

Two paintings, thirty years apart, give an idea of the persistence of certain themes and beliefs in his life and work as well as the changes he wrought in his painting. *Hidden Treasure* (1917) and *Hidden Treasure* (1947) show how he remained enamoured of the idea of "treasure". In the 1917 painting, the slopes look like they have been formed over centuries; in the 1947 work, the slopes have been created by slabs of paint. The layers of colourful paint draw one's attention. In both paintings, there is a lone boatsman who has either found a treasure and is picking it up, or is lowering the treasure into water. These paintings, like *Karakirghizes*, capture the ambivalent moment. *Chintamani* (1924) is another painting on the same theme.

In *Treasure of the Mountain* (1933) and *The Vault* the theme is repeated, albeit with a difference. The interior of the mountains are precious, for they contain civilizational treasures. These interiors are the object of several of Roerich's paintings. They have chiseled stones within them and a depth in which men (as in *Treasure of the Mountain*), whose calling seems to be that of monks, are gathered. The interior of *The Vault* is of a different order; part evoking rough stone slabs, that are worked upon in part by human hand and in part by the forces of nature, creating geological layers. The third kind of interior we see is that of jagged hanging rock formations like stalactites and stalagmites, as in *Buddha the Conqueror* and *Chud the Subterranean* (1929). The underground of the mountain ranges, holding secrets within them of civilisations past and to come, was an integral part of Roerich's Eurasianist thinking.

Beyond synthesis

Roerich moves beyond synthesis and syncretism in his paintings on women figures into the realm of the hybrid. *Sophia and the Wisdom of the Almighty* (1932), *Madonna Laboris* (1933), *Madonna Protectoris* (1933), *Mother of Chinghiz Khan*

(1931), *She Who Leads* (1943) and *Agni Yoga* (1927) are some of his drawings on women. The women are shown nurturing and protecting humankind. Sophia is astride a horse, protecting the city; the Madonnas too are saving people. *Mother of Chingiz Khan* depicts the mother of a king who created and ruled over one of the biggest empires in world history on the Eurasian continent. She is all alone, unafraid, riding high on the mountains with a transparent white light gleaming behind her. The Eurasian vision of the importance of Chingiz Khan and his empire, discussed earlier, finds its reflection in two paintings – one dedicated to Chingiz Khan's mother and the other to his campaign (1937), in which the army with its flags and soldiers is seen descending the mountain slopes in a long curve deep into the distance. In his paintings on the Mother of the World, she is represented in a celestial realm, with symbols evoking various religions. It is in these paintings that hybridity is posited over synthesis as in, for instance, *Crossroad of Christ and Buddha*. In the last named painting, the synthesis is one of the salad-bowl variety, with the architectural symbols of both coexisting side by side.

The Roerich Pact

The Roerich Pact (Pax Cultura), prepared in collaboration with George Callaver, was signed on 15 April 1935 by the United States and twenty Latin American countries. It was ratified by ten countries. It was meant to be like the Red Cross. Just as the Red Cross operated in a zone of neutrality, so were objects of cultural heritage meant to be protected even in times of war. The preservation of cultural artifacts was to be prioritised over military considerations. The Roerich Pact did not become international law, but has remained an important aspiration and document for the preservation of museums, historical monuments, educational institutions and cultural artifacts, above all considerations of "one's own" and "otherness" during times of armed conflict. Nikolai Roerich also designed the Banner of Peace that was to be displayed over the cultural objects that were to be protected and preserved. This was a symbol of three dots in a circle. The three dots were a "synthetic/syncretic" symbol, representing the concept of trinity present in many religions, representing the highest achievements of humankind – religion, art and science, representing past, present and future. This was a symbol that was found in Stone Age drawings. The circle represented infinity and eternity. This flag was to fly over scientific, artistic and cultural institutions during times of peace and war for their protection. The symbol finds its representation in many of Roerich's paintings, including *Sophia, Stones of Mongolia* (1933), *White Stone* (1933), *Madonna Oriflamma* (1932), and *Chingiz Khan's Campaign* (1937). Roerich was nominated for a Nobel Peace Prize in 1929, 1932 and 1935. Of *Madonna Oriflama*, Lokesh Chandra writes:

> This intellectual strand added to the urgency of his Pax Cultura. In 1929 he published the complete text of the Pact to ensure the protection of monuments, museums, institutions and their personnel during war. He designed the distinctive "Banner of Peace" to be placed on objects to be protected. In 1931

he envisioned a new goddess devoted to the Pact, and called her Madonna Oriflamma. Oriflamma is the ancient battle standard of the kings of France, the banner of St. Denis, Ori is Latin aurum "gold" and flamma "flame". St. Denis was the first bishop of Paris and the patron saint of France. He had come to France during the reign of Roman Emperor Decius (AD 201–251). The goddess is reminiscent of the agniyoga of Roerich. Her counterpart in Buddhism is Marici "Lady of Sunrise Splendour" who travels before the sun and moon, is inescapable, unerring, unassailable by weapons. She is radiant and golden. She is a powerful protectress: simply calling her to mind elicits her protective powers. What an evocative Madonna was envisioned by Roerich in a spontaneous configuration.[10]

Conclusion

Roerich's travels in Eurasia led to many different kinds of painting of this space. There were paintings of mountain ranges and storms, paintings of peaks and passes; there were paintings of myths and legends from this continent; there were paintings of religious leaders; there were paintings of mythical and real women. What endured through all these registers was the love of the mountains. What was important for Roerich was the rarified atmosphere of the mountains, seen from the heights parallel to the heights of the mountains. This is what makes his works unique even today, in an age when aerial views of mountains and panoramic views are easily available in photographic imprints. The majesty of the mountains and the point of view of the mountains is possible only for a traveller of the mountains, one who knows them firsthand and has traversed their heights. This is neither an aerial view nor a view from the plains. What makes Roerich's mountains distinctive is also that the mountains are "real" but also transcendental at the same time. This is achieved very often through the creation of a cloud line in lieu of a horizon line. The horizon line is usually cut (off) by the mountains. The clouds create a kind of a wispy wafting horizon line. They serve to "lift" the mountains from the earth they are embedded in, giving the ranges a transcendental feel. The cloud line replaces the horizon line in paintings such as *Path to Kailash* (1932 and 1933), *Path to Shambala* (1933) and *Mountain of Five Treasures* (1933). L. Shaposhnikova states "the Central Asian itinerary was laid along the cosmic evolution of mankind. The earthly and cosmic as if came into contact on it".[11]

Apart from the heights of the mountains, the two other spaces that emerge in his paintings of this period are the rich interiors of the mountains, with a secret life of their own, and the lower reaches of the mountains, with plains and deserts.

The "moment" that the painter captures is as important as the horizon line. The moment of action is rarely captured by Roerich. He does it once in a while, the portrayal of the cause-effect moment as in *Empathy* (1936), *Remember* (1924), *He Who Hastens* (1924), or *Pearl of Searching* (1924). *Empathy* embodies the godlike in man, who shows compassion for the deer hit by the arrow of the hunter. Likewise, *Remember*, in a rare case, has the traveller (whom we see in so many other paintings) cast one look back at the dwelling he is leaving behind. These moments of emotion were not usually part of Roerich's repertoire. But by and large, he spurns the moment of reaction. His is the moment of ordinariness, when the legendary is subsumed by the landscape, as in *Confucius, the Just One*, or *Oirot*. In the latter, the horse with the messenger is above the clouds on a non-material plane.

Although he was fascinated by anthropology, ethnography and folklore, Nikolai Roerich's greatness lies in the fact that he eschewed any form of Orientalism. This remains his greatest contribution to the Eurasian worldview. The mountains deterritorialise nation-states with their very specific temporal issues and conflicts. Mountains act as a bridge between countries, and in Roerich's worldview, as repositories of spiritual values. They are sources of material and spiritual energy that have lasted centuries. They eschew narrow ethnocentricity and thus nationalism of any kind. They outlast kingdoms, empires and nations. To Roerich also goes the credit of the secularization of all religious imagery and the valorisation of the figure of the seeker and the searcher, who treads fearlessly, alone, at these heights. The horizon line, which often has a proxy in the cloud line, is ambivalent, creating upper and lower spaces in the composition, but simultaneously also pointing to the possibility of this and other worlds.

Notes

1 Madhavan K. Palat, "Eurasianism as an Ideology for Russia's Future". *Economic and Political Weekly*, 8 December 1993. p. 2799.
2 Martin Beisswenger, "Eurasianism: Affirming the Person". In: *A History of Russian Philosophy 1830–1930: Faith, Reason, and the Defense of Human Dignity*. Edited by G.M. Hamburg and Randall A. Poole. New York, Cambridge University Press, 2010. p. 365.
3 Slawomir Mazurek, "Russian Eurasianism – Historiography and Ideology". *Studies in European Thought*, Vol. 54, 2002. p. 112.
4 Judith Deutsch Kornblatt, "Eschatology and Hope in Silver Age Thought". In: *A History of Russian Philosophy 1830–1930: Faith, Reason, and the Defense of Human Dignity*. Edited by G.M. Hamburg and Randall A. Poole. New York, Cambridge University Press, 2010. p. 299.
5 Palat, "Eurasianism as an Ideology for Russia's Future", p. 2805.
6 D.S. Mirsky, "The Eurasian Movement". *Slavonic Review*, Vol. 6, No. 17, December 1927. pp. 313–14.
7 Ibid.
8 Suchandana Chatterjee, "Glimpses of Inner Asia". In: *Nicholas Roerich: A Quest and a Legacy*. Edited by Manju Kak. New Delhi, Niyogi Books, 2013. pp. 48–9.
9 Nikolai Roerich, *Heart of Asia*. www.roerich.org/roerich-writings-heart-of-asia.php.
10 Lokesh Chandra, *Pax Cultura of Nicholas Roerich*. www.roerichs.com/Lng/en/Publications/book-culture-and-peace-/Pax-Cultura-of-Nicholas-Roerich.htm.
11 L. Shaposhnikova, *Great Travel: Master* (Book 1). Quoted on the webpage of the International Centre of Roerichs in Moscow. http://en.icr.su/museum/layout/expedition/05.php.

8 Shamanism in Eurasia

V. N. Tuguzhekova

Shamanism is the most ancient religion for most people in Central Asia. Shamans did not have specially constructed temples. They deified nature, were eager to keep balance in nature and not hurt it by their actions. Nature was a single divine temple, which they treated with due care. In the shamans' view, the whole of Asia is inhabited by spirits. Every valley, every mountain has its own spirit or master. Every place is a living body.

Places where gods and spirits came out or where they acted were marked as holy space. This tradition has been preserved since antiquity. At such places – "a contact zone" between worlds – they constructed simple chancels of wood, stones and clay for sacrifice and prayers, erected columns (*sarchins*) and tied ribbons (*chalama*) to the branches of trees. A place was proclaimed holy and people came there especially for performing their rites. Offering to masters of locality is a common practice in Siberia, Tibet, Mongolia and Buryatia. Thus, in Mongolia once a year, usually in summer, the ritual *oboo takhilga* is carried out. All the local population comes to participate in this ritual; they bring treats to a spirit-master of the locality. According to the tradition, which is especially observed by the local population, one cannot pass by such place without favoring a spirit-*ezhin* – a master of this place. In the seventeenth and eighteenth centuries in Mongolia and Buryatia, many shamanist rituals were influenced by the religion of the lamas, and Buddhist rites started to be performed on them.

A general characteristic, common to all these places, is natural beauty, which emphasizes these natural objects among the surrounding landscape. It is considered that at these places meditation is most productive for attaining enlightenment, energy and vivacity. Solitude at such desolate places is an essential part of mystical education. The main aim of solitude is to deflect attention away from objects of the external world and direct it to spirituality. At places, where a cult systematically takes place, big *obos* appear after some time.

Shamanism has an ancient history on the territory of Central Asia. Old Chinese chronicles preserved the description of the religion and shamans of Xiongnu tribes who had been living in Mongolia. The Mongols' "Black faith" was a religion of Genghis Khan, the founder of the Mongol empire. Genghis Khan was proclaimed as the great ancestor of a kin of Mongolian Khans. In his honor a sanctuary in the Ordos Desert, famous under the name "Eight White Pavilions", was erected. Many mythological tales and connected with these cult beliefs had existed in Central Asia long before the appearance of the historical Genghis Khan. The mythological Genghis Khan entered the Mongols' tradition of honoring ancestors' spirits (expressed in the making of *ongons*, mentioned in invoking and in sacrificial offerings). The Genghis Khan-deity became a patron of a kin of Mongolian Khans. Originally it was a cult of privileged ones – members of the imperial family and their relatives. Any attempts by strangers to enter the sanctuary were punished by death. Within Genghis Khan's cult there was a cult of his *sulde* – his military spirit (genius), embodied in a *gonfanon*. According to the Mongols' beliefs, a *sulde* of a great person became a genius-guardian of his kin, tribe, people. Genghis Khan's *sulde* became a *gonfanon* of all Mongols. They created a special ceremony for invocation of *Sulde-tengri*, which according to a belief in case of the exact execution made a man an owner of *sulde* power. After that, he was not afraid of wars or enemies. Consecration ceremonies of a *gonfanon* and its *boncuks* and sacrificial offerings to them in connection with military marches were of horrendous, bloody character. However, from the sixteenth century the position of Mongol shamanism weakened greatly.

In modern times, following the crash of the communist ideology after the fall of the Soviet Union (1991), an intensive process of shamanism's rebirth started in Eurasia and Central Asia. At the same time the process of deideologization such as globalization, ecological problems, local wars leading to destruction of monuments of world culture, emerged as a global process. From 1990 onwards, scholars from all over the world began taking interest in shamanism. The notion of shamanism figured in the Russian scientific literature in the eighteenth century, when Siberian shamans were mentioned in written sources.[1] Giving a classification of early religious forms, outstanding ethnographer S.A. Tokarev referred shamanism to a religion which had appeared during the breakup period of communal-generic structure.[2] A majority of the Soviet scholars referred shamanism to religion. Speaking about shamanism, L.P. Potapov considered it a traditional national religion of Siberian peoples.[3]

It was for the first time in 1997 that in Khakassia, KhRILLH headed by G.G. Kotozhekov organised an international seminar, "Traditional Worldview of the Khakass: Past, Present and Future".[4] It led to the study of shamanism and revival of shaman practices in Khakassia. In the same year L.V. Anzhiganova's monograph *Traditional World View of the Khakass* was published.[5] Later KhRILLH made close scientific contacts with the Institute of Ethnology and Anthropology, the Russian Academy of Sciences and scholars like V.I. Kharitonova and D.A. Funk. In 2001 together with them an international interdisciplinary scientific seminar was held: "Ecology and Traditional Religious-Magic Knowledge".[6] A center for the study of shamanism and other traditional beliefs and practices was created in the Institute of Ethnology and Anthropology headed by V.I. Kharitonova. It began studying the state of modern shamanism and Siberian shamans and publishing scientific works and results of research.[7] Works devoted to a shaman's personality began to be published. Thus, famous ethnographer Anna Vasilyevna Smolyak's monograph *Shaman: Personality, Functions, World View* (*Peoples of*

Nizhny Amur)[8] and V. I. Kharitonova's edited volume *Shamanistic Gift* were published.[9] After the foundation of this center, ethnologists, ethnographers, culture experts and folklorists as well as representatives of different fields of science such as physicists, biophysicists, specialists of technical sciences, parapsychologists, neurophysiologists, psychiatrists and hypnologists participated in the study of shamanism. For the first time such widespread scientific collaboration was undertaken and the very owners of unusual powers – shamans, magicians, quacks, folk healers and intuitives also participated. The experiment appeared to be timely as participants of this center carried out joint investigations in this sphere.[10] Khakass shamans V. S. Topoyev and L. V. Kobezhekova often take part in its work.

Modern shamans, like their predecessors in ancient times, continue practicing traditional ceremonies connected with the cult of the sky, fire, water, mountain, earth.[11] It is noteworthy that ancient shamanistic worldview is preserved in shamans' practices. It is handed down from generation to generation often through genetic memory. Shamans take part in the renewal and carrying of national and calendar festivals such as *Chyl Pazy, Chir Ine, Tigir taiyɜ, Taɜ taiyɜ, Suɜ taiyɜ, Pai khazyң, Ÿren Khurty, Tun Airan*, etc.

Shamans play an important role in the ecological education of population. Thus, in 2009 shamans of Tuva and Khakassia participated in the campaign, "Tambourine of the World". The idea of this campaign belonged to shamans of the Scandinavian Sami who had decided to send a tambourine as a sacred shamanistic attribute on a journey around the world with the slogan "Stop the war between man and nature". The main idea was to return to humankind life in harmony with nature. In Russia "Tambourine of the World" as a symbol of Earth Mother's care took place in the territory of Tuva from 22 May to 24 July 2009 and in Khakassia from 9 to 15 August 2009. In all populated places of Khakassia where "Tambourine of the World" took place, ceremonies were held by Khakass shamans and their helpers: V. Chebochakov, T. Kobezhikova, G. Kostyakova, R. Nasibulin, N. Sagalakova, M. Sagalakova, L. Asochakova, G. Kuzhakova, M. Cherpakov, V. Mindibekov and others, and also Tuvinian shamans V. Nursat and D. Markov.[12]

Khakass shamans take an active part in the revival of traditional sacral and kin places, in the reconstruction of ancient *menhirs* and steles. L. R. Kyzlasov has stated that the village Sinyavino stone statue Chelgus Oba lay abandoned for long time on the left bank of the river Ninya, not far from the rock Tarbakh khaya.[13] According to L. R. Kyzlasov this *menhir* had been an ancient sanctuary, where sacrificial offerings were made.[14] In 2013 shaman Valery Chebochakov together with friends put back Chalgus oba (*menhir* standing alone). Shaman Leonid Gorbatov worked at ground zero to organize the museum *Khurtuyakh tas*. Now he works there as a scientific officer. Famous shaman Tatyana Kobezhekova conducted a worshiping ritual to a stone statue *Inei tas* in Ordghonikidze district after its reconstruction.

Shamanistic society, headed by shaman Natalia Sagalakova, regularly performs various rites at sacral places of Khakassia. On 28 February 2014, at the initiative of shaman Svetlana Butusova together with Tuvinian, Khakass and Slavic shamans of Khakassia a rite of purification, called by them "Mystery of Purification", was performed for the citizens of Abakan. Hundreds of people took part in this ritual.

This author travelled to Mongolia, Tibet, Nepal, Bhutan and Northern India, and it is worthy to note that despite the domination of Buddhism in these countries in ceremonial practices, the presence of shamanism is still felt. For example, in Tibet, Indian Buddhism mixed with ancient local shamanism and heathenism, which imparted a unique color to Tibetan Buddhism. Tibetan healers cure not only the body but the soul too. A shaman was not only a healer but a spiritual tutor for his tribe. A shaman gave help to a dying person so that a soul would go the right way in its last trip. In Mongolia and Tibet one finds offerings being made to spirits and deities especially on passages and sacral localities.

At such places different chancels of wood and stones for sacrificial offerings and blessings are constructed. Columns are erected and ribbons are tied on the branches of trees. The Khakass call them *chalama*. According to shamanistic traditions by deifying the nature people try to keep balance in the nature. For a shaman, nature has always been the unique Divine Temple which needs careful attention.

In East Tibet every summer in the sixth month according to the Moon calendar a festival of shamans is held. This old tradition was inherited from followers of Bon religion which had reigned in Tibet long before the coming of Buddhism. The shamans' festival is held with the purpose of appeasing the local spirits. A good harvest and the well-being of local residents depend on these spirits. In Tibet, Mongolia and other regions where Buddhism is widespread, researchers notice the modernization of shamanism. Thus shamans and attendants at ceremonies say the Buddhist mantra *Om mani padme hum*. And often there is also substitution of shamanistic rituals by blessings.[15]

In Mongolia revival of shamanism has been noticed after 1990. Shamanism is more widespread in northern and north-western regions of Mongolia. According to researchers' opinion, the oldest variant of shamanism is widespread among the *Tsaatans* (Turkish-speaking group) of Khövsgöl Aimag. In Mongolia there are 282 *Tsaatans*.[16] The *Tsaatans* not only worship their shaman but know by themselves a range of sacred shamanistic incantations which are used in their everyday life (during hunting, for invoking rain, etc.).

It is worthy to note that in old traditional beliefs of both the Mongolian and Sayan-Altaian Turkic peoples a cult of fire and sacred mountains dominated. The paradigm Sky-Earth played an important role.[17] Shamans call upon people to live in harmony with nature, to understand and listen to nature, take good care of their spiritual roots with the help of their attention to nature, their old roots and ancient monuments. Its understanding will help humanity to prevent ecological catastrophe.

Notes

1 S.A. Tokarev, *Early Forms of Religion*. Moscow, 1990. p. 267.
2 Ibid., p. 50.
3 L.P. Potapov, *Altaian Shamanism*. Leningrad, Science, 1991. p. 11.
4 *Traditional World View of the Khakass: Past, Present and Future*. Materials of the International Seminar. Abakan, 25 September 1997. Under the editorship of G.G. Kotozhekov. Abakan, 1997. 115 pp.

5 L.V. Anzhiganova, *Traditional World View of the Khakass: Reconstruction Experience*. Abakan, Zentaurus, 1997. 128 pp.
6 *Ecology and Traditional Religious-Magic Knowledge*. Materials of International Interdisciplinary Symposium. Moscow, Abakan and Kyzyl, 9–21 July 2001. 2 vols.
7 *Ethnological researches on shamanism and other traditional believes and practices. A series of scientific works*. V.I. Moscow, Institute of Ethnology and Anthropology, Russian Academy of Sciences, 1995, 272 pp.
8 A.V. Smolyak, *Shaman: Personality, Functions, World View (Peoples of Nizhny Amur)*. Moscow, 1991. 277 pp.
9 V.I. Kharitonova, *Shamanistic Gift* (To 80th anniversary of Doctor of historical sciences Anna Vasilyevna Smolyak). Moscow, 338 pp. (Ethnological researches on shamanism and other traditional beliefs and practices. Volume 6).
10 Ibid., p. 33.
11 V.N. Tuguzhekova and I.K. Kidiyekova, "Man and Nature: Ceremony Sur taiyr". In: *Current Problems of History and Culture of Sayan-Altai*. Seventh Edition. Abakan, 2006. pp. 125–31.
12 V.N. Tuguzhekova, "Tambourine of the World in Khakassia". In: *Current Problems of History and Culture of Sayan-Alatai. A Series of Scientific Works*. Eleventh Edition. Abakan, 2010. pp. 125–9.
13 L.R. Kyzlasov, *The Oldest Khakassia*. Moscow, 1986. pp. 87–91, fig. 17–19.
14 Ibid., p. 91.
15 N.L. Zhukovskaya, "Shamanism Modernization in Circumstances of Buddhist Expansion Among the Mongolians and their Neighborhood". *Ethnographic Journal*. Edition No. 5. Ulan-Ude, 1969. p. 178.
16 Data of Population Census in Mongolia of 2000, 2010: The Turkomen of Mongolia. turak.info>forum/showthreat (Accessed on 7 August 2013).
17 N.V. Abayev, *Early Forms of Religion and Ethnic and Cultural Genesis of Turkic-Mongolian Peoples*. Kyzyl, 2005. p. 103.

9 The Eurasian factor in Russian foreign policy
Implications for India

Tatiana Shaumyan

The new concept of the foreign policy of the Russian Federation approved by President of the Russian Federation V. Putin on 30 November 2016 identifies the main priorities and objectives of the foreign policy of Russia. The priority directions of foreign policy of the Russian Federation are the development of bilateral and multilateral cooperation with states-participants of the Commonwealth of Independent States and further strengthening of operating in the space of the CIS integration structures with Russian participation. The Russian Federation is stepping up its cooperation with CIS states-participants in the field of security, including a joint fight against common challenges and threats, primarily international terrorism, extremism, illicit trafficking in narcotic drugs, psychotropic substances and their precursors, transnational crime and illegal migration.[1]

Paragraph 53 of the new version of the concept states that Russia is working on further realization of the potential of CIS, strengthening of the Commonwealth as an influential regional organization, a forum for multilateral political dialogue, as a mechanism of multifaceted cooperation in the sphere of economy, humanitarian interaction, combating traditional and new challenges and threats. In paragraph 97 the authors of the concept focus on the continuing instability in Afghanistan, which

> poses a serious threat to the security of Russia and other CIS States-participants. Russian Federation in cooperation with the Islamic Republic of Afghanistan, other interested States and using the abilities of the UN, CIS, SCO and other international structures will consistently make efforts for an early resolution of the problems of this country . . . An integral part of such efforts is the implementation of comprehensive measures to reduce the terrorist threat emanating from Afghanistan and directed against others, including Afghanistan's neighboring States, as well as on the elimination or significant reduction of illicit production and trafficking of drugs.[2]

After the collapse of the Soviet Union, Russia found that not all of the "near abroad" states were enthusiastic on integration processes in the CIS space: these states feared Russia's domination in the Commonwealth; they did not trust Russia and didn't demonstrate interest to deepen the integration process. At the turn of the millennium, the Russian leadership gradually came to realize that the CIS has not met completely the goals that were set during its formation.³

On 3 October 2011 Vladimir Putin published an article in *Izvestia* on the Eurasian Union concept, which involves the creation of confederation of states which share political, economic and military customs and cultural space. He suggested

> a powerful supranational association capable of becoming one of the poles in the modern world and serving as an efficient bridge between Europe and the dynamic Asia-Pacific region. Its natural resources, capital, and potent reserve of human resources will combine to put the Eurasian Union in a strong competitive position in the industry and technology race, in the struggle for investors, for the creation of new jobs and the establishment of cutting-edge facilities. Alongside other key players and regional structures, such as the European Union, the United States, China and APEC, the Eurasian Union will help ensure global sustainable development. The Eurasian Union will become a focal point for further integration processes since it will be formed by the gradual merging of existing institutions, the Customs Union and the Common Economic Space.⁴

In the analysis of the Eurasian factor in Russian foreign policy, it should be noted, first of all, that geographically Eurasia covers the geopolitical space of Suez to Tibet, from the Caspian Sea to western China, from the Urals to Altai, Tien Shan, the Pamir, the Hindukush and the Kopet Dag. Eurasia has an overwhelming majority of the world population and exceptional natural resources. The important trend here is the shift of the global economic and political centre to the "New Asia" – or to the East and Southeast Asia and India.⁵ Given the characteristics of a new stage of development of the world economy and politics, including the military-political confrontation, in the words of Zbigniew Brzezinski, "Eurasia is the world's axial supercontinent. A power that dominated Eurasia would exercise decisive influence over two of the world's three most economically productive regions, Western Europe and East Asia".⁶ He wrote further: "Eurasia is the 'chessboard', which is the struggle for world domination, and this struggle affects geostrategy – strategic management of geopolitical processes".⁷

It is impossible not to take into account the importance of the largest countries of the world, with influence not only in this area but also in the world politics. These are Russia, India and China, Kazakhstan, the Central Asian states, the authority and influence of which is increasing steadily. It is no accident that the United States and its allies are taking extraordinary measures to strengthen its influence in the Eurasian countries, bearing in mind both the political and strategic interest, and the need to secure raw materials. Apparently, the United States is interested in containing the geopolitical ambitions of China, which is now strengthening its position in the oil-producing regions of Eurasia.

In the opinion of Russian analysts,

> Russia's economic and political advantage in the Asia-Pacific region is a prerequisite for its internal stability and international competitiveness. Only by

balancing its Western and Eastern Development vectors and system of foreign relations can Russia become a truly modern global power.[8]

The strengthening of the Eastern vector should be based on measures to accelerate the development of Siberia and the Russian Far East on the basis of improving trade, economic and political relations with the leading Asia-Pacific countries.

Russia possesses the most important competitive advantage, as the central geopolitical, historical and civilizational position in Eurasia. Historically, Russians aggressively moved from west to east Eurasia, opening up new territory, until they reached the shores of the Pacific Ocean and crossed it, establishing settlements in Alaska and California. Thus, by the eighteenth century, Russia had shifted to the East not only its geographic center, but also the influence of Russia in Eurasia.

According to analysts, the focus of Russia's Eurasian policy should be the priority development of the eastern regions of the country, "the Russian core" of Eurasia, for which there are huge opportunities. The underdevelopment of the Trans-Baikal area and the Russian Far East and the flight of the population from there will create a sense that the region is vulnerable and in a security vacuum.[9] On this largest continent of the planet is housed the essential part of the world's natural resources. Here is Siberia, "the main storehouse of the Earth". Siberia and the Russian Far East should become full-scale economic participants of the Eurasian Union.

Close cultural and economic ties have existed between India and Central Asia, Caucasia and Russia from time immemorial. The historical experience of the Russian people gives them the opportunity to become a real bridge and the shortest route from Europe to the rapidly developing Asia-Pacific countries. This experience is of paramount importance at a time when not only the center of the world economy, politics, but also the center of the military-political confrontation has shifted to Eurasia.

Eurasian Union project has significant potential for implementation. The Eurasian countries represent about 20 percent of the world's natural resources. In contrast to the BRICS countries, they represent a single geopolitical space, essentially a state-continent. Eurasia is home to most of the world's population, representing the five Eurasian civilizations: Hindu, Confucian, Islamic, Western Christian and Orthodox-Slavic. New independent states of Central Asia have a special place in the geopolitical space of the Eurasian region.

In these circumstances, it is quite understandable that the United States is strengthening its activity in Eurasia and in the post-Soviet space, and establishing bilateral relations with countries such as China, Russia and India, while ignoring the existing multilateral institutions such as the Shanghai Cooperation Organization (SCO), Collective Security Treaty Organization (CSTO) and others, thus preventing the creation of a Eurasian security system. At the same time, Eurasia accounts for about 80 percent of all international conflicts and local wars, among which are the Arab-Israeli conflict, the India-Pakistan confrontation and the tensions in and around Afghanistan. The relationship between the two giants – China and India – has in store controversial and unresolved issues.

Strengthening Russia's presence in the Asia-Pacific region (APR) is becoming increasingly important since Russia is an integral part of this fastest-developing geopolitical zone, towards which the center of world economy and politics is gradually shifting. Russia is interested in participating actively in APR integration processes, using the possibilities offered by the APR to implement programs meant to boost the Siberian and Far Eastern economy, creating transparent and equitable security architecture in the APR and cooperation on a collective basis. In this context, special emphasis is placed on enhancing Russia's role in regional and global affairs of the SCO, whose constructive influence in the region as a whole has significantly increased.

Russia is committed to strengthening its privileged strategic partnership with India, improving collaboration on relevant international issues and enhancing mutually beneficial bilateral ties in all areas, primarily in military-technical cooperation, the nuclear energy sphere and trade, bearing in mind the implementation of long-term cooperation programs approved by the countries. Cooperation between Russia and India in Eurasia should be seen, first of all, in the context of the huge natural, economic, political and cultural potential of the region.

The main factors determining the interaction of Russia and India in the Eurasian geopolitical space are the following:

1 Bilateral Russian-Indian relations developed under the influence of historical, economic, political, cultural and civilizational factors, notably the centuries-old ties between the Buddhists of the Russian Siberia and Baikal region with their co-religionists in India, China, Mongolia and Tibet. It is no coincidence that this region was the scene of the "Great Game" – Anglo-Russian rivalry in Central Asia – which determined the fate of the entire region.

2 One should keep in mind the interests and policies of newly independent states of Central Asia, which are based on centuries-old cultural, trade and economic ties between Russia and India with Central Asia. If Russia and the Central Asian states for decades constituted an entity, then India for centuries traditionally developed trade, economic and cultural relations with them, as evidenced, for instance, by the materials of archaeological excavations.

3 It can be noted that the region faced the interests of major international players like Russia, India, China and the United States, whose relations are based on the principles of "cooperation-competition". The United States used the fight against the terrorists and drug trafficking threat from Afghanistan to strengthen its own position in Central Asia, including the establishment of US military facilities on Asian territories. The United States also used the separatist movements to destabilize the situation in the region.

4 In the analysis of the positions and policies of Russia and India in regional, sub-regional and inter-regional organizations and associations, such as the SCO and BRICS, it is necessary to take into account the factor of China, which is not merely a part of these associations, but also occupies the leading position, at least in the SCO.

5 Relations between India and China have a special character: between them remain unresolved border issues and the obvious geopolitical rivalry in parts of Asia, but at the same time trade and economic relations are developing very actively. The trade turnover is close to 100 billion dollars. Apparently,

the pragmatic interests of the two countries prevail over ideology and politics: geo-economics prevails over the geopolitics.

> Thereupon Russia will promote cooperation with India and China in various areas, including seeking ways to address new threats and challenges, finding solutions to urgent regional and international problems, cooperating within the UN Security Council, G20, BRICS, SCO and other multilateral formats. Russia attaches great importance to the further development of the mechanism of effective and mutually beneficial cooperation in foreign policy and economy between Russia, India and China.

6   The situation on the Eurasian geopolitical space is characterized by the persistence of unresolved conflicts and problems in bilateral relations between India and China, India and Pakistan, Russia and the European Union, but there are common interests of countries in Eurasia: the stability, economic development, combating Islamic extremism. While countries in the region do not realize the commonality of interests at the Eurasian level, the risk for the entire continent will continue. Therefore, for the countries of Eurasia it is time for giving up old political stereotypes and develop a new Eurasian continental thinking. Hope that all the troubles will cause more damage to the neighbor, not to you, may turn into a disaster for Eurasia.

The SCO has decided to admit two more major Asian countries, with Moscow and Beijing supporting the requests of India and Pakistan. Indian and Pakistan's participation in the SCO may contribute to the normalization of relations between them, and at the same time it is a signal that the organization will support the normalization of Pakistan-India relations. In the 1960s, the USSR acted as the arbiter between the two countries, but now the SCO can take on this function.

India has wanted to join the organization almost since its inception, and it has held observer status. But as soon as full-fledged membership was brought up for India, Pakistan was also immediately engaged. In this situation, Russia was ready to support India's bid for membership and China expressed interest in Pakistan. In the end, it was decided to admit both countries.

Strategic analysts note that the SCO is becoming an increasingly significant player in the global arena. On 2 October 2013, after negotiations with the Indian External Affairs Minister Salman Khurshid, his Russian counterpart Sergei Lavrov said that Moscow supports India's bid for membership in the organization and believes that the SCO "will benefit from the membership of countries such as India and Pakistan". There is no doubt that this issue was agreed to by both China and Russia. For Russia, admitting India to the SCO was a very positive step, but now the question of mending Russian-Pakistani relations will certainly come up but definitely not at the cost of Moscow's relations with India. Russia is now trying to build a relationship with Pakistan in the context of the new geopolitical situation following the partial withdrawal of US and NATO troops from Afghanistan in 2014.

At a summit held in Minsk, Russia, Belarus and Kazakhstan confirmed their intention to form the Eurasian Economic Union in 2015 on the basis of the

Customs Union. Turkey, India and Syria could join the new alliance, but this project was seriously criticized by Kazakhstan's president, N. Nazarbayev. In his opinion, the three countries should solve the existing problems and then deepen the integration, and after that the Customs Union and the Eurasian Economic Union could accept new members.

Russia is an Asian country, and the security of Asia is vital for the country. It declared India and China as strategic partners, as well as important military partners. It is in the interest of Russia to make sure that the SCO becomes a platform for these three major powers, Russia, China and India, to come together. Analyzing the prospects for further development of the situation in Eurasia and Russia's policy in the region in the context of Russia-India relations, the following factors may in future have an impact on the evolution of the situation in this vast geopolitical space.

Development of the situation in and around Afghanistan after the withdrawal of coalition troops and the possibility of activating the Taliban and al-Qaeda in the region

Russia and India occupy similar or common position in respect of the Afghan problem, and both have demonstrated their willingness to participate in the restoration of peace and stability in Afghanistan, contribute to the solution of internal economic and political problems, and take special measures to prevent the spread of terrorism and drug trafficking from the territory of Afghanistan.

As regards Russia, China and India will be crucial for stability in Afghanistan after the withdrawal of US and NATO troops, as well as the balance of political forces that are most likely to fight for power in Afghanistan. It should be borne in mind that the central government exercises control over Kabul and only a small part of the territory of Afghanistan, while the Taliban controls the rest of the country. The question may arise about the threat to the territorial integrity of Afghanistan, and Russia, China and India are highly interested in preserving the country's unity.

On 16 January 2014, at the trilateral meeting in Beijing of the three major powers in the region, India, China and Russia agreed that Afghanistan's stability and security are important to the region against the backdrop of the US plan to remove its troops from Afghanistan, raising fears of the reemergence of Taliban and other al-Qaeda–linked elements. The three sides exchanged views on the situation in Afghanistan and agreed that security in Afghanistan is important to the country and the region. "They reiterated support for a strong, united, stable, peaceful and prosperous Afghanistan. They also agreed to meet again". Replying to a question on the meeting, Chinese Foreign Ministry spokesperson Hong Lei said: "The development of situation in Afghanistan is closely related to the peace and stability in the region".[10] Hong Lei said that China recognized that security outcome in Afghanistan would affect broader regional security and stability. He added,

> As a close neighbor of Afghanistan, China is ready to work with countries in the region and the international community to support the peaceful

reconstruction and reconciliation process in Afghanistan and jointly maintain peace, stability and development of Afghanistan and the whole region.

Beijing recently held a trilateral meeting with Pakistan and Russia on the same matter, and also met with Pakistani and Afghan officials on a number of occasions. China has also pushed the matter of Afghanistan to the top of the Shanghai Cooperation Organization's (SCO) agenda.

In early 2013, Moscow hosted a trilateral dialogue on Afghanistan with India and China. The logic of the trilateral discussion is simple on its face: India, China and Russia all have an important stake in Afghan stability after the withdrawal of US and NATO forces, and want to see a turbulence-free election this year. China has invested over $3 billion in Afghanistan, and India over $2 billion.[11]

Russia, India and China all supported the Bilateral Security Agreement, which Afghan President Hamid Karzai was reluctant to sign, arguing that his successor would be best left to handle the issue.[12]

Prospects for the development of relations between India and China in the Eurasian context

The relationship between the two major Asian powers traditionally determines the level of stability and security in the Eurasian geopolitical space. At the moment one can say that, despite the persistence of unresolved contentious issues in bilateral relations, the two sides promote bilateral economic and political cooperation, as well as interact through such associations as RIC, BRICS and SCO. Russia is involved in the activities of these organizations and also develops political and trade relations with India and China, at the bilateral level. The three countries hold common or similar positions on the issues of stability and security in Eurasia, on resolution of the situation in and around Afghanistan, combating international terrorism and so forth. Cooperation on Afghanistan could serve to bring India and China closer in terms of their mutual contributions to security in Asia. Both India and China, and Russia to a lesser degree, will be important sources of investment for Afghanistan in coming years.

Russia, India and China as the Eurasian powers can pursue economic and scientific and technical cooperation in the exploitation of natural resources of Eurasia, including in Siberia and the Far East, including joint construction of oil and gas pipelines linking the three countries.

Afghanistan-Pakistan-India trilateral ties

If Russia, India and China begin to frame the discussion about Afghanistan in counterterrorism terms, that would inevitably involve Pakistan. India uniquely faces the threat of Pakistan-bred Islamist terrorism. Pakistan's status as an "all-weather" partner of China complicates this reality. However, Beijing gives cause for optimism on this matter as it so far has succeeded in avoiding any linkages between its relationship with Islamabad and its interests in Kabul.

Chinese analysts realize that Pakistan's military and Inter-Services Intelligence (ISI) have a major stake in destabilizing Kabul. Beijing doesn't seem to be interested in reigning in Islamabad on this matter, and instead prefers to deal with Afghan security as a separate issue altogether. Ultimately, cooperation between Russia, China and India on Afghanistan will be a net positive for regional security, provided that India and China can successfully navigate their respective relationships with Pakistan in the process. De-linking Afghan policy from other competitive impulses will only be beneficial for Afghanistan and the region.

Great powers will continue to pretend to be the "center" of Eurasian integration. It is primarily about China, the European Union, and the United States, as well as a group of Islamic states. Former US Secretary of State Hillary Clinton stated in December 2012 that the United States will oppose the Eurasian integration in any form. At the same time, the United States is expected to build bilateral relations with China, Russia and India, ignoring the existing institutions (SCO, CSTO, etc.) and preventing the creation of a Eurasian security system.

According to some analysts, the objective process of Eurasian integration is only about one thing – under whose control it will pass. Under the control of the United States, which will inevitably grow from Southeast Asia to the Antarctic, or under the control of China, to create its own "*Velikokitaysky*" (Great Chinese) Eurasian union", or under the control of Russia (and possibly India), which can unite Eurasian powers.

In this regard, the question arises: will the future Eurasian Union be monocentric or polycentric? Today there are different opinions, though by and large, the choice may be between American-centric, China-centric or Russia/India–centric projects.

Notes

1 *Foreign Policy Concept of the Russian Federation.* Approved by the decree of the President of the Russian Federation from November 30, 2016, No. 640.
2 *Toward the Great Ocean, or the New Globalization of Russia.* Moscow, Valdai Discussion Club Analytical Reports, July 2012. p. 5.
3 See Levan Kakhishvili, *Assessing Russia's Policy Towards its "Near Abroad"?* www.e-ir.info/2013/06/17/assessing-russian-policy-toward-its-near-abroad/.
4 *Izvestia*, 3 October 2011.
5 *Toward the Great Ocean.*
6 See: *Executive Intelligence Review* Vol. 24, No. 49, 5 December 1997.
7 See Zbigniew Brzezinski, *The Grand Chessboard: American Primacy and Its Geostrategic Imperatives.* New York, Basic Books, 1997.
8 Ibid., pp. 8–9.
9 Ibid., p. 47.
10 http://afghanistan.ru/doc/71073.html; http://news.outlookindia.com/items.aspx?artid=825014.
11 *Is Trilateral China-India-Russia Cooperation in Afghanistan Possible?* http://the diplomat.com/2014/01/is-trilateral-china-india-russia-cooperation-in-afghanistan-possible/.
12 http://economictimes.indiatimes.com/.

10 The Eurasian vector of Kazakhstan's policy
Relevance for India

Fatima Kukeyeva

The Eurasian vector of Kazakhstan's foreign policy is relevant for India, as it allows solving a number of geopolitical, geo-economic and geo-cultural challenges. It would strengthen India's position in the competition with China for influence in Central Asia and Eurasia as a whole. Today, researchers state the gap between the significant potential for the creation of an Indo-Central Asian and Indo-Eurasian alliance and of the weakness of its presence in the region, which Delhi demonstrated by the end of the first decade of the twenty-first century.

From geo-economics India could join the ranks of the powers using economic instruments to influence the European Union, South Korea and Japan. Indian cultural relations with Central Asia and Russia would modernize the mechanism of historical ties corresponding to the twenty-first-century demands. In general, three states – India, Kazakhstan and Russia – could constitute a successful triangle.

The Eurasian vector of Kazakhstan

The Eurasian vector can allow Kazakhstan to increase its sovereignty and strengthen its position in the international arena. Eurasian integration is a strategic choice of Kazakhstan, which is developing cooperation within the framework of the most complex and deep integration formats – the Customs Union and Common Economic area of Russia, Belarus and Kazakhstan. These three countries have become the core of the Eurasian integration.

The Eurasian vector could replace the previous strategy of unstable balance between Russia and the West in order not only to avoid the conflict with the Russian strategic interests but also to strengthen Kazakhstan's sovereignty and international positions. In fact, it is the unique possibility to combine (reconcile the irreconcilable) and to develop real "multi-vector foreign policy" within the priority of the Russian vector.

Such a policy can be defined as a strategy of "sustainable multi-vector" or "Eurasian". Eurasianism and multi-vector policy being the alternative trend will turn to be a complementary vector of development. The situation currently developing in Eurasia gives a quite real chance for this policy. The new foreign policy concept of Kazakhstan, 2014–2020, emphasizes:

> Considering the Eurasian economic integration as one of the most effective ways to promote the country's strong position in the world economic system, Kazakhstan will strengthen the Customs Union and the Common Economic Space in order to build on this basis, the Eurasian Economic Union.[1]

Growing Chinese influence in the region certainly troubles India. But the question – will it lead to cooperation or conflict? – is still open. Creation of strong economic ties in Eurasia is an integral part of the rise and strengthening of Chinese power. All states concerned should consider the Chinese expansion in Central Asia and Eurasia in long-term strategic planning, as it will inevitably affect both themselves and the balance of power in the Eurasian continent. Considering that India and China are involved in the processes of Eurasian cooperation, it could be said that Kazakhstan is located in the center of the "great circle", which consists of both competing and cooperating states

India and Kazakhstan

For Kazakhstan, India is of great pragmatic interest. The dynamics of events taking place in South Asia, namely the economic and political potential increase, strengthening regional integration trends, indicates the priority of building stable and mutually beneficial relations between India and Kazakhstan. The Republic of Kazakhstan holds a special place in Indian regional policy. In 2009, President Nursultan Nazarbayev announced a "strategic partnership" which was promoted widely during his official visit to India as the chief guest at India's Republic Day.[2]

The Joint Action Plan signed in 2011 started the "road map" which defines bilateral cooperation in various areas. India and Kazakhstan share the same views on the most topical global problems. Both countries develop important investment projects. There is also an agreement to explore the possibility of establishing direct trade and energy routes between India and Kazakhstan. In support of this position, there are enough strong arguments:

> First, similar foreign policy priorities make mutual interest more stable.
> Second, political stability, high economic and scientific-technical potential of Kazakhstan and the emerging confidence level of bilateral relations.
> Third, existence of significant reserves of hydrocarbons and other natural resources in a favorable investment climate in Kazakhstan market.
> Fourth, the support of Kazakhstan's initiatives by India in the international arena.

Eurasian vector of Kazakhstan's foreign policy is an important factor for Indian geopolitical and geostrategic activities, apart from geo-economic and geocultural activities based on competing interests in the region.

Presently India demonstrates an interest in shaping and organizing the Eurasian space for the following reasons:

1 India's big strategy includes so-called extended neighborhood in Asia (including Central Asia) where India is trying to balance the influence of other powers, and not allow them to overstep upon its interests.

Indian policy makers are working tirelessly to improve the status of India both in regional and global realms. Delhi is doing its best to adjust relations with its direct neighbors, to find ways of coexistence with China and Pakistan (their main competitors in the region) and to restore its position in the Near Abroad, in some parts of Africa, Central and South East Asia, the Gulf and the Indian Ocean. At the same time India has developed its relations with the great powers, especially with the Russian Federation and the United States.

India's participation in the strategic alliance or unions with one or even a few neighbors is the way to increase its role and importance in the global community. Considering the fact that India has serious tensions with Pakistan and China, the absence of any major contradictions with Kazakhstan and Russia and in the future with the Eurasian Union makes them "natural ally states".

2 India's interests in the energy sector, while ensuring political stability, are the main factors in encouraging India to strengthen its influence in the Central Asian region.

India's interest in Eurasia is now obviously based on the fact that being rich in natural resources, Kazakhstan has oil-exploration and other energy contracts with Chinese companies. Kazakhstan was reportedly initially wary of allowing a Chinese company to take over its strategic oil assets for fear that China could control its energy resources. CNPC eventually managed to reassure the Kazakh government, and acquired the company. The deal has not only added to CNPC's existing share in Kazakhstan's petroleum sector, but also moved China into a better position to expand into other oil projects in the country.[3]

In order to diversify energy flows, Kazakhstan welcomes the active introduction of the Indian ONGC oil company to the Kazakh market. Today, India is seriously considering the prospects for its own energy security with the countries of Central Asia and Eurasia. That is why India seriously correlates its own energy security perspectives with Central Asia and Eurasia. The global energy security in the long term will be of great relevance for India. The intensive Indian energy diplomacy aims to create a new world energy structure, which is based on the so-called pan-Asian solidarity. Its proponents believe that this structure will provide producing countries guaranteed energy markets and importing countries guaranteed supply on a long-term basis.

According to the statements of the Indian minister of petroleum and natural gas, India has the intention to participate in the exploration of Kazakh oil and gas fields as well as in the works to expand oil and gas in the well-known and long- exploited fields. India is also interested in cooperation with Kazakhstan companies to upgrade existing refineries and creating new ones.

The Indian side is also interested in the development of the "North-South" transport corridor at Aktau on the Caspian Sea through Iran to the Arabian Sea. The design of this corridor requires a railway from Europe through Russia, Azerbaijan and Iran to India and Southeast Asia. There is the possibility of connection of Kazakhstan and other Central Asian oil fields in Aktau with India through a pipeline route, possibly through Turkmenistan and Iran.[4]

However, even if India gets access to the oil and gas fields in the region, a serious problem for the implementation of energy interests is the lack of pipeline between the two countries. The project of the Turkmenistan-Afghanistan-Pakistan pipeline could become a possible solution to the issue of providing oil and gas supplies to India. According to calculations of the profitability, the project requires India's gas market connection to it to justify the development of major projects. India initially refrained from confirming its participation in the project, considering the complicated political situation in the region. But in 2005 India began actively participating in the member countries' negotiations. The alternative is a proposed Russian project to build a gas pipeline from Iran to India through Pakistan's territorial waters.

Anyway, India has actively participated in the discussion of the two projects, which have developed the feasibility study. In general, the energy policy of India is designed for the longer term. Now India is fully provided with oil and gas supplies from the Persian Gulf. Central Asian importance as a source of energy will increase as resources from geographically close regions are exhausted and difficulties with the supply of oil and gas of the more affordable places will increase.

However, India's energy strategy in Central Asia remains modest compared to China, Russia and the United States. Virtually all researchers have noted the weak presence of India in Central Asia. China successfully went ahead of India in obtaining contracts for hydrocarbon production and delivery from Kazakhstan. China, despite the growing Indian economy, is undoubtedly ahead in the region in terms of energy imports, transport infrastructure construction and building trade. But India's energy needs are increasing. That is why for India it is extremely important to develop new energy sources. India started negotiations with Kazakhstan on the issue of purchase of the Kazakh Kashagan share for about $5–6 billion.[5]

India is also trying to expand cooperation in the field of nuclear energy with Russia and Kazakhstan, and at the same time negotiating with Rosneft to buy a share. Such large investment projects cannot solve the problem of "energy shortage" of India. The country is the fourth largest consumer of oil and the seventh largest gas consumer in the world. It is expected that oil demand in the country will grow to 200 million tons by 2025.[6] India will have to remove quotas on oil and gas imports from any country and buy energy anywhere it can find at the best price. In this context, the Caspian basin is considered to be an important source of hydrocarbons.[7] It is for this reason that India's ONGC bought a 8.42 percent share in Conoco Phillips in Kazakhstan, as well as in the Azerbaijan sector of the

Caspian Sea. Former Indian Prime Minister Manmohan Singh's visit to Astana in 2011 helped India gain access to areas of the northern Caspian Sea, where there are reserves of oil, gas and uranium. In 2012, India's ONGC was allowed to take over in future 25 percent stake in an offshore oil block Satpayev owned by KazMunaiGas.[8]

Holding shares in energy projects, India has problems with the extraction of oil resources and use them for production purposes or sell. The main obstacles for India are its geographic location, the instability in Afghanistan and the complex relationship with Pakistan. Another problem is its relations with China, which obviously does not want to have a competitor in the region. China's success in Central Asia is incomparable with any other country. China has already received 40 billion cubic meters of natural gas per year from Turkmenistan, and this figure is projected to increase to 65 billion cubic meters after the accession of the Uzbek and Kazakh pipeline. According to experts, India is a secondary force in Central Asia, which cannot compete with either China or Russia.

China very successfully competes with India in Central Asia. In this resource-rich region, China is building roads, railways and pipelines. Kazakh oil, Turkmen natural gas and Afghan copper is sent directly to China through a newly built eastward network, contributing to the rapid development of China. Pipelines from the Caspian Sea through Kazakhstan and planned roads and railways across the entire territory of Russia to the port of Gwadar in Pakistan are part of China's efforts to turn Central Asia into the transit region between East and West.

Therefore, India plans to send the increased goods flow through an international "North-South" transport corridor. The opening of the last Turkmen section of the line Zhanaozen-Golgan (under construction since 2007), will shorten the distance of the international trade corridor "North-South" by 600 km.[9]

3   Eurasian vector of Kazakhstan's policy allows India free access to the vast markets for Indian exports (including Russia). India is interested in Central Asia because of trade and economic cooperation. This region is considered as a market for Indian products and promising source of natural resources (gold and energy resources), as well as a transit corridor for Indian goods in the CIS countries and Europe.

At the same time, India is seeking ways to expand economic ties with the region, to create conditions for solving its political problems. It is obvious that the incentives for the development of economic ties originate mainly from the Indian side, by organizing international industry expeditions, business meetings and so forth. The Indian government is investing in the Central Asian economies and is encouraging private sector investment in the region. India, by developing trade and economic cooperation, is trying to gain a foothold in those niches where it is traditionally strong: information technology and software, pharmaceuticals and medical equipment, textiles and tea.

Kazakhstan is one of the main economic partners in the region. Indian business is present in the field of pharmaceuticals, agricultural products processing and textile manufacturing. But the main reason for the weak presence of Indian companies in the Central Asian market are direct transport and communication difficulties. These are caused by the lack of a common border with the Central Asian republics which lack access to the ocean, besides the absence of well-developed transport infrastructure. India's presence in Central Asian markets requires the development of the "North-South" transport corridor, designed to connect the countries of South and Southeast Asia to Europe via Iran, the Caspian Sea and Russia by creating a network of rail, sea and road links.

However, the growth of the Kazakh-Indian trade and strengthening bilateral political cooperation suggests that India can play the role of a counterweight to China, thereby reducing the factor of the "China threat" in the region. According to Kazakhstan experts, India could stand in one line with the powers like the European Union, South Korea and Japan that use economic leverage to influence.

Kazakhstan is the largest Indian trading partner in Central Asia (bilateral trade in 2011 amounted to $291.4 million, and for 2012 it was $525 million). It is evidence of the great opportunities for Indo-Kazakh business cooperation.[10] It is, therefore, necessary to harmonize the trade dynamics in tune with the potential of the two countries. Kazakhstan and India have agreed to cooperate in the field of nano and information technologies. Taking into consideration that India has a well-developed science and modern technology, it is the second (after the United States), a worldwide developer of computer programs, there exist good opportunities for investment projects in the fields of IT technologies, and also in pharmaceuticals and textiles.

India has always been one of the Russia's closest and most reliable friends and partners. Trade and economic cooperation between Russia and India is developing dynamically. The Federal Customs Service of Russia reported a 7.5 percent increase in Russian-Indian trade between 2008 and 2009, to US$7.46 billion. In January-February 2010, it grew by 40 percent, with a 40 percent increase in Russian exports and imports.[11]

According to Ajay Bisaria, former head of the Eurasian Department of the Indian Foreign Ministry, India needs to develop a number of mechanisms at the intergovernmental level that could contribute to the growth of trade between the countries. The free trade agreement or an agreement on comprehensive economic cooperation with the joint Eurasian space will change the situation for the better. India is willing to consider the issue about joining the Customs Union. Speaking at a seminar, Ajay Bisaria described economics as the weakest link in India-Russia and India-Kazakhstan strategic ties which could be fortified with a Free Trade Agreement (FTA) or a Comprehensive Economic Cooperation Agreement (CECA).[12] Both sides are following multi-vector policies. India is negotiating FTAs or CECAs with several trading blocks and countries (Russia, Belarus and Kazakhstan). But hotbeds of instability, underdeveloped transport networks and rugged mountains located between the territory of the Customs Union and India pose a challenge to establish closer trade relations between the two sides.

4   The development of the Eurasian vector and the creation of the Eurasian Union will enable India to strengthen its economic presence in the region.

India, in the absence of a land border with Kazakhstan, is losing in comparison with China's economic presence in Kazakhstan and the region as a whole.

However, in the case of accession to the Customs Union, India can bypass China and gain a foothold in the region of its strong interest. India is interested in establishing a Free Trade Zone to gain access to the energy resources of Central Asia and Russia. In a joint statement, the leaders of the Customs Union member states stated that the parties agreed to explore the possibility of direct ground transportation of hydrocarbons from Russia to India and also expressed support for India joining the Shanghai Cooperation Organization (SCO).

Rapprochement between India and the Customs Union is a very important political maneuver. If the Customs Union will develop a pace commensurate on a similar model as China's, it naturally will create a powerful economic center. There is a view that India does not seek Customs Union membership, but only expressed a desire to create a Free Trade Zone with the Eurasian Economic Community. Indian entry into the Customs Union is unrealistic, but the alignment of special economic relations with this country in the former Soviet space is quite real. This opinion was expressed by Azhdar Kurtov, "Rosbalt" correspondent expert with the Russian Institute of Strategic Studies.[13]

5   India supports Kazakhstan's foreign policy Eurasian vector in the hope to play a greater role in the SCO. India would like to expand regional cooperation. China is well ahead of India in the creation of such an influential regional political structure as the SCO. China clearly intends to use the SCO to strengthen its influence in Central Asia and was thus opposed to India's membership in the organization.

According to Indian analysts, SCO has emerged as a highly active and leading organization in the region. "SCO was able to solve the task of maintaining stability and security in Central Asia". Significance of the SCO also increased because the focus of international politics gradually moved from Western Europe to Eurasia. Eurasian continent attracts a lot of attention because of its natural resources, including large energy reserves. It caused serious rivalry between the major powers for control on this territory.[14]

India, like other SCO member states, is facing security problems that have an inter-ethnic character. Non-traditional threats require concerted and joint action of SCO's almost ready mechanism. Thus, India supports the concept of "common geopolitical space" in security matters.

India and Kazakhstan have a common interest in fighting against Islamic extremism, terrorism and drug trafficking, and stabilizing the situation in Afghanistan and regional security. By promoting regional cooperation with Central Asian countries in this field, India is trying to indirectly limit the influence of Pakistan, which is considered by India as the base of international terrorism and Islamic extremism in the region.

Strengthening the Eurasian vector prevents the Islamization of Kazakhstan and Central Asia on the whole and creation of an "Islamic belt" associated with

Pakistan. Central Asia is an important security element in Indian relationship with Pakistan, and in the stabilization of Afghanistan. Possible threats from Islamic extremist groups could also invigorate elements active in Kashmir. As regards the balance of power among the great powers in the Central Asian region, India has to restructure the India-Russia partnership, remain alert to China's penetration in Central Asian, forge a cooperation framework with the United States and address its historical rivalry with Pakistan.

6   Kazakhstan and Central Asia are an area of vital importance to India, not only on account of its geographical proximity and India's historical and cultural links with the region, but also because of the common challenge they all face from extremism and terrorism. Thus, India has a common interest with Central Asian governments in stopping the spillover of Islamic fundamentalism from Pakistan and Afghanistan into Central Asia and preventing the region from becoming a conduit for radical religious ideologies with the potential to destabilize the border regions of Uzbekistan, Tajikistan, Kyrgyzstan, China and India.

Considering the intense power play taking place between Russia, China, the United States and other Western countries in the strategic arena of Central Asia, India emphasises its soft power and its positive experience. In spite of the factors contributing to the growth of India's importance for Kazakhstan, experts do not exclude the possibility of stagnation of geopolitical situation in the region and worse, events can develop not in favor of India. The most negative consequence will be the establishment of Chinese economic protectorate in the region or the Islamization of Central Asia.

Security is an important issue of the Indian and Central Asian authors' research, including the problem of Islamisation and as a consequence Islamist extremism. Professor K. Warikoo of Jawaharlal Nehru University analyses the Central Asian religious agenda through expanded regional one, considering the region in the light of the growing threat of radical Islam.[15] The threat of Islamisation comes from the fact that the Islamists fundamentally disagree with the concept of democracy and secularism. Warikoo opines that the rhetoric of political Islam is a response to growing economic inequality, corruption and political impotence within Muslim societies, as well as the moral bankruptcy of modern Western materialistic culture and its value system. Central Asian countries could not stay away from these processes. But the main cause of instability with Islamist overtones is the region's proximity to Afghanistan, and for this reason, Islamisation is a threat for India. The Indian researcher reasonably assumes that India, China, Russia and its Central Asian allies should unite against a common threat. The Eurasian vector of Kazakhstan will certainly contribute to this.

In conclusion, it should be noted that the development of the Eurasian vector of Kazakhstan's foreign policy and the future of the Eurasian Union can strengthen Indian position in Central Asia and Eurasia. India considers the Eurasian space as its extended neighborhood and attaches high importance to its geopolitical and strategic environment in Central Asia and Indian geo-economic interests. India's support to the anti-terrorist and Islamist movements has made it a closer partner of Russia and the Central Asian states. An active Chinese presence in Kazakhstan and Russia is an obvious fact, posing a challenge to the Indian policy makers and business. India, with its civilizational and cultural links to the region, combined with its approach based on soft power, can play the role of a balancer.

But Indian preference to negotiate with the United States all important strategic issues is the challenge for Kazakhstan and especially for Russia. This may affect the geopolitical plans of partners. Over the past few years, the United States developed a consistent policy of rapprochement with India. In 2009 Hillary Clinton, US Secretary of State during her visit to the Indian capital announced: "A new era begins in the relations between India and the United States".[16] The starting point of this new era was the signing of a bilateral agreement on the US export of the modern weapons for the Indian armed forces. Today, Indo-US bilateral trade volume exceeds $100 billion, and US investment in India has exceeded $25 billion. While Kerry stressed that this is not the limit, the United States seeks to maximize their business presence in India, which in the next ten years is poised to become a third world economy.[17]

In contemporary international relations Russia and India have common interests. Both countries are concerned about Central Asian security and counterbalancing China's growing power. For many years, regardless of changes in government leadership, well-developed economic cooperation (especially in the arms trade) and energy projects looked promising. For a long time, Russia and India spoke in one voice in international forums and regularly consulted with each other during periods of crisis and tension. Delhi has been a key ally for Moscow not only in Asia but also in the whole world.

In the context of the increasing importance of Asia in world politics and the necessity to find its place in the new global configuration, Russia used its successful cooperation with India as a valuable asset for the future. That is why a gradual drift of India toward the United States is causing anxiety in Moscow. In the new balance of power India operates by the old principles of geopolitics. By partnering, and in any future alliance with the United States, India pushes the objective logic of maintaining balance. On the one hand, the United States and India desperately look for allies to hold Beijing and limit its ability to implement imperial appetites. From this perspective, "gendarme of the world democracy" and "the largest democracy of the world" are as if made for each other.

In addition there is justification to the pragmatic alliance against China: support for its citizens and the international community's favor can be achieved by emphasizing the similarity of the domestic policy of "democratic" and "peace-loving" states and the contrast between them and the "authoritarian", "aggressive" China.

Thus, Russia and Kazakhstan should strengthen the Indian vector in foreign policy in order to maintain the balance of power between China and other Asian partners.

India, from its side, should activate its foreign policy in Central Asia in general and Kazakhstan in particular. The period when India explained its passive policy in Central Asia and Eurasia due to absence of geographical boundaries is coming to an end. In this context, the views of experts, as well as the policy makers and business, have changed significantly.

Notes

1 www.zakon.kz/4599704-utverzhdena-koncepcija-vneshnejj.html.
2 *Казахстан-Индия: Н. Назарбаев завершает государственный визит в Дели* ["Kazakhstan-India: Nazarbayev Completes State Visit to Delhi"]. www.fergananews.com/news.php?id=11143.
3 *О деятельности CNPC на территории Казахстана* ["About Activities of CNPC in Kazakhstan Territory"]. http://expertonline.kz/a10113.
4 *Энергетическое сотрудничество Индии и стран Центральной Азии* ["Energy Cooperation Between India Vestnik KazNU and Central Asian Countries"]. Вестник КазНУ. No. 1. 2013.
5 www.ia-centr.ru.
6 *Индия подключается к российскому шельфу* ["India Secures Russian Shelf"]. www.gazeta.ru/business/2012/08/20/4731313.shtml.
7 www.ia-centr.ru.
8 Ibid.
9 www.wok.kz/search?find_str.
10 http://infoshos.ru/ru/?idn=3573.
11 *О состоянии российско-индийского Торгово-экономического* ["About Russia-India Trade Economic Cooperation"]. сотрудничества//www.economy.gov.ru/wps/wcm/connect/ . . . /tes_ru_india.doc?MOD
12 Ibid.
13 A. Ivanovsky, *Россия теряет Индию на рынке вооружений* ["Russia Losing Indian Arms Market"]. http://vpk-news.ru/articles/16804.
14 www.ia-centr.ru.
15 K. Warikoo, ed., *Religion and Security in South and Central Asia*. London and New York, Routledge, 2011. 217 pp.
16 Ibid.
17 Ibid.

11 Eurasianism and Kazakhstan's foreign policy

Angira Sen Sarma

"Eurasianism" as a concept

The genesis of "Eurasianism" has its roots in the works of the Russian emigrants of the early twentieth century, who took refuge in various Western countries after the October Revolution and the subsequent civil war. This ideology since then has been debated to explain the rich heritage and uniqueness of the vast Eurasian region. Eurasianism has been variously interpreted depending on circumstances prevailing at a particular historical juncture. It is associated with geopolitics, history, geography, culture and so forth.

Broadly speaking, the ideology has seen two phases in its evolution: the classical period of the early twentieth century and Neo-Eurasianism that started from the late 1980s. The main ideologues in the classical period were Nikolay S. Troubetzkoy, a linguist and philologist; Peter N. Savitsky, a geographer and economist; George Vernadsky, a historian; G. Florovskii, an Orthodox theologian; P. Suvchinski, a musicologist and art historian; and L. Karsavin, a philosopher. The idea of Eurasianism during the classical period was linked to culture and geography, associating Russia with "neither European nor Asian culture".[1] Rather for the Eurasianists, Russian identity was embedded in the Turko-Mongol heritage.[2] The concept of Eurasia as described by Troubetzkoy was that

> the territory of Russia . . . constitutes a separate continent . . . which in contrast to Europe and Asia can be called Eurasia. . . . Eurasia represents an integral whole, both geographically and anthropologically. . . . By its very nature, Eurasia is historically destined to comprise a single state entity. From the beginning the political unification of Eurasia was a historical inevitability, and the geography of Eurasia indicated the means to achieve it.[3]

The Eurasian movement that one witnessed in its classical phase gradually started losing its vigour. Because of differences among scholars and Soviet repression, an "organizational and ideological crisis" gradually surfaced.[4] Despite facing repression during the Soviet period, works of scholars like L. N. Gumilev kept the ideology alive. Gumilev, a Russian historian and ethnologist, greatly influenced the post-Soviet Eurasian movement. In the latter part of the 1980s and following the post-Soviet disintegration, the ideology witnessed a revival, primarily through the works of Alexander S. Panarin and Alexander G. Dugin. This period of discourse on Eurasianism is known as the era of Neo-Eurasianism, which is still continuing. For Panarin and Dugin, Eurasianism is a doctrine that relates to geopolitics, tradition, opposes globalization, is close to Orthodox Christianity and stands for a multipolar world order.[5] The Eurasian philosophy includes

> differentialism, pluralism of value systems against obligatory domination of a single ideology (in our case and first of all, of the American liberal democracy); traditionalism against destruction of cultures, beliefs and rites of the traditional society; world-state, continent-state against both bourgeois national states and the "world government"; rights of nations against omnipotence of the "Golden Billion" and neo-colonial hegemony of the "Rich North"; an ethnos as a value and subject of history against depersonalization of nations and their alienation in artificial socio-political constructions; social fairness and solidarity of labour people against exploitation, logic of coarse grain, and humiliation of man by man.[6]

For Dugin,

> Eurasianism is a very large set of ideas, attitudes, approaches and concepts, which represent a complete model of world outlook, applicable to different levels. Eurasianism also contains, along with the political component, the purely philosophical, historic-cultural, historical, sociological and geopolitical ones.[7]

From time to time, different interpretations of Eurasianism have developed, but the common thread is that the ideology constitutes "some unique synthesis of European and Asian principles".[8] Both classical and Neo-Eurasianists viewed Russian-Eurasian civilization as antithetical to the West.[9] However, the classical Eurasianists and Neo-Eurasianists differ on four main issues: the definition of Eurasia, the location of Eurasia, the definition of the West and the place of Eurasia in the world.[10] Classical Eurasianists see Eurasia as a "specific civilizational zone" within a "more or less clearly demarcated geographical region".[11] Their description of geographical boundaries of Eurasia was limited within the demarcated boundaries of Russia-Eurasia at the start of the twentieth century and later incorporated those areas which were included under the former USSR by the middle of the 1920s.[12] The Neo-Eurasianists, on the other hand, identify Eurasia as "political and ideological principle" that is opposed to the US efforts of creating a unipolar world order.[13] Eurasia for Neo-Eurasianists like Dugin includes any region and people opposing American hegemony.[14] His concept of geographical extent of Eurasia is not limited to post-Soviet space and moves beyond "geographical boundaries altogether to become a genuinely global project".[15] According to Dugin, Eurasianism portrays "a special civilizational, cultural, philosophical, and strategic choice, which can be made by any member of the human race, regardless of what [specific] national and spiritual culture they may belong to".[16] An important aspect of the ideology in the classical period was its opposition to Western European civilization and its efforts to build Eurasia as an alternative to Europe.[17] They believed in the uniqueness of the Russia-Eurasia space, which they believed constitutes a world in itself.[18] Now, for the Neo-Eurasianists, West means the United States and not Europe. They are opposed to the United States/ Atlanticism, and this opposition is an offshoot of "global geopolitics" and does not arise from an "unbridgeable moral and historical-civilizational divide" as was seen during the classical period.[19]

Having looked at the basic tenets of the ideology, this chapter discusses its expansion beyond Russia after the Soviet disintegration. The interest in the ideology is growing. Generally associated with Russia, Eurasianism today has received a lot of support from other countries too. In the post-Soviet period, one of the main proponents of Eurasianism outside Russia is President Nursultan Nazarbayev of Kazakhstan. President Nazarbayev's support for the idea of Eurasianism has given a new dimension and momentum to the Eurasian movement.

Eurasianism and Kazakhstan

Support from President Nazarbayev gave Eurasianism the status of a state ideology. Back in 1994, President Nazabayev took the initiative to revive the idea of Eurasian integration, which he proposed in a speech delivered on 29 March at the Lomonosov Moscow State University. In his speech, President Nazarbayev outlined his vision for Eurasian integration in the following words:

> How do I see the future of that space that used to be one country? Nowadays, in the conditions of sovereignty, recognising equal rights of all, respecting the sovereignty and independence of each state, we could create a completely new unity. I would call it the Eurasian Union. The basic principle is ensuring equality and respect for the sovereignty and independence of the states, for individual rights and the identity of each state. Only those states which recognise these principles should be accepted into the Eurasian Union. We would work on the basis of bilateral agreements with those which do not accept or are not yet ready to observe these principles. Naturally, for member states of such a union, special conditions will be created.[20]

However, at that point of time, there was not much enthusiasm for the idea and nothing much progressed. The situation since then has changed significantly. The concept is gradually gaining salience in Kazakhstan's foreign policy. Economic integration features prominently in Nazarbayev's vision of Eurasianism. The emergence of the Customs Union, culminating gradually to Eurasian Union reflects the ongoing Eurasian integration process in the Eurasian region. Before going into the Eurasian vector of Kazakhstan's foreign policy, a look into the dynamics of the country's foreign policy, especially Kazakhstan's relationship with Russia, China, the United States and the European Union deserves attention. Diversification under the framework of "multi-vector" foreign policy has been a key pillar in Kazakhstan's foreign policy. Understanding the trends in Kazakhstan's relationship with these countries is critical to assess the implications of Kazakhstan's Eurasian vision.

Foreign policy dynamics

Abundant natural resources, economic growth, relative political stability and its location at the crossroad between Asia and Europe makes Kazakhstan an important country in the Eurasian region. Post-independence, Kazakhstan's willingness to take up greater international responsibilities has boosted its international image. It was the first Eurasian country to hold the chair of the Organization of Security and Co-operation in Europe (OSCE) in 2010. It held the chair of the Organization of Islamic Conference (OIC) in 2011 and was instrumental in changing the name of the group to Organization of Islamic Cooperation (OIC). Kazakhstan has been an active member of various regional groups dealing with different issues like the Shanghai Cooperation Organization (SCO), the Collective Security Treaty Organization (CSTO), the Commonwealth of Independent States (CIS), the Conference of Interaction and Confidence-building Measures in Asia (CICA) and so forth. Kazakhstan has initiated the Assistance Programme on Reconstruction of Afghanistan; it is the only country in Central Asia to have a programme earmarked for Afghanistan. President Nazarbayev's nuclear diplomacy immediately after independence won him accolades. As part of the Soviet legacy, Kazakhstan inherited huge nuclear arsenals, but Kazakhstan voluntarily renounced nuclear weapons after independence. It is a signatory to the Nuclear Non-Proliferation Treaty (NPT) and has been a supporter of nuclear disarmament. Kazakhstan banned nuclear testing in the country and with help from the United States under the Nunn-Lugar Cooperative Threat Reduction Programme cleaned Kazakhstan of any nuclear weapons and its infrastructure.[21]

The document "Strategy Kazakhstan 2050" of 2012 outlines the country's foreign policy priorities as strengthening regional and national security, promoting economic and trade diplomacy, boosting international cooperation in cultural, humanitarian, scientific and education sectors and increasing legal protection of citizens.[22] It also indicated Kazakhstan's continuing emphasis on diversification of its foreign relations: "our aims are to diversify our foreign policy and develop economic and trade diplomacy to protect and promote national economic and trade interests".[23]

Kazakhstan since independence has been making efforts to diversify its relations by reaching out to the wider international community. The multi-vector diplomacy coined by Nazarbayev became a cardinal principle in Kazakhstan's foreign policy. The term is used to describe Kazakhstan's "foreign policy balancing act, which seeks to position Kazakhstan as an even-handed ally of Russia, China, the European Union and the United States".[24] Kazakhstan has successfully practiced its multi-vector policy. It has managed its relations well with not only big countries like Russia, China and the United States but also developed close relations with various other countries across the globe. This has been an astute move by a country that was born only twenty-five years ago in a region witnessing tough competition among various players trying to create their spheres of influence. Balancing its relations with different countries has helped Kazakhstan to avoid dependence on any one particular country. Although Kazakhstan's relations with other countries were determined under the broader concept of multi-vector diplomacy, the way its bilateral relations emerged with the four main players (Russia, China, the United States and European Union) is critical to its foreign policy objectives. Over the years, Kazakhstan has developed a "nuanced foreign policy" that in the initial years emphasised on foreign investments, particularly in the hydrocarbon sector to boost economic development and later focussed on enhancing the country's role in regional and international affairs.[25] Following is a brief description of Kazakhstan's relations with Russia, China, the United States and the European Union.

Russia

Kazakhstan shares the longest border with Russia; a sizeable population of ethnic Russians resides in Kazakhstan, and strong energy and trade linkages with Russia make Russia an important pillar of Kazakhstan's foreign policy structure. Geography and a long history further link Kazakhstan with Russia. In 1998, the Treaty of Eternal Friendship and Cooperation was signed between the two countries, and in the same year an agreement was signed to demarcate their sectors of the Caspian seabed. It formulated a legal basis for the joint development and exploitation of oil fields lying in the Kazakhstan-Russian sectors.[26] Both sides have peacefully resolved their border issues and ratified the treaty demarcating the common land border in 2005.[27] Defence cooperation has been another benchmark in the bilateral relationship. In 2006, an agreement was signed to rent four training and testing grounds to Russia and the two countries have been hosting joint exercises.[28] They amicably resolved their differences on the Baikonur space centre and in 2005, Kazakhstan extended the Russian lease for Baikonur till 2050.[29] The Soviet-era oil and gas pipelines till recently served as the only means for Kazakhstan to access international markets. A common economic space created by the Customs Union increases the scope for greater engagement between the two countries. Moscow remains an important partner of Kazakhstan and the bilateral relationship is a determining vector in Kazakhstan's foreign policy objectives.

China

China is yet another powerful neighbour of Kazakhstan. China's growing profile in the region, especially economic engagement has made it an important partner of Kazakhstan. The completion of the Kazakhstan-China oil pipeline in 2009 has strengthened China's position in the region. It gave Kazakhstan an alternative pipeline route and access to a new market, thereby reducing its dependence on Russia. Bilateral trade is increasing, which is further bringing the two countries closer. In 2013, 2014 and 2015, the bilateral trade was around US$22.4 billion,

US$17.2 billion and US$14.6 billion, respectively.[30] By comparison, in 1995 bilateral trade was only US$331.7 million.[31] In 1995, the two sides signed the agreement for the "long term neighbourly and stable relations", and in 1999 they amicably resolved their border disputes.[32] China gave a loan of US$10 billion to Kazakhstan in exchange of access to oil fields in Kazakhstan under the "loan-for-oil" deal of 2009.[33] China is also investing in building infrastructure, especially in the transport sector in Kazakhstan. Under the China Gateway Project, China is building railway network in southern Kazakhstan.[34] In addition to the economic considerations, another factor determining the bilateral relationship is the issue of ethnic Chinese and Kazakhs residing in each other's countries. The two countries have tried to avoid any differences arising from this ethnic settlement. China agreed to allow ethnic Kazakhs willing to return to Kazakhstan to go back to their country, and Astana in return promised that it would not allow Kazakhstan to be used by any Uyghur separatist movement groups against China.[35]

United States

Kazakhstan's relation with the United States is another important vector in Kazakhstan's multi-vector diplomacy. With US cooperation, Kazakhstan in the 1990s dismantled its nuclear warheads. Cooperation in the energy sector is an important component of the bilateral relationship. In 2001, the US-Kazakhstan Energy Partnership was established to enhance cooperation in this sector. US companies are engaged in Kazakhstan's hydrocarbon sector. Chevron and ExxonMobil operate two largest hydrocarbon projects in Kazakhstan: Tengiz and Kashagan. In 2010, the US Foreign Direct Investment in Kazakhstan was about US$9.6 billion, which was mainly concentrated in the oil and gas sector, business services, telecommunications, and electrical energy.[36] Kazakhstan is a recipient of US assistance through development projects, training and education.[37] In 1994, Kazakhstan joined the NATO's Partnership for Peace (PfP) programme and in 2002 began participating in the PfP Planning and Review Process (PARP). In 2004, Kazakhstan developed its first Individual Partnership Action Plan (IPAP). Kazakhstan allowed its airspace to be used by the US military aircraft for their operations in Afghanistan and also permitted emergency landings of these aircrafts in Kazakhstan.[38] Later, it also allowed the transit of non-lethal cargoes through its territory for the NATO-ISAF mission in Afghanistan under the Northern Distribution Network plan.[39] Under the platform of Strategic Partnership, Kazakhstan and the United States started the Annual Bilateral Consultations in 2010. Although the relationship is growing, the US insistence on progress in democracy and human rights records remains a sore point in the bilateral relationship.

European Union

The European Union (EU) is another important partner of Kazakhstan. Energy has been a focal point in Kazakhstan's relationship with the EU. In 1995, Kazakhstan and EU signed the Partnership and Cooperation Agreement, which came into effect in 1999.⁴⁰ France, Italy, the Netherlands and UK have invested in oil and gas projects in Kazakhstan.⁴¹ In 2008, in order to improve its relationship with Europe, Kazakhstan drafted a special programme, Path to Europe, which included improving economic cooperation, bringing technology and management experience of Europe and so forth.⁴² With Europe, too, promotion of democracy and poor human rights records are sources of irritation.

Kazakhstan's relations with the aforementioned entities reflect the delicate balance which Kazakhstan has maintained since independence through its reliance on multi-vector diplomacy. However, it is not to suggest that its multi-vector diplomacy is limited to these countries only. The multi-vector policy of Kazakhstan has helped it to develop relations with countries like Turkey, Iran, Japan, South Korea, Brazil, Egypt, Qatar, Syria, Pakistan, India and many others. Kazakhstan's willingness to further expand its diplomatic network is evident in some of the initiatives taken in the recent past. In 2013, Kazakhstan announced to set up embassies in South Africa and Ethiopia in its efforts to develop cooperation and tap the economic potentials of Africa.⁴³ It is also reaching out to Latin American countries. Kazakhstan opened its embassy in Brazil and Mexico in 2012 and 2016, respectively.

Kazakhstan's foreign policy objectives acknowledge the importance of developing a vibrant relationship with other Central Asian countries too. The Foreign Policy Concept for 2014–2020 reiterated the need for a stable Central Asia:

> the development of multifaceted relations of the Republic of Kazakhstan with Central Asian states . . . will focus on strengthening regional efforts to jointly counter internal and external challenges and threats, enhancing political, economic and cultural cooperation on a mutually beneficial and parity basis.⁴⁴

The essence of Kazakhstan's foreign policy is stated in the document "Strategy Kazakhstan 2050":

> our priorities remain unchanged – development of partnerships with our neighbours – Russia, China, Central Asian countries as well as the USA, European union and Asian countries. . . . we are developing friendly and predictable relations with all states and playing a significant role in the global agenda that represents the interests of all Kazakhstan.⁴⁵

Nazarbayev's interpretation of "Eurasianism"

President Nazarbayev's Eurasian vision has assumed a special place in present-day discourse on Eurasianism. The former ambassador of Kazakhstan to the United States, Erlan Idrissov (now the foreign minister) explained Kazakhstan's vision and rationale for supporting Eurasian integration at a conference in October 2007:

> Kazakhs had resolved not to take as a "curse their country's landlocked status", but instead to "turn it into an opportunity" and a benefit by leading the

drive for regional integration. . . . Kazakhstan operates on the principle that "one cannot prosper without being surrounded by prosperous countries".[46]

Kazakhstan's foreign policy has always emphasised on widening its horizon of engagement. Eurasianism as viewed by President Nazarbayev is based on the "principles of economic benefits and multi-vector integration".[47] Within the framework of the idea of Eurasianism, Kazakhstan benefitted in developing "balanced and friendly relations with all major states and blocs", strengthening the "integration process at the post-Soviet space" and in sustaining national unity.[48]

Although developed on the broader framework of the concept of Eurasianism as debated in Russian intellectual circles, Nazarbayev's vision of Eurasianism has its own distinct features. Unlike in Russia, Nazarbayev does not see Eurasianism as an ideology but as an outline for foreign policy and international cooperation.[49] It supports cooperation with the West, favours modernization and emphasizes economic integration.[50] Nazarbayev's variant of Eurasianism has been termed as "pragmatic" and economic oriented.[51]

The idea of Eurasianism has long been in international discourse. Since the time President Nazarbayev first mooted the idea in 1994 in the draft "On the Formation of the Eurasian Union of States", the Eurasian integration vision of Nazarbayev has made considerable progress. The creation of the Customs Union (CU) gave a practical shape to the vision of Eurasian integration. Nazarbayev's continuous emphasis on the Eurasian vision of the country and Kazakhstan being a founding member of the CU, calls for a deeper understanding of the CU/Eurasian Union. Despite challenges, CU has set the stage for Eurasian integration. The *raison d'état* for Kazakhstan to join the CU/Eurasian Union and the challenges it faces needs to be analysed. President Nazarbayev in an article published in *Izvestia* in 2011 explained the fundamental principle behind the creation of the group:

> economic interests, rather than abstract geopolitical ideas and slogans are the main driving force of integration processes. Therefore, the fundamental principle of the future of the Eurasian Union is common economic space our peoples need for development.[52]

Also the Foreign Policy Concept of 2014 takes note of the rising significance of the Eurasian integration process and the broad principles to be followed within the Eurasian Economic Union (EAEU) structure. It says:

> Viewing Eurasian economic integration as an effective tool for the promotion of a sustainable position in the modern world, Kazakhstan will strengthen the Customs Union and the Common Economic Space in order to build the Eurasian Economic Union on its basis. During the course of implementing the process the following principles will be observed: inviolability of the political sovereignty, economic rationalization of the decisions, gradual approach, pragmatism and mutual benefit, equal representativeness of parties in all integration organs and consensus at all levels of collaboration.[53]

The CU came into existence in 2010 with Russia, Kazakhstan and Belarus as the founding members. The precursor to the CU was the Eurasian Economic Community (EurAsEC) which was established following an agreement signed in 2000 and ratified in 2001. The signatories of the treaty for EurAsEC were Belarus, Kazakhstan, Kyrgyzstan, Russia and Tajikistan. Uzbekistan joined the group in 2006 but withdrew its membership in 2008. Article 2 of the EurAsEC founding document states that "EurAsEC is established in order to effectively advance the process of the formation by the Contracting Parties of the Customs Union and Common Economic Space".[54] The Joint Declaration by the Heads of EurAsEc members in the tenth anniversary of the group noted: "recognising the strategic importance of integration for achieving a new level of development, the Community member states began the 21st century with the creation of an international organisation, the 'Eurasian Economic Community' ".[55] The EurAsEc institutionalised the Eurasian integration process. The CU was established in 2010 and the EurAsEc Common Economic Space (CES) in 2012. The final stage is the creation of the Eurasian Economic Union (EAEU), which became operational in January 2015.

With the creation of the CU, a common customs territory is formed that allows for free movement of goods within the common space. After paying customs duty at the entry point, goods from other countries also freely circulate within this common territory. The Customs Union Commission (CUC) is the main regulatory body of the CU with one member from each member country of the CU.

The next milestone in the integration process was the creation of the CES in 2012. The work for the creation of the CES began in 2009 when the presidents of Russia, Belarus and Kazakhstan approved the Plan of Action for creating a CES. Another landmark in the integration process was the signing of the Treaty on establishing the EAEU on 29 May 2014 at Astana. The EAEU became functional on 1 January 2015 after the parliaments of the three CU members ratifies it. Back in November 2011, the three members of the CU agreed to create an EAEU. The new group would comprise a market of 170 million people and a total GDP of US$2.7 trillion.[56] The EAEU members would enjoy free movement of goods, services, capital and labour within the common space, while under the CU only free movement of goods is permitted. Hailing the decision of 29 May 2014, President Nazarbayev said that the signing of the treaty for the EAEU is a "qualitatively new development stage of integration on the Eurasian space . . . the EEU is based on the principles of economic pragmatism, equality and respect for the sovereignty of member states".[57]

Moscow will host the EAEU headquarters, Minsk the Eurasian court and Almaty the financial capital, thus each country will share equal administrative responsibilities. President Nazarbayev has suggested that May 29 is celebrated as the Day of the Eurasian Integration to mark the significance of the integration process.

The Eurasian Commission was established in July 2012 as the nodal agency of the EAEU. It replaced the earlier body CUC. The main function of the commission is to look after tariff and non-tariff regulation, customs and facilitate the integration process and functioning of the EAEU.[58] EAEU membership doesn't come with any baggage like promotion of democracy and improving human rights records that are associated with EU. There would be equal representation from member countries at all levels in the EAEU.

Kazakhstan benefits in a number of ways form the integration process in the region. Kazakhstan's trade with Russia and Belarus has increased by 88 percent, which amounts to US$24 billion; exports to Russia and Belarus have gone up by 63 percent, which is about US$6 billion.[59] Pointing at the benefits of the integration process, President Putin while addressing the guests after signing the treaty for EAEU in May 2014 said that Russia's "annual trade with the EU is $440 billion, while with China it is $87 billion. Belarus and Kazakhstan have far smaller economies than those two colossuses of the world economy, yet they are Russia's third largest trading partner".[60] The integration gives Astana access to Russian market. It also gets access to sea and the transport infrastructure of the member countries.[61] Because of the integration Kazakhstan would benefit from the free movement of goods, capital, labour and joint ventures within the common space.[62]

Although the EAEU holds great prospects for the member countries, there are a few concerns. Kazakhstan has been one of the main advocates for economic integration in the region but it too has expressed some doubts. There has been scepticism about the utility of the new body. Mostly, critics see this as a Russia-dominated group and an attempt by Russia to create its zone of influence. Kazakhstan's domestic market has to face stiff competition from Russian products as a result of the integration. For example, the farmers in Kazakhstan are worried that they would incur losses because of competition from low-priced food products from other countries, and entrepreneurs in Kazakhstan are concerned that Kazakh industrial growth would be hampered making Kazakhstan only a supplier of raw materials within the Union.[63]

Within Kazakhstan also there are debates on the advantages and disadvantages of the EAEU.[64] The main argument of the proponents of the integration is that it would help in addressing economic challenges facing the country.[65] At the initial stage there would be some temporary difficulties, which can be overcome through negotiations.[66] Some sectors of the economy have welcomed the integration. The domestic car industry of Kazakhstan is optimistic that the integration would result in modernisation.[67] On the other hand, the opponents of the integration see it as a challenge to the country's sovereignty, giving Russia a special place and thereby challenging Kazakhstan's multi-vector foreign policy.[68]

The government has refuted claims that the integration would be harmful for Kazakhstan's independent stand. In an interview with the newspaper *Vremya*, Deputy Foreign Minister of Kazakhstan Samat Ordabayev stated that the EAEU will not jeopardise its national sovereignty and that all non-economic issues have been removed from the draft. He reiterated President Nazarbayev's view: "political sovereignty in our integration association is immutable, and this is an axiom.... Economic integration strengthens national statehood, to make it more sustainable through the development of the economy".[69] Moreover, Article 3 of the Union Treaty outlines principles of sovereign equality, territorial integrity, respect for each other's political systems, mutually beneficial cooperation, and equal treatment of members and respect for each other's national interests.[70] Decision in the Union depends on a majority of votes.[71] The EAEU will not be a political union as clearly stated in the Article 1 of the Treaty, which says that the Union is to be an "international organisation of regional economic integration".[72] Nothing in the EAEU treaty prevents Kazakhstan from interacting with the international community. Article 30 of the Treaty deals with "relations of this Treaty with other international agreements", which states that countries are free to engage and enter into agreements with third countries.[73] Allaying fears that the integration would erode Kazakhstan's multi-vector foreign policy approach, President Nazarbayev stated that "as sovereign states, we actively cooperate with various countries and international organizations, without prejudice to mutual interests. The Union should not hinder us in this direction".[74]

In addition to the economic aspect, President Nazarbayev has expressed his Eurasian vision through various other projects. The opening of the L. N. Gumilev Eurasian National University at Astana, named after the famous scholar on Eurasianism, L. N. Gumilev is a subtle exposition of Nazarbayev's emphasis on Eurasianism. Numerous other institutes exist in Kazakhstan with the name "Eurasia", like the mining company, the Eurasian Natural Resources Cooperation (ENRC), Eurasian Bank, Eurasia Logistics (now closed), property development company, the Eurasian Association of Universities and so forth.[75]

The Eurasianism ideology is gaining prominence in the region. The emphasis Kazakhstan gives on economic integration in Eurasia reveals Kazakhstan's main focus area. This would also shape Kazakhstan's foreign economic policy goals. The success of the EAEU would leave a deep impression on the future of the Eurasian integration process. Equal power sharing among the EAEU member countries is crucial for the success of the group and the future of the integration process. Will the proximity with Russia affect Kazakhstan's relations with other countries? Where will Kazakhstan-China relations figure in Kazakhstan's Eurasian vision? Giving a definite answer to these issues at this moment is difficult. It is to be seen with what fineness Kazakhstan balances the two approaches in its foreign policy: multi-vector policy and Eurasiansim.

India and Eurasian integration project

Having discussed the concept of Eurasianism, it is important to see where India stands in Kazakhstan's Eurasian vision. India has been keenly watching the developments in the region. Will the Eurasian integration project open avenues for greater engagement between the two countries?

Kazakhstan has emerged as an important partner for India in the region. The two countries have signed the Strategic Partnership Agreement in 2009. Kazakhstan is India's largest trade partner in the region. In 2013–2014, the bilateral trade was US$917.84 million and in 2014–2015 it was US$952.35 million.[76] However, the potential for trade is much higher. The relationship got a major impetus after Nazarbayev participated as the chief guest of India's Republic Day function. It was for the first time that a president from Central Asia was invited as the Chief Guest for the event.

India until recently had no place in the region's energy sector. India's effort to gain a foothold in the region's energy sector received a blow in 2005 when it lost to China in the PetroKazakhstan deal. The situation today looks brighter with India gaining 25 percent stake in the Satpayev block in Kazakhstan. Agreement between India's ONGC Videsh Ltd. and Kazakhstan's National Company "Kazmunaigas" for joint exploration of the Satpayev block was signed during Prime Minister Manmohan Singh's visit to Kazakhstan in 2011. The Satpayev block located in the Caspian Sea is close to some of the prime hydrocarbon discoveries in Kazakhstan.

Encouraging bilateral relations with the Central Asian States would help India to make a footprint in the region. Kazakhstan in the past few years has emerged as India's most important partner in the region. It is one of the energy rich countries in the region. The republic has been relatively stable politically and economically. Efforts have to be made at the bilateral level and at multilateral fora to build closer ties with the countries in the region.

With the economic integration already in progress in Eurasia, India needs to prepare herself for the new developments in the region and tap the opportunities. Within the Custom Union members, India has strategic partnership agreement with Russia and Kazakhstan. The EAEU would give India access to wider Eurasian market. Indian goods entering a member country would then be able to access markets of other member states.[77] The Connect Central Asia policy launched in 2012 shows India's interest in participating in the Eurasian integration process. It highlights India's willingness to cooperate with the countries of the region within the multilateral framework like SCO, the Eurasian Economic Community and the Custom Union. A larger economic role for India in the region is possible once direct transport linkages are established. Availing all possible opportunities to engage with the region is in India's interest.

Notes

1 Evgeny Vinokurov and Alexander Libman, *Eurasian Integration: Challenges of Transcontinental Regionalism*. UK, Palgrave Macmillan, 2012, p. 21.
2 Ibid.
3 Ibid.
4 Ryszard Paradowski, Liliana Wysocka and Douglas Morren, "The Eurasian Idea and Leo Gumilev's Scientific Ideology". *Canadian Slavonic Papers* Vol. 41, No. 1, March 1999. p. 22.
5 Vinokurov and Libman, *Eurasian Integration*, p. 22.
6 Alexander Dugin, "Multipolarism as an Open Project". *Journal of Eurasian Affairs*, Vol. 1, No. 1, 2013. p. 13, www.eurasianaffairs.net/category/journal-of-eurasian-affairs-vol-1-num-1-2013/ (Accessed on 15 June 2014).
7 Alexander Dugin, "Eurasian Keys to the Future". *The Fourth Political Theory*. www.4pt.su/en/content/eurasian-keys-future (Accessed on 12 August 2014).
8 Mark Bassin, "Eurasianism 'Classical' and 'Neo': The Lines of Continuity", p. 281. https://src-h.slav.hokudai.ac.jp/coe21/publish/no17_ses/14bassin.pdf (Accessed on 18 June 2014).

9 Ibid., p. 284.
10 For details see ibid., pp. 285–94.
11 Ibid., p. 286.
12 Ibid., p. 287.
13 Ibid., p. 286.
14 Ibid.
15 Ibid., p. 288.
16 Quoted from ibid., p. 294.
17 Ibid., p. 289.
18 Ibid., p. 291.
19 Ibid., p. 290.
20 Altair Nurbekov, "Eurasian Economic Integration 'Will Continue', Nazarbayev says". *Astana Times*, 2 April 2014. www.astanatimes.com/2014/04/eurasian-economic-integration-will-continue-nazarbayev-says/ (Accessed on 1 August 2014).
21 For details of the negotiations on the nuclear issues see Jonathan Aitken, *Nazarbayev and the Making of Kazakhstan*. London and New York, Continuum, 2009. pp. 129–48.
22 Address by the President of the Republic of Kazakhstan, Leader of the Nation, N. Nazarbayev, *'Strategy Kazakhstan-2050': New Political Course of the Established State*, 14 December 2012, p. 34. www.akorda.kz/en/page/page_address-by-the-president-of-the-republic-of-kazakhstan-leader-of-the-nation-n-nazarbayev-%E2%80%9Cstrategy-kazakhstan-2050%E2%80%9D-new-political-course-of-the-established-state%E2%80%9D_1357813742 (Accessed on 12 August 2014).
23 Ibid.
24 Aitken, *Nazarbayev and the Making of Kazakhstan*, p. 208.
25 Shirin Akiner, "Evolution of Kazakhstan's Foreign Policy: 1991–2011". *OAKA*, 2011. p. 18. www.turkishweekly.net/files/other/eGs8SfrqpCGYkCKOTFrkIpXQhB5L2d.pdf (Accessed on 11 July 2014).
26 Ibid., p. 4.
27 Ibid.
28 Ibid.
29 Ibid., p. 5.
30 Asian Development Bank, *Key Indicators for Asia and the Pacific 2016*. www.adb.org/publications/key-indicators-asia-and-pacific-2016 (Accessed on 5 December 2016).
31 Asian Development Bank, *Key Indicators for Asia and the Pacific 2013*. www.adb.org/publications/key-indicators-asia-and-pacific-2013 (Accessed on 1 August 2014).
32 Akiner, "Evolution of Kazakhstan's Foreign Policy", p. 5.
33 Ibid.
34 Ibid.
35 Aitken, *Nazarbayev and the Making of Kazakhstan*, p. 181.
36 US Department of State, Bureau of South and Central Asian Affairs, *US Relations with Kazakhstan*, 10 February 2014. www.state.gov/r/pa/ei/bgn/5487.htm (Accessed on 15 August 2014).
37 Akiner, "Evolution of Kazakhstan's Foreign Policy", p. 6.
38 Ibid.
39 Ibid.
40 Ibid., p. 8.
41 Ibid.
42 Address of the President of the Republic of Kazakhstan Nursultan Nzarbayev to the People of Kazakhstan, *Official Site of the President of the Republic of Kazakhstan*, 6 February 2008. www.akorda.kz/en/allNews?category_id=338 (Accessed on 14 August 2014).
43 *Kazakhstan to Open Embassies in Mexico, Ethiopia and South Africa*, 16 October 2013. http://en.trend.az/casia/kazakhstan/2201570.html (Accessed on 16 July 2014).
44 *Foreign Policy Concept, Embassy of the Republic of Kazakhstan, United States*, www.kazakhembus.com/page/foreign-policy-concept (Accessed on 10 August 2014).

45 Address by the President of the Republic of Kazakhstan, Leader of the Nation, N. Nazarbayev, *Op. cit.*, p. 33.
46 Richard Weitz, "Kazakhstan and the New International Politics of Eurasia". *Silk Road Paper, Central Asia-Caucasus Institute Silk Road Studies Program*, July 2008. p. 13. www.silkroadstudies.org/new/docs/Silkroadpapers/0807Weitz.pdf (Accessed on 12 July 2014).
47 Sadykova Raikhan, "Eurasian Idea of N.A. Nazarbayev as the Basis of Modern Integration". *Procedia-Social and Behavioral Sciences*, Vol. 89, 2013, p. 382. http://ac.els-cdn.com/S1877042813029947/1-s2.0-S1877042813029947-main.pdf?_tid=c40e9f22-2eac-11e4-a043-00000aab0f6b&acdnat=1409228208_777b3eb72d01d2ed4 42fdc216b70681c (Accessed on 10 June 2014).
48 Golam Mostafa, "The Concept of 'Eurasia': Kazakhstan's Eurasian Policy and Its Implications". *Journal of Eurasian Studies*, No. 4, 2013, p. 169, http://ac.els-cdn.com/S187936651300016X/1-s2.0-S187936651300016X-main.pdf?_tid=7c818e66-2ead-11e4-abec-00000aab0f02&acdnat=1409228518_4dce96988d23eb78d485fcd7a978f 7cc (Accessed on 10 June 2014).
49 For details see Vinokurov and Libman, *Eurasian Integration*, pp. 24–9.
50 Ibid., p. 25.
51 Ibid., p. 24.
52 "Eurasian Union: Front Idea to the History of the Future". *Izvestia*, 26 October 2011. http://personal.akorda.kz/pda.php?r=page/category&sefname=statyi&page_id=158& language=en (Accessed on 12 August 2014).
53 *Foreign Policy Concept, Embassy of the Republic of Kazakhstan, United States*, www.kazakhembus.com/page/foreign-policy-concept (Accessed on 10 August 2014).
54 Integration Committee Secretariat of the Eurasian Economic Community (EurAsEC), *EurAsEC Today*, Moscow, 2011. www.evrazes.com/i/other/EurAsEC-today_eng.pdf (Accessed on 10 July 2014).
55 Ibid.
56 Ministry of Foreign Affairs and Central Communication Service for the President of Kazakhstan, Republic of Kazakhstan, "Kazakhstan, Belarus and Russia Sign Eurasian Union Treaty". *Astana Calling*, Issue No. 356, 30 May 2014. http://ortcom.kz/media/upl oad/1/2014/05/30/1fb48956099b09c20e6d3dc7f74b0d53.pdf (Accessed on 10 August 2014).
57 Ibid.
58 Andrei Akulov, "What the Eurasian Union Is About". *Strategic Culture Foundation*, 14 July 2013. www.strategic-culture.org/news/2013/07/14/what-the-eurasian-union-is-about.html (Accessed on 15 July 2014).
59 Ministry of Foreign Affairs and Central Communication Service for the President of Kazakhstan, Republic of Kazakhstan, "Kazakhstan, Belarus and Russia Sign Eurasian Union Treaty". *Astana Calling*, Issue No. 356, 30 May 2014. http://ortcom.kz/media/ upload/1/2014/05/30/1fb48956099b09c20e6d3dc7f74b0d53.pdf (Accessed on 10 August 2014).
60 Ibid.
61 "Kazakhstan to Greatly Benefit From the Eurasian Economic Union: President Nazarbayev". *Tengri News*, 29 May 2014. http://en.tengrinews.kz/politics_sub/Kazakhstan-to-greatly-benefit-from-the-Eurasian-Economic-Union-President-253824/ (Accessed on 18 June 2014).
62 Ibid.
63 Askar Nursha, "Evolution of Political Thought in Kazakhstan on the Problems of Eurasian Integration: 'Eurasia-optimists' and 'Eurasia- skeptics'", *Working Paper*, The Institute of World Economy and Politics (IWEP) at the Foundation of the First President of the Republic of Kazakhstan–The Leader of the Nation, Almaty, 2014. p. 17.
64 For details see ibid., pp. 16–32.
65 Ibid., p. 24.

66 Ibid., p. 25.
67 Ibid., p. 17.
68 Ibid., pp. 21, 26.
69 Malika Orazgaliyeva, "Integration Without Insinuations: Kazakhstan's Deputy Foreign Minister Says Eurasian Economic Union to Become "An International Organisation of Regional Economic Integration". *Astana Times*, 29 May 2014. www.astanatimes.com/2014/05/integration-without-insinuations-kazakhstans-deputy- foreign-minister-says-eurasian-economic-union-become-international-organisation-regional-economic-integration/ (Accessed on 18 June 2014).
70 Ibid.
71 Ibid.
72 Ibid.
73 Ibid.
74 Ibid.
75 Vinokurov and Libman, *Eurasian Integration*, p. 21; Raikhan, "Eurasian Idea of N.A. Nazarbayev as the Basis of Modern Integration", p. 384.
76 Government of India, Ministry of Commerce and Industry, Department of Commerce, *Export-Import Data Bank*. http://commerce.nic.in/eidb/default.asp (Accessed on 6 December 2016).
77 Ajay Patnaik, "Customs Union and Eurasian Union: Implications for India". In *Perspectives on Bilateral and Regional Cooperation: South and Central Asia*. Edited by Rashpal Malhotra, Sucha Singh Gill and Neetu Gaur. Chandigarh, Centre for Research in Rural and Industrial Development (CRRID), 2012, p. 86.

12 International transport corridors of Eurasia

History, problems and prospects

Marina Baldano

Russia's geopolitical position between two fast-growing world business centers – Europe and Asia – predetermines its key role in the securing of Eurasian connections. International transport routes criss-cross Russia in shortest distances with minimal crossing of state borders. They run on the territory with the same legal system, which assures the fastest delivery speeds. Besides, Russia has an extensive railroad and waterway network with a capacity reserve and a developing highway network, which would save large investments into the development of international transport corridors. Within the formation of new development model of world economy, transportation is considered an instrument of national interests and a tool allowing Russia's integration into the world economy. In Russia's Transportation Strategy for the period up to 2030, considerable attention is paid to problems of forming a basic transportation network on the principles of transport corridors.

In Western and Central Europe, where communications are better developed in comparison with East Asian states, the development of the basic system of transport corridors has largely been completed by now. However, the system of pan-European corridors does not fully correspond to geopolitical and economic interests of Russia. In their present form they do not provide transport access to a number of regions and large participants of international trade and economic links with the Asia-Pacific region – one of the business centers of the world. They do not allow actively using transportation networks of Russia to provide international trans-continental links. Despite lagging behind the majority of European countries in the field of shipping, Russia has developed multimodal systems. The system of international transport corridors through the Russian territory is formed in accordance with geography and structure of existing and prospective international transport connections.

Historically, transport communications between various states, peoples and civilizations ran through Russia's territory at all times. It can be concluded that as a "geopolitical project" Russia emerged, formed and reached imperial status as a transit territory on the age-old trade routes "from the Varangians to the Greeks" and the routes "from the Varangians to the Persians" are still in existence nowadays, almost precisely corresponding to the international transport corridors No. 9 and "North-South".

Contemporary geopolitical position of Russia predetermines its special key role in the provision of Eurasian transit ties. The Russian system of international transport corridors (ITC) includes the Northern Sea Route as well as two Eurasian corridors, such as "North-South" and the Trans-Siberian railroad, which partially overlap with the Pan-European ("Cretan") corridors No. 9 and No. 2.

The "North-South" transport corridor connects the Baltic Sea with the Persian Gulf. Its history extends back over centuries. Having defeated the Khazar Khaganate in the middle of the tenth century, Kievan Prince Svyatoslav established control over the trade route "from the Varangians to the Persians", which later was named the Khazar-Hanseatic route. Later, as a result of the Mongolian invasion this control was lost. A merchant from the city of Tver, Afanasii Nikitin, attempted to restore the trade route in the late fifteenth century. The attempt was quite successful, but soon Vasco da Gama's caravels came to anchor in Indian Kalicut seaport. A sea route around Africa was laid from Europe to Persia and India. Goods were transported in the cargo holds of Portuguese, Dutch and English vessels after the creation of the East India Company. A shortened version of this sea route via the Suez Canal is used as the main sea route nowadays.

The inner continental route over which Russia regained control in the mid-sixteenth century could not compete with it. Thus it was used mainly for internal needs of the empire. Only by the end of the twentieth century the development of transportation network allowed speaking about the creation of a full-fledged transport corridor. On 12 September 2000, in the course of the second Eurasian transport conference, an inter-governmental agreement was signed between Russia, Iran and India about the "North-South" international transport corridor. In May 2002, transport ministers of the participant countries signed an official opening protocol. A coordinating council chaired by the participant states on a turn-based principle became the authority of the "North-South" ITC. Azerbaijan, Armenia, Belarus, Kazakhstan, Oman and Syria joined the agreement. Until recently ten more states were ready to join it.

This project widely discussed in the early 2000s attracted lot of attention and evoked much interest. The Russian leadership made grandiose plans about the "North-South" project. It had to connect Northern and Central Europe with Persian Gulf states and India. The use of these directions for shipping of international transit cargo through the Russian territory could significantly reduce delivery time due to being two or three times shorter routes in comparison with the southern sea route via the Suez Canal.

However, later the Russian government's interest in this project sharply decreased. In 2006 the head of the Strategic Planning Service Alexander Sobyanin noted,

> The reason for absence of interesting results, as strange as it may appear, is in the absence of interest of Russia and India. Without the highest interest of these two countries the ITC "North-South" will not survive because it is practically considered only as a Caspian-Central Asian regional corridor.[1]

The transport project initiated on political grounds finally never became fully functional. The Russian-Iranian trade cargo turnover remains the basic cargo traffic on the Caspian site of the "North-South" corridor. From the south there is mostly Indian cargo, but the return cargo flow is practically absent. In this connection a large number of empty Indian cargo containers are concentrated in Russia. Their return has over time turned into a separate problem. Besides, at present the need to carry out cargo handling in Indian, Iranian and Russian ports and its high cost is an obstacle for the development of the corridor.[2]

Why did the project not work with maximum performance? There are political and economic reasons for this. The main Russian mistake is that in the "North-South" ITC a stake was made on cargo transit to Europe, whereas there are more comfortable and better equipped routes, such as via the Suez Canal. As the analysts argue, another direction should have been prioritized. It is the cargo traffic between the main Russian industrial regions in the Volga area, the Urals and Siberia on one side and Iran, India and Persian Gulf states on the other side.

Defense enterprises in the Urals cater to Indian military orders, such as T-90 main battle tanks, multiple rocket launchers, tank engines, "Ural" trucks and civic goods, such as trucks, heavy machinery, in particular, metallurgic plant equipment produced by Uralmash. Cooperation between the largest Russian producer of titanium, Avisma, and India to process Indian titanium ore was envisaged. Besides, Indian goods such as tea and spices go to the Volga, Urals and Siberian regions. However, now these goods are delivered via a long way through Far Eastern sea ports. The "North-South" ITC could have sharply reduced these distances.

Despite today's complicated international situation the transportation infrastructure needs improvement. Prospectively, it will allow gathering cargo from Central Asia, Siberia and even Xinjiang for shipping via the Caspian route. The Trans-Siberian corridor is also an alternative to the traditional sea route from Southeast Asia around India and via the Suez Canal to Europe. According to professional estimates the development of transport ways and modernization of seaports in the Far East and north-western region provide linking of this corridor with the international communications. International cargo transit in a latitudinal direction along the Trans-Siberian railway will not only allow earning additional money, but will also contribute to the growth of inner shipping and development of eastern regions of Russia.

The Northern Sea Route is an international transport corridor providing the shortest shipping distances between Western Europe and the Asia-Pacific countries. The role of the state in the formation of an Arctic transportation system is to create favorable conditions for reliable functioning of the Northern Sea Route and formation of a transportation infrastructure for this process. This need is dictated by prospective development forecasts of large-scale crude hydrocarbon projects on Arctic deposits and their transport links.

The route of a future Eurasian transcontinental railway runs through the main regions of Russia with high concentration of fuel and energy, mineral and timber resources. In its influence zone there are Timan-Pechora and West Siberian Oil and Gas Basins, Lower and Middle Angara regions with their various natural resources, a unique Udokan copper and other mineral deposits, forming Bratsk-Ust-Ilimsk, Upper Lena and South Yakutia regional production complexes, and new centers of oil and gas extraction on the Sakhalin and its shelf.

One of the main sites of transport corridor creation is the construction project of a railroad between the Baikal-Amur Railway and Trans-Siberian Railway on the territory of Buryatia. In this case the ITC gets linked with the railroad system of Mongolia and China. This corresponds to the provisions of Russia's Transportation Strategy about the development of transit corridor projects jointly with the subjects of the federation in addition to the basic international transport corridors. Hence, improvement of the transportation system becomes one of the key steps in the development of Russian economy. The same applies to the fulfillment of a powerful transit potential of the country to support Eurasian links.

As for Siberia and the Far East, which occupy over 70 percent of Russian territory and have a huge and unique natural resource potential, the problem of state support is most topical here. The bulk of Russia's hydrocarbons, coal, non-ferrous and precious metals, timber, water and hydro energy resources is situated in Siberia and the Far East. The extracted explored oil reserves account for 77 percent of Russia's total reserves, while natural gas and coal reserves account for over 80 percent. Over a half of Russia's total timber reserves are in Siberia. The construction of new transport route plays a key role in the rise of Siberian and Far Eastern economy, settlement of underpopulated areas and increase of living standards. Though it requires large lump-sum funds, it is highly effective economically. This is proved by, for example, the construction of the Trans-Siberian Railway, development of transport and formation of West Siberian Oil and Gas Complex (WSOGC).

Construction of the Trans-Siberian Railway helped the mass resettlement of people in Siberia, created the first Siberian universities and built large mining and metallurgical centers in the 1930s. The railway allowed evacuating many enterprises to Siberia during the Second World War and assured seamless operation of the home front. This contributed a lot to the Soviet victory in that war.

However, at the very beginning of the construction, along with laudatory comments, it was also heavily criticized especially after it was known that the Siberian railway would be built in its southern variant, via Omsk to Krasnoyarsk, Irkutsk and further to Vladivostok via Chita and Chinese territory. Business representatives considered that as a result of such corrections the Pacific gates would still remain closed to Siberian trade. In the wake of an emerging armed conflict with Japan, some specialists insisted that the Chinese Eastern Railway may play a role of a stabilizing factor for international situation in the Far East. It was also noted that this was not only dictated by military and strategic considerations, but also by prospective meaning of the Chinese Eastern Railway in the international cargo and passenger transit as well as the key position of Russia in the Eurasian transportation networks.

The war against Japan was lost. Only afterwards in 1907 a decision was made to build the Amur line of the Siberian railway, but the real construction dragged on for almost ten more years. At the project stage of the Trans-Siberian Railway considerable attention was concentrated on the issues of significant broadening of active economic development of Siberia. In the tideway of these plans, large-scale field studies of Siberian natural resources were carried out. Special and general geological studies, geophysical and topographic mapping, and systematic study of hydrological regime of Siberian rivers encompassed huge spaces. As a result a number of new coal deposits were found, including Ekibastuz, Karaganda, Sudzhenskoe, Antropovskoe, Kubekovskoe, Kuskunskoe, Cheremkhovskoe, Malinovskoe, Khara-Norskoe and Suchanskoe. Some of them were previously unknown, while on the others commercially exploitable resources were measured. In Cisbaikalia, geological studies of oil fields were financed by the Siberian railway. Despite being incomplete, their results were the first experience of the geological study of oil fields of Siberia.

From its first days, the committee of the Siberian railway insistently underlined that the expedition results would be used for feasibility studies and ensuing development opportunities of iron works and casthouse production, as well as creation of construction materials industry, primarily concrete production. However, the promised state subsidies for a comprehensive economic development of Siberia were not allocated with the exception of 30 million roubles for the creation of production structures (open pits, quarries, brick, limestone and cement factories, timber mills, tie saws, etc.) directly connected with the construction of the railway between 1893 and 1902. Thus, the plan of a comprehensive economic development turned out to be just an illusion.

In the late 1920s an issue of super trunking of the Trans-Siberian railway was raised. The proponents of this project proposed to increase the carrying capacity by constructing additional railways all along the Trans-Siberian Railway. According to the professional estimates, turning the railroad into a ten-track railway could be cheaper than building a new railway through thinly populated or unpopulated and inaccessible northern regions. This was despite the fact that the North-Siberian Railway or the Great Siberian Way that could link three ocean shores – the Pacific, Arctic and Atlantic – opened a broad and politically invulnerable access possibility to oceanic communications. Based on mineral, fuel and energy resources in the zone of the prospective Northern Trans-Siberian Railway it was planned to construct large industrial enterprises, which in case of war would form a strategic industrial rear inaccessible to any potential aggressor.

However, the domestic tradition according to which high-cost railroads should be constructed only after the potential of other and cheaper transportation networks is exhausted, manifested itself in full in the counter-arguments against the Great Siberian Way.[3] Nevertheless, the directive solution of a latitudinal railway construction became a point of departure of a new stage in the working out of the formation of railroad network in North Siberia and the Far East. With all its feasibility, there were discrepancies too. The most significant one was that the railway to be built had no transport access to the Arctic coast. A choice between Arkhangelsk and Indiga had to be made according to the criteria derived from the really existing technical and economic potential, which was determined by the operational port facilities and Northern Sea communications in Arkhangelsk and

Murmansk. The construction of a new port in Indiga was to start at the end of the second five-year plan, or the third five-year plan in the last resort.

Yet the beginning of the Second World War disrupted all that, and Murmansk seaport together with the railroad grew dangerously close to the battlefield. Desperate efforts were made to prevent enemy breakthrough to the Murmansk railroad and seaport. However, there was no full guarantee against catastrophic development of events. Naval communications in the Baltic Sea were paralyzed in the first months of the war. The Arkhangelsk seaport, second after Murmansk in the list of priority port construction objects in the north, did not have real reserves to compensate a possible loss of Murmansk despite all facilities created during the pre-war years.[4]

In this situation an idea of building a seaport in the Indiga Bay popped up again, but the works that started were soon stopped. The extreme military situation too distinctly denoted bottlenecks of communication hubs of the domestic transportation system with the outer world. Railroad connections, traditionally developed westward, were disrupted during the first days of the hostilities. Both Baltic and Black Sea communications were disrupted in a similar manner. Caspian sea and land routes could not compensate the Black Sea and Baltic connections. The Trans-Siberian Railway hub was the only relatively open access to the outer world through oceanic communications.

History demonstrates that when geopolitical and socio-economic interests of the state competed against each other, the former would usually outweigh. The geopolitical position of Russia in the late twentieth century from the viewpoint of economic and geographical potential of the transportation system appeared much similar to historical situations that temporarily emerged during the wars. Russian borders were altered in the south and west. Siberian boundaries to the east of Kazakhstan, Pacific and polar coasts and northern territories of European Russia remained untouched by national and political transformations.

A way out was needed in such conditions. In his address at the Baikal Economic Forum in 2000, Governor of Tomsk region V. M. Kress stated that

> it is necessary to reconstruct the Trans-Siberian railroad to make its technical equipment level to the international standards; form a basic thoroughfare of federal highways and have here not just one, but several highways; organize a system of international airlift between the Asian Pacific countries and European subcontinent; expand and bring to contemporary standards communication networks and pipeline transport.[5]

In autumn 2010 Russian Minister of Transport Igor Levitin stated, "A significant increase of cargo shipments to the Far East seriously affects the Trans-Siberian railway. Its capacities are practically exhausted. The Baikal-Amur Railway soon will also work at the end of tether".[6]

Nevertheless, today there are four international routes that use the Trans-Siberian Railway. The first two can be determined as transit routes, because the cargo traverses the territories of the former Soviet republics. Two other routes may be determined as two-sided. The European transit connects East Asian states (Japan, Korea and China) with Finland by railroad and sea transport. For instance, such goods as household electronic appliances are temporarily stored in Finnish customs warehouses and are then exported mainly to Russia, including the Russian Far East. The most interesting fact is that their cost is much lower than those that get to the Far East by sea directly from Japan. This can be explained by higher custom clearance tariffs. This route can correctly be called the Finnish transit. Cargo shipping from Japan and Republic of Korea takes thirty to thirty-five days by sea, whereas it takes only twenty days via the Trans-Siberian Railway. In 1998 a demo container train ran via the Trans-Siberian Railway, and it completed the journey (10,538 km) in 9.3 days, which is more than twice as short as the existing sea route shipping schemes.

The advantage of the Trans-Siberian Railway over the sea route is in speed, but naval shipping is much cheaper. This is gained by the size of sea containers. The Afghan transit connects Japan and Korea with Afghanistan via the Trans-Siberian railroad and railway systems of Central Asian states. The Iranian route, cheaper in comparison with the Trans-Siberian one, is its main competitor. The Iranian route runs by sea to Bandar Abbas and then by land into West Afghanistan. The main cargo is various tubing and automotive spare parts. The Central Asian two-way route connects Japan and Korea with Kazakhstan and Uzbekistan by sea and railroad using the Trans-Siberian Railway and Central Asian railroads. Korean-made goods exported to Central Asia form the main cargo on this route. An alternative route through China, the "Trans-Asia Railway", connects the Chinese port of Linyangang with Kazakhstan via a Chinese railroad. This route is widely used for shipping from Japan (transportation time is three weeks compared to two months on the Trans-Siberian Railway and has cheaper tariffs). Russian two-way transit connects Japan and Korea with Russian regions.

As for the frequency of Japan's use of the Trans-Siberian Railway, if Japanese ports and Vostochny seaport were used earlier three times a month, now they are used twice a month. Japanese companies use the sea route virtually every day. Unlike their Japanese counterparts, the Koreans use the Trans-Siberian Railway much more often. The cargo volume of Korean and Chinese shipping is growing (chemical produce: rubber, plastics, consumer goods and goods invested in Central Asia), whereas the volume of Japanese cargo is shrinking. The Japanese are not content with the absence of security guarantees, high tariffs with no normal shipping conditions (containers) and poor Russian management of cargo. Besides, Japanese companies have recently started having their branches in China, Malaysia and other Southeast Asian countries because of cheap labor. From there it is much cheaper to ship goods to Europe by sea.

The Trans-Siberian Railway is a two-track railroad on reinforced-concrete sleepers with automatic block signal system and all-electric interlocking, Caucasus Transit Corridor (CTC), optical carrier which is duplicated by the aeronautical communications satellite system. Creation of an international transport corridor and further modernization of the Trans-Siberian Railway should foster the development of industrial infrastructure of fourteen districts, three regions, two republics and one autonomous district of Russia. The Trans-Siberian Railway runs through eighty-seven cities including the largest industrial centers and transportation hubs such as Moscow, Yaroslavl, Perm, Ekaterinburg, Omsk, Novosibirsk, Krasnoyarsk, Irkutsk, Ulan-Ude, Chita, Khabarovsk and Vladivostok. On the adjacent territory of Siberia, 62 percent of all natural resources of Russia are concentrated. Siberia provides 50 percent of Russian exports. The main timber enterprises are located along the Trans-Siberian Railway. The development of East Siberia's economy, namely, the territories adjacent to the Baikal-Amur Railway, is connected with the development of the Chineiskoe titanium and magnesium, vanadium containing, copper and platinum ore deposit, development of Udokanskoe copper deposit and Elginskii coal deposit. Such large-scale international projects should lead to the growth and integration of economic systems of Russia, Europe and the Asia-Pacific region.

To secure a rightful place in the world, Russia should use all available possibilities. Creation of intercontinental transport corridors provides opportunities for the growth of industrial infrastructure, development of cutting-edge technologies in the project, and in the use of benefits from the functioning transport corridor to raise the material and spiritual culture of Russia in the twenty-first century.

Notes

1 *Container Business*. 2006. No. 1 (2). p. 16.
2 I. Polyakova, "Roads and Corridors". *Za rulyom*. 7 May 2013. www.zr.ru/content/articles/539962-dorogi_koridory/.
3 V. Alexeyev, M. Bandman and V. Kuleshov, eds., *Problem Areas of Resource Types: Economic Integration of the European North-East of the Urals and Siberia*. Novosibirsk, Publishing House of SB RAS, 2002. p. 81.
4 A. Dolgoliuk, V. Ilyin, V. Lamin, V. Plenkin and A. Timoshenko. *Siberia: The Projects of the Twentieth Century (the Beginnings and the Reality)*. Novosibirsk, Publishing House of SB RAS, 2002. p. 146.
5 Bulletin of the Council of Federation. 2001. No. 1. p. 53.
6 News of the World Railways. November 2010. p. 19.

13 Eurasian regional economic cooperation
Opportunities and challenges

Gatikrushna Mahanta

Economic cooperation is an integral part of the regional integration process. The Eurasian region since Soviet disintegration is also trying to promote economic integration to address the numerous economic challenges facing the countries of the region. The economies of the former Soviet countries went through a difficult phase after the disintegration of the Soviet Union. These nascent independent states are facing numerous challenges in their path to economic development. During the Soviet period, the economies of the countries within the Soviet bloc were mutually dependent and complementary to each other. Since the disintegration of the Soviet Union, most of the post-Soviet states have been trying to diversify their economies. In the post-Soviet space, regional economic cooperation is steadily gaining momentum, which if successful could bring major transformation in the Eurasian region. Understanding these initiatives of regional economic integration in the Eurasian space is important to assess the trends, developments and geo-politics prevailing in the region.

This chapter discusses the major groups formed after Soviet disintegration to promote regional economic cooperation, namely, Central Asia Regional Economic Cooperation (CAREC), Eurasian Economic Community (EurAsEC), EurAsEC Customs Union, EurAsEC Common Economic Space and Eurasian Economic Union (EAEU). A brief background of these groups has been discussed herein to reflect the origin, progress and politics involved. The chapter assesses the status and potential of these economic organisations in the Eurasian region. An attempt is made to examine how far these organisations are benefitting the economies of the member countries. It is significant to understand the challenges faced by these groups to comprehend the future prospects of these organisations. In the Eurasia region, Russia is the biggest economy and Russia's economic engagement with the former Soviet countries remains substantial. Except CAREC, Russia is a member of the other groups. Will the smaller countries in these groups be overshadowed by Russia? Is Russia trying to counter European Union's eastward expansion and whether it is trying to restrict China's growing influence in the Central Asian region through these economic groups? These are some of the pressing questions that need attention. The chapter also analyses the benefits and challenges for India in joining the EAEU. India's trade with the Central Asian region is abysmally low. Will joining the EAEU help India in developing robust economic ties with the region?

Central Asia Regional Economic Cooperation (CAREC)

The CAREC Programme, supported by the Asian Development Bank (ADB), was established in 1997 to promote economic cooperation among countries in the Central Asian region. CAREC's vision, "Good Neighbours, Good Partners, Good Prospects", reflects the rationale behind its formation. The member states are Afghanistan, Azerbaijan, China, Georgia, Kazakhstan, Kyrgyzstan, Mongolia, Pakistan, Tajikistan, Turkmenistan and Uzbekistan. In addition to ADB, other multilateral institutions involved in the project are European Bank for Reconstruction and Development (EBRD), International Monetary Fund (IMF), Islamic Development Bank (IsDB), United Nations Development Programme (UNDP) and the World Bank. CAREC partners with other key regional groups like the Shanghai Cooperation Organization (SCO).

The prime focus of the project is financing infrastructure projects and improving the region's transport facilities, trade facilitation (especially customs cooperation), trade policies and energy (including water energy). The project aims to foster effective regional economic cooperation, thereby promoting economic development and alleviating poverty in these countries.

CAREC member countries are meeting regularly. The tenth and eleventh Ministerial Conferences were held in Baku (Azerbaijan) and Wuhan (China) in 2011 and 2012, respectively. In the eleventh Ministerial Conference, the member countries agreed to invest more than US$23 billion in building new regional transport infrastructure projects, along with energy and trade initiatives to boost connectivity with Central Asia.[1] The Wuhan Action Plan was introduced in the eleventh Ministerial meeting, which identified sixty-eight transport priority projects for six major corridors linking the ports in eastern China with Caucasus and beyond, and connecting northern Kazakhstan to the trading hubs in Karachi and Gwadar in Pakistan, improving border and customs services and allowing easy movement of people and goods.[2]

The theme of the twelfth Ministerial Conference held in Astana, Kazakhstan, on 23–24 October 2013 was "Integrated Trade and Transport". The main objectives were to (1) review the progress of cooperation in the CAREC Programme during 2013, and (2) consider further improving the Transport and Trade Facilitation Strategy and Implementation Action Plan (TTFS) 2020 and the Trade Policy Strategic Action Plan (TPSAP) 2013–2017.[3] It was also decided that the CAREC programme will develop new road and rail routes linking Central Asia to China and South Asia by 2020 to tap the trade potential between the three regions.[4] Investments worth US$38.8 billion till 2020 were agreed for developing road, rail, logistics and border facilities in priority corridors.[5] ADB President Takehiko Nakao, in his address at the twelfth CAREC meeting at Astana, said: "To increase trade outside the region, CAREC will need to align its corridors to new routes, and develop long distance multimodal transport services combining road and rail".[6] However, more integrated approach for greater transport and trade linkages are required. It could be achieved by improving logistics services supporting manufacturing networks, installing more modern and integrated customs and border controls, and linking roads and railways to key ports.[7]

CAREC is a project-based programme in the field of transport, trade and energy infrastructure. The investment in CAREC has grown from six projects worth US$247 million in 2001 to 146 projects worth US$22.4 billion in 2013.[8] ADB, so far, has approved and implemented a number of regional investment projects. An important project was the construction of the 75 km rail line connecting Mazar-e-Sharif in Afghanistan to Uzbekistan, which was inaugurated in December 2011. The rail line has helped in boosting commerce and enhancing the flow of humanitarian assistances to Afghanistan. There are also plans to connect northern Afghanistan with other parts of Afghanistan, as well as with other countries like Pakistan, Tajikistan and Turkmenistan.

In 2013, some of the important programmes that were started include Facilitation of Regional Transit Trade in CAREC, Coordinated Border Management for Results in CAREC, Aligning Customs Trade Facilitation Measures with Best Practices in CAREC, Modernization of Hydropower Stations in Tashkent, Shakhrikhan and Kadirya, Energy Sector Development Investment Programme – Tranche 5, North-South Power Transmission Enhancement Project (formerly Power Distribution Project), CAREC Corridor 3 (Bishkek-Osh Road) Improvement Project – Phase 4, Energy Efficiency Project–Kazakhstan, Additional Financing Energy Efficiency for Industrial Enterprises, CAREC Regional Improvement of Border Services Project and so forth.

In Central Asia, six CAREC corridors link the region's economic hubs to each other and also connect most of the landlocked CAREC countries to other Eurasian and global markets. The Implementation Action Plan for the CAREC Transport and Trade Facilitation Strategy plans to upgrade the six transport corridors to international standards by 2017, the work for which has already started.

The most active of the six corridors is the CAREC Corridor-1 that links Europe to China and East Asia through Russia, Kazakhstan and Kyrgyzstan, which comprises 13,600 km of roads and 12,000 km of railways, one logistics centre and three airports.[9] The CAREC Corridor-2 connects the Caucasus and Mediterranean to East Asia. The route travels through Azerbaijan, Kazakhstan, Turkmenistan, Uzbekistan, Tajikistan, Kyrgyzstan and China, comprising 9,900 km of roads and 9,700 km of railways.[10] The CAREC Corridor-3 has 6,900 km of roads and 4,800 km of railways, extending from west and south of the Siberian region of Russia through Afghanistan, Kazakhstan, Kyrgyzstan, Tajikistan, Turkmenistan and Uzbekistan to the Middle East and South Asia.[11] The CAREC Corridor-4 connects Russia to East Asia via Mongolia and China. The route comprises 2,400 km of roads and 1,100 km of railways.[12] The CAREC Corridor-5 connects East Asia to the Arabian Sea through Central Asia. The route covers China, Kyrgyzstan, Tajikistan and Afghanistan, and covers 3,700 km of roads and 2,000 km of railways.[13] The CAREC Corridor-6 includes three routes linking Europe and Russia to the Arabian Sea port of Karachi and Gwadar or Bandar Abbas in the Persian Gulf. The route has 10,600 km of roads and 7,200 km of railways.[14]

The thirteenth Ministerial Conference of CAREC was held in Bishkek, Kyrgyzstan in November 2014 and the focus was "linking connectivity with economic transformation in CAREC". It was announced that the CAREC Institute would be established in Urumqi, Xinjiang Uyghur Autonomous Region. The first city-level cooperation in the CAREC region to coordinate urban development planning between Almaty and Bishkek was also initiated. The fourteenth Ministerial Conference took place in Ulaanbaatar, Mongolia, in September 2015 and the theme of the Conference was same as the last one. It discussed issues like the Almaty-Bishkek Corridor Initiative, cooperation in sanitary and phytosanitary measures, and road safety in CAREC.

The fifteenth Ministerial Conference was held in Islamabad, Pakistan, in October 2016. It noted the progress achieved so far by the CAREC Programme and proposed measures to further boost regional cooperation. In the meeting, CAREC countries adopted a "Road Safety Strategy (2017–2030)" that aims to halve road fatalities in the region by 2030. CAREC ministers also endorsed the "Railway Strategy 2017–2030", which prioritizes six designated railway corridors aligned with trade routes. The meeting also highlighted the need for modernization of customs and coordinated border management initiatives, such as joint customs control between Mongolia and China, to improve regional transit and information exchange. It discussed progress in the implementation and investment framework of the Almaty-Bishkek Corridor Initiative (ABCI), a pilot economic corridor development initiative of the CAREC Programme.

Since 2001, the CAREC Programme has attracted investments worth US$28.9 billion, of which over one-third (US$10.1 billion) has been financed by ADB.[15] As of 2015, 166 CAREC-related projects (worth about US$27.7 billion) have been implemented in the four core areas – transport, trade facilitation, trade policy, and energy.[16] The sixteenth Ministerial Conference will be held in 2017 in Tajikistan.

Eurasian Economic Community (EurAsEC)

Another significant initiative to boost regional economic integration in the Eurasian space is the EurAsEC. The group originated in 1995 and the treaty for EurAsEC was signed on 10 October 2000 in Astana by Belarus, Kazakhstan, Kyrgyzstan, Russia and Tajikistan. After ratification by the member states, the treaty came into force on 30 May 2001. In January 2006, Uzbekistan joined the group but suspended its membership in October 2008 due to differences with other member countries. Uzbekistan's decision to suspend its membership from the organization is seen by many analysts as a response to its improving relationship with the West. On the other hand, Uzbekistan claimed that the EurAsEC duplicates other organizations such as CIS (Commonwealth of Independent States) and CSTO (Collective Security Treaty Organization), and was critical of the clause of "automatic joining of all EurAsEC member-states to the Customs

Union".[17] Ukraine, Moldova and Armenia enjoyed observer status in the organisation. EurAsEC was established to promote economic cooperation and trade, facilitate the process of the formation of the Customs Union and Common Economic Space, and coordinate member states with the international trading system and world economy.

The main aims of the EurAsEC were completing formalisation of the free trade regime; creating a unified customs tariff and a unified system of non-tariff regulation measures; ensuring free movement of capital; forming a common financial market; coordinating the principles and conditions for transition to a common currency within the framework of EurAsEC; establishing common rules for trade in goods and services, and their access to internal markets; creating a common unified system for customs regulation; drawing up and implementing interstate targeted programmes; creating equal conditions for industrial and entrepreneurial activities; forming a common market for transportation services and a unified transport system; forming a common energy market; creating equal conditions to access foreign investments by the member states; ensuring free movement of citizens within the community; coordinating social policy with the aim of forming a community of social states that allows for a common labour market, common educational space, coordinated approaches in resolving questions of healthcare and labour migration and so forth; coordinating and harmonising national legislation; and ensuring coordination of the legal systems of EurAsEC member states to create a common legal space within the Community.[18]

The EurAsEC covers a territory of 20,374 million km^2 with about 180 million inhabitants (2.7 percent of the global population) and produces 3.5 percent of the world's gross domestic product.[19] EurAsEC countries are endowed with vast resources of minerals and raw materials. In 2010, EurAsEC countries constituted 9 percent of the global oil resources, 25 percent of gas and 23 percent of coal; their share in the generation of electrical energy amounted to 5.5 percent globally; steel production was 5.4 percent and grain production 5.7 percent.[20] The EurAsEC also has vast reserves of uranium, raw diamonds, platinoids, gold, silver, zirconium, rare metals, rare-earth elements and many other minerals. EurAsEC countries are major exporters of mineral resources and metals in the world, such as oil and gas, chrome and manganese resources, aluminium, nickel and copper, platinoids and raw diamonds.

Within the framework of the EurAsEC, there are four bodies: Interstate Council, Integration Committee, Inter-Parliamentary Assembly and Community Court. For addressing specific issues, EurAsEC has different Integration Committee Councils and Commissions like Council of Heads of Tax Services, Council of Heads of Customs Services, Transport Policy Council, Energy Policy Council, Council on Border Issues, Financial and Economic Policy Council, Council of Ministers of Justice and so forth. The EurAsEC Interstate Council is the supreme body of the Eurasian Economic Community, which is composed of heads of state and heads of government. The EurAsEC Integration Committee is a standing body of the Eurasian Economic Community accountable to the EurAsEC Interstate Council. The Integration Committee is composed of deputy heads of government of member states.

In January 2008, Russia, Belarus and Kazakhstan signed nine trade agreements, which included customs duties, unified customs and tariff regulations, unified rules to determine the countries of origin of goods, unified measures of non-tariff regulation, anti-dumping and protective measures, determination of customs values, customs statistics, technical and sanitary controls, and taxation of imports and exports.[21] Kyrgyzstan, Tajikistan and Uzbekistan did not sign these agreements.

Some of the major initiatives of the EurAsEC by the end of 2010 were 120 international treaties adopted and implemented, including 55 within the framework of the Customs Union; 33 meetings of the Interstate Council held (at the level of heads of state and heads of government); 22 Councils and Commissions formed; 31 memorandums of cooperation with international organisations and financial and economic organisations signed; 12 meetings of the Interstate Council (supreme body of the Customs Union) held; 55 meetings of the Integration Committee held; 21 meetings of the Customs Union Commission held; 68 meetings of the Permanent Representatives Commission held; and 284 meetings of Councils and Commissions held.[22]

The EurAsEC Anti-crisis Fund was established in 2008 to grant loans to participating countries to address the impact of the global financial crisis; allocate stabilization credits; and finance interstate investment projects. The fund has helped many member countries during crisis situations. For example, it gave a US$70 million loan to Tajikistan in 2010 from the US$10 billion anti-crisis fund created in 2009.[23]

In accordance with the principles of the EurAsEC, Belarus, Kazakhstan and Russia created the Customs Union and systematically moved ahead with the next stage of integration – the EurAsEC Common Economic Space.

EurAsEC Customs Union

The Customs Union is a trade bloc consisting of a free trade area, where member countries share a common external tariff, external trade policy and competition policy. The main purpose behind the Customs Union was to boost economic integration among the member countries. The Customs Union attempts for free movement of goods produced in the territory of the Custom Union member countries but also of goods produced in countries outside the common zone after paying the customs duty at one entry point.

Geopolitics has also influenced economic integration process in Eurasia. The Customs Union gained priority among the EurAsEC member countries after the European Union (EU) announced its Eastern Partnership Programme (EPP) with six post-Soviet states – Armenia, Azerbaijan, Belarus, Georgia, Moldova and Ukraine in 2008. The EPP was initiated to improve political and economic relations between the EU and the aforementioned six states. The EPP policy was a source of irritance between EU and Russia, each accusing the other of trying to interfere and influence the aforementioned six countries. Other reasons of Russia's concern were the US plan to deploy NATO's missile defence system in Poland and the Czech Republic, and China's growing economic presence in Central Asia. The Kazakhstan-China oil pipeline and Central Asia-China gas pipeline have strengthened China's position in the Central Asian region. Further, China is also investing in building infrastructure in the region like road networks, etc. Economic integration in the region would strengthen Russia's position in the post-Soviet space, an area too important for Russia to ignore. The West and China have been pursuing their own initiatives to revive the old Silk Route and make Central Asia the bridge for trade with Europe and China, respectively. Efforts by the West and China to develop economic engagement with the region is challenging Russia's stronghold in the region. The creation of the Customs Union and subsequently the EAEU is seen as Russia's attempt to dissuade the CIS countries from moving close to the United States, the EU and China.[24] Also, Russia receives a large number of migrants from the former Soviet countries, which in future could emerge as a contentious issue in Russia. Russia seeks to form "ethnic unity" of the Soviet people through a common economic space.[25]

The resolution on establishment of the EurAsEC Customs Union was adopted by the heads of six EurAsEC states at a EurAsEC Interstate Council meeting on 6 October 2007. It was decided that at the initial stage, Belarus, Kazakhstan and Russia will join as members of the Customs Union. Other EurAsEC members would join gradually as and when the economies and legislative systems of these countries are prepared. In 2009, Kazakhstan, Belarus and Russia agreed on a unified customs tariff and customs code.

The unified customs tariff and custom code came into effect from 1 January 2010 and 1 July 2010, respectively. Common measures to determine the country of origin of goods, non-tariff regulation with respect to third countries, special anti-doping and compensation measures for third countries had been outlined by the Union. The customs control within the borders of the three member countries was abolished in July 2011. After the removal of the customs control, the total trade among the three countries increased by 35 percent in 2011–2012.[26] Eliminating customs formalities at borders saves time and is cost-effective. More than 50 percent of the time taken for transportation is saved by removing customs formalities at borders and 15 percent of the cost of the products by eliminating customs duties and other formalities.[27]

The Customs Union Commission is the apex management body of the Union. The commission has the power to determine rates of tariff and supervise customs administration of the Union. Russia has 57 percent, Belarus 21.5 percent and Kazakhstan 21.5 percent of votes in the Union.[28]

The Customs Union covers a population of 170 million in Eurasia, US$2 trillion worth of GDP and US$900 billion worth of trade turnover.[29] Its place in the world oil and grain market is remarkable; total oil reserves is worth about 95 billion barrels and grain export contributes about 18 percent of the global market.[30] It is assumed that Customs Union will gradually constitute about 15 percent of GDP growth of the member countries.[31] The major trading partners of the Customs Union countries in 2013 were the EU (52.86 percent), the APEC countries (26.5 percent), China (12.3 percent), Ukraine (5.38 percent), Japan (3.8 percent), the United States (3.3 percent) and South Korea (2.9 percent).[32] The total trade volume of the Customs Union outside the member countries amounted to

US$681.2 billion in 2013, in which export and import were US$429.5 billion US$251.7 billion, respectively.³³

It was expected that other CIS countries might also join the Customs Union and eventually the EAEU. Main attractions for these countries in joining the Custom Union were easy access to Russian technology, Russian resources, the large common market, a way to develop their manufacturing sector, infrastructure and so forth, and thereby reducing their dependence on natural resources.³⁴ However, there is another view that by giving economic concessions to smaller countries, Russia is trying to create a bloc of its own.³⁵

The major obstacle that the Customs Union faced was the WTO membership of the members of the Customs Union. Initially, the three members of the Customs Union decided to join WTO together, but because of differences during the negotiation process opted to join WTO separately but on common terms and conditions.³⁶ Russia and Kazakhstan joined WTO in 2012 and 2015, respectively, and Belarus is also negotiating with the WTO. The common tariff adopted by the Customs Union was fixed at the prevailing rate in Russia that was higher as compared to the rates in Belarus and Kazakhstan.³⁷

There are other issues the group had to address to make it effective like resolving issues of certification, quota and granting of licenses; resolving state subsidy and tax policy; and identifying the list of sensitive goods for each member country and giving them a transition period to adopt new conditions and establish temporary tariff.³⁸ The advantages and disadvantages of each of the three member countries faced by joining the new group are discussed as under the following sections.

Russia

The Customs Union gives Russian products easy access to wider markets. Moreover, Russia gains from cheaper products and labour from Belarus and Kazakhstan. A number of Russian enterprises have re-registered in Kazakhstan to benefit from the cheaper tax rates. Russia gets the major share of the collected customs duty. The distribution is as follows: Russia gets 87.97 percent of the collected duty, while Kazakhstan and Belarus receive 7.33 percent and 4.70 percent, respectively.³⁹

Russia as a member of the Customs Union faces a few problems at least in the short run. For instance, Russian farmers face competition from subsidised agricultural products of Belarus and Russian steel industries from steel producers of Kazakhstan.⁴⁰

Kazakhstan

Kazakhstan has its own share of advantages and disadvantages in joining the Union. Its agricultural, automobile and airline sectors benefit by the policies of the Union.⁴¹ Kazakhstan products now have access to the large Russian market. Kazakhstan uses Russia and Belarus to transit goods without any customs duty. For example, Kazakhstan exports grain via Russia to other countries without paying duty to Russia, and Kazakhstan now supplies electricity for its power deficit industries in the western part through Russia.[42] By joining the Union, Kazakh industries have access to raw materials at concessional rates from Russia and by exporting their final products to Russia earn profits.[43] Another factor is the growing concern in Central Asia of China's economic presence. The Kazakh markets were abundant with low-cost Chinese goods, which had earlier entered the country through Kyrgyzstan. From Kazakhstan, Chinese goods entered Russian markets without any customs duty. Unified rules under the Customs Union help in addressing this concern.

There are challenges too. The majority of Kazakh imports had lower duty, and hence Kazakhstan now receives minimum dividend on these goods.[44] Kazakhstan relies on Russia for 40 percent of its imports.[45] The consumers and the entrepreneurs engaged in the consumer goods sector in Kazakhstan are worried over the unified customs tariff. The common customs tariffs would make imported garments, agricultural products, medicines, cosmetics, construction materials, aviation techniques, automobiles, electrical goods, mobile phones and many other imported industrial products from outside the Union expensive in Kazakhstan.[46] The rise of speculative business practices due to abolition of inter-state customs barriers is another problem arising out of the formation of the Customs Union, causing public dissatisfaction. Russian entrepreneurs bring cheaper Kazakh products at lower domestic prices and sell these goods as Russian products in Kazakhstan at higher prices after minimum processing, like changing the packaging.[47] As a result of this practice, the food market in Kazakhstan has been affected. For instance, in 2001 the sugar price in Kazakhstan doubled, beef increased by 40 percent and mutton increased by 33 percent.[48]

Belarus

Belarus is a landlocked country and dependent on Russia for trade. It mainly imports raw materials from Russia and also uses Russian territory to export goods to other markets. Russia-Belarus relations have gone through difficult phases. Gas dispute has been a major irritant in the bilateral ties. Back in 2004, Russia stopped the supply of gas for six months, and later it was resumed after resolving the differences on price rates. There were other differences too. Russia in 2009 banned import of dairy products from Belarus, as it did not meet Russian packing standards. Belarus incurred a loss of about US$1 billion and reacted by banning the sale of Russian agricultural machinery in Belarus.[49] The real reason for this action, however, was different. Because of subsidies, the cost of milk production in Belarus was cheaper than in Russia, which hit Russian dairy producers hard.[50]

In 2012, both sides fixed the price of gas at US$164 for a thousand cubic metres, which is near the Russian domestic gas price.[51] Russia has also agreed to supply about 21 million tons of oil to Belarus without customs duty, which means about US$4.3 billion subsidy to Belarus.[52] In return, Russia gained control over the Belarussian gas major, Beltransgaz. By joining the Union, Belarusian products now have access to a large market, and it exports products through Russia to other countries without paying duty to Russia. It gains because of discounts on hydrocarbon prices by Russia, which is agreed after mutual understanding and does not fall under the provisions of the Customs Union. It reflects Russia's favourable gesture to member countries to promote the integration process.

EurAsEC Common Economic Space (CES)

A common economic space created by the Customs Union in January 2012 has opened a new chapter in the Eurasian economic regional integration process. The CES ensures a region of the Customs Union countries that practice uniform market mechanisms: coordinated tax, monetary, currency and finance, trade and customs policies; common legal norms, integrated infrastructure; and free movement of goods, services, capital and human resources.

In December 2009, at an informal summit in Almaty, Belarus, Kazakhstan and Russia approved the Plan of Action for 2010–2011, which laid the outline for the formation of a common economic space including the three countries. The CES came into effect on 1 January 2012. Besides free movement of goods and services, this body seeks greater economic integration by ensuring free movement of labour and capital among the member countries, taking the integration process in the Eurasian region a step ahead. The progress of the integration is visible from the expansion of areas included at different levels of the integration process. The extent of economic cooperation in the Customs Union is greater than it is in the EurAsEC, and the level of cooperation is more in the CES than in the Customs Union and EurAsEC. These bodies merged with the EAEU on 1 January 2015.

Eurasian Economic Union

The final stage of the integration process in the Eurasian region is the creation of the EAEU, which became operational on 1 January 2015. In November 2011, Belarus, Kazakhstan and Russia signed an agreement to create EAEU. On 29 May 2014, Kazakhstan, Russia and Belarus signed the Treaty establishing the EAEU in Astana, which has been ratified by the parliaments of the three countries in October 2014. It has been a long journey since the idea was first put forward by President Nazarbayev in a speech at Lomonosov Moscow State University in March 1994. Its objective is to create a larger market, specialise in goods based on comparative advantage, and rebuild some of the Soviet manufacturing chains.[53] The organization aims at closer coordination of economic and monetary policies, enhancing regional economic integration, including introduction of a single currency and deepening Eurasia's relationships with Europe and Asia. EAEU is not a political body but purely an economic union,[54] a factor vital for its effective functioning.

The group has a common market of 182.7 million people and its combined GDP is worth US$1.6 trillion.[55] The common space created by the formation of the Union is rich in hydrocarbon reserves, consisting of about one-fifth of the globe's natural gas reserves and 15 percent of oil reserves,[56] making it a very significant area. Of the total world production in 2014, the group occupies first place in oil production (14.6 percent) and second place in gas production (18.4 percent).[57]

The primary regulating institution of the EAEU is the Eurasian Economic Commission (EEC), launched in July 2012, that replaced the Customs Union Commission. Earlier, it was decided that the body would comprise 350 members; 84 percent from Russia, 10 percent from Kazakhstan and 6 percent from Belarus on the basis of the population of the three countries.[58] Foreign Minister of Kazakhstan, Yerlan Idrissov, however, in a speech after signing the Treaty in May 2014, stated that the different bodies of the Union would have equal representations from each member country.[59] This was a significant step in ensuring equality in the group. This body is entrusted to enforce rules and regulations and administer initiatives for further integration. The main functions of EEC are to implement coordinated macro-economic policy, create unified trade regimes with third countries, administer activities of natural monopolies and form a unified approach to support industry and agriculture.[60] It was also the permanent regulatory agency of the EurAsEC, Common Economic Space and the Customs Union. The apex body of the EEC is the Supreme Eurasian Economic Council represented by the heads of state and government of the member countries. The EAEU's headquarters is in Moscow and the Eurasian court is at Minsk. However, so far, no decision has been taken on the formation of the Currency Union. Initially, the union was to have a single market for energy, finance and other areas by 2015. But the new agreement, which mentions of a single market by 2025, is silent about regulation of the financial market and hydrocarbon market.[61] A unified market for medical products/pharmaceutical and electricity is also planned for by 2016 and 2019, respectively.[62]

Russia's interest in EAEU is for various reasons. Russia would like to raise its international image, expand its market and maintain its influence in the former Soviet republics by dissuading them from engaging with the West and China. Russia is keenly watching China's growing economic presence in Central Asia and would not like to lose the economic influence it enjoys in Central Asia. This vision of Russia was indicated by President Putin in an essay published in *Izvestia* in December 2011: "We suggest a powerful supranational association capable of becoming one of the poles in the modern world and serving as an efficient bridge between Europe and the dynamic Asia-Pacific region".[63] However, Russia has always denied the West's criticism that through the EAEU, it is trying to rebuild Cold War–style blocs. Critics of EAEU have pointed out the dominant position that Russia would enjoy in the group might sideline the interests of smaller nations. Russia's share of GDP in the EAEU (including Belarus, Kazakhstan, Kyrgyzstan, Tajikistan and Armenia) would be more than 85 percent, and Russia's population is more than eight times that of Kazakhstan, the next largest member of the group.[64]

Kazakhstan, a strong supporter of the EAEU, has of late expressed some concerns. President Nazarbayev in a speech in 2013 at the Higher Eurasian Economic Council in Minsk, highlighted the difficulties faced by Kazakh entrepreneurs in exporting their products (particularly Kazakh meat), especially to Russia because of different technical and sanitation standards for imported products in the member countries: "Technical barriers on our exports still remain, including sanitation requirements, difficulties with licensing and certification".[65] Moreover, Kazakhstan is concerned over Russia's statement of protecting ethnic Russians living outside Russia, as Kazakhstan has a sizeable ethnic Russian population.[66]

Notwithstanding these concerns, Kazakhstan has placed its faith in the economic integration process in Eurasia, which is reflected in President Nazarbayev's statement at the Nuclear Security Summit in The Hague on 24–25 March 2014. He reiterated Kazakhstan's interest in greater Eurasian economic integration with Russia and Belarus, but at the same time stressed that it will not compromise on its political sovereignty.[67] A week before the signing of the EAEU treaty on 29 May 2014, President Nazarbayev stated that the EAEU should be a self-sufficient regional financial institution which can address global crisis.[68] After signing the treaty, President Nazarbayev expressed his optimism about Eurasian economic integration, in the following words: "the treaty is well-balanced and responds to all interests of the new union member states and the EAEU is based on the principles of economic pragmatism, equality and respect for the sovereignty of member states".[69] The decision-making process at all levels of the EAEU is based on consensus. Moreover, the EAEU treaty is not inimical to member countries' signing other international agreements.[70] President Nazarbayev also stated that there would be no de-industrialization as a result of the integration in any of the member countries.[71]

With the integration processes in practice, Kazakhstan's trade with Russia and Belarus has increased by 88 percent, reaching US$24 billion, exports to Russia and Belarus have grown by 63 percent, increasing exports to US$6 billion.[72] Trade within the Customs Union members grew almost 50 percent (by US$23 billion) during 2011–2013 and in 2013 it reached US$66.2 billion.[73] Belarus and Kazakhstan together constitute Russia's third largest trading partner following the European Union and China. Although Kazakhstan and Belarus are much smaller economies than the EU and China, their emergence as the third largest trading partner of Russia does reflect the progress in the economic integration process in the region.[74]

Addressing the concerns of the members about their sovereignty, President Putin has said:

> It is important to note that providing certain authorities to supranational bodies brings absolutely no harm to the sovereignty of our countries. . . . We are creating the largest common market on the territory of the CIS with huge industrial, scientific and technological potential and colossal natural resources.[75]

He also said "gradual harmonization of our countries' monetary policies will improve stability of the financial systems of the member-states, make the national currency markets more predictable and better protected from exchange rate fluctuations. This will enhance our sovereignty".[76]

Aleksandr Lukashenko, president of Belarus, also pointed out the opportunities that would arise after formation of the Union: "We believe that the economic union will become a basis of our political, military and humanitarian unity in future".[77] Prior to the signing of the treaty, Belarus received a US$2 billion loan and energy concessions from Russia.[78] Trade in hydrocarbons with Russia constitutes 10 percent of its economy, and once the concessions are included, it would rise to 15 percent of gross domestic product.[79]

Belarus has its own concerns too. Energy is not included as an item in the common market, and hence Belarus will have to pay duties to Russia for its export of oil products produced from imported oil from Russia. However, Belarus receives large concessions from Russia on its oil purchases. Belarus purchases crude oil from Russia at domestic rate prevailing in Russia, which is about half the price that Russia receives for its oil in the international markets. Belarus's customs duties on oil imports from Russia is about US$4 billion per year, but after negotiations with Russia for discounts, it was decided that US$1.5 billion would be deducted from the total from 2015 onwards.[80]

By 2015, EAEU plans to expand its membership. The presidents of Armenia and Kyrgyzstan attended the EAEU meeting at Astana in May 2014. Armenia and Kyrgyzstan signed the accession treaty to the EAEU on 10 October 2013 and 23 December 2014, respectively. Armenia joined the EAEU on 2 January 2015. However, Armenia does not share its border with any of the member countries. Armenia has strong economic linkages with Russia. Russia is the largest trade partner of Armenia and is the prime foreign investor of the country. Also, Armenia is dependent on Russia for security in its conflict with Azerbaijan over the Nagorno-Karabakh issue. Earlier, President Serzh Sargsyan stated that "Armenia's membership in the Russian-led Collective Security Treaty Organization (CSTO) necessitates joining the economic structure that covers the same geographic space, under Russian leadership".[81] Moreover, there is a sizeable Armenian diaspora in Russia. Oil and gas politics have shaped Armenia's decision to join the EAEU. Armenia earlier had shown keenness to join the EU. However, it shelved off the idea after Russia offered gas at the price Belarus pays – about US$170 to US$180 per thousand cubic meters in early 2014.[82]

Kyrgyzstan joined EAEU on 12 August 2015. As the new economic organization is based on WTO principles, Kyrgyzstan's membership in the WTO did not pose a problem in its accession to EAEU. In May 2013, the first deputy prime minister of Kyrgyzstan had stated that Kyrgyzstan was "taking steps to mitigate any negative effects of entering a customs union with Russia, Kazakhstan and Belarus, and was hoping to use the end of a United States military airbase as an opportunity to re-energize the civil aviation industry".[83]

There are pros and cons of Kyrgyzstan joining the Union. By joining the EAEU, it has now access to cheaper oil, gas and other refined fuel products from the member countries. Kyrgyzstan is one of the two Central Asian countries not having oil and gas reserves. EAEU also facilitates easier movement of labour force among the member countries, which is crucial for Kyrgyzstan as a large number of labour migrants from Kyrgyzstan go to Russia and Kazakhstan for work. Remittances from these migrant workers are vital for the Kyrgyz economy. However, a common tariff rate among the member countries increases the prices of several goods in Kyrgyzstan. Earlier, Kyrgyzstan had a low import tariff, a position it lost after joining the EAEU. Earlier, Kyrgyzstan imported cheaper goods from China and re-exported these products to other Central Asian and CIS countries. With Kyrgyzstan entering the EAEU, this practice came to an end. Similarly, prices of medicines will increase as Kyrgyzstan earlier received duty-free medicines.

It is too early to assess the future of the integration process expected to come after the EAEU is formed. However, the way it has been moving ahead in the past few years raises hope for greater regional economic integration.

Eurasian Economic Union and other post-Soviet states

With the Eurasian economic integration making steady progress, a number of countries have shown interest in participating in the new group. Ukraine, Moldova and Georgia had earlier shown interest in joining the EAEU. But having signed the Association Agreement with the EU on 27 June 2014, they have now decided to stay away from the EAEU. A brief overview of the position of the countries willing to join the group is discussed later to better understand the prospects and challenges the new group holds in future.

Tajikistan has also expressed its interest in joining the EAEU. Earlier, one of the major issues of Tajikistan joining the EAEU was that it did not share a border with any of the EAEU member countries. However, with Kyrgyzstan joining the EAEU this problem has been resolved. A large number of migrant labourers from Tajikistan go to Russia and Kazakhstan for work. Joining the EAEU would thus be beneficial to Tajikistan. About 40 percent of Tajikistan's GDP comes from Russia as remittances.[84] Like Kyrgyzstan, Tajikistan is also not blessed with hydrocarbon reserves, and thus joining the EAEU would give it access to cheaper oil, gas and other refined fuel products from within the member countries.

Ukraine's decision whether to join the EU or EAEU has been a controversial issue. With the signing of the pact with the EU, it has taken its stand. Ukraine is an important country in the Eurasian region, and its inclusion in the EAEU would have been a boost to the integration process. Hence, it is important to study what would have been the impact if Ukraine would have been part of the EAEU. Historical ties and strong economic linkages with Russia were important considerations for Ukraine to join EAEU. However, it has failed to do so. Tension in Russia-Ukraine relations has always been there. Politics over gas has often hampered the bilateral ties. The bulk of Russia's gas is transported to European markets through Ukraine. The Ukraine-Russia-Turkmen gas pipeline is the main conduit. About 50 percent of Russia's gas export to EU passes through Ukraine.[85] Often, there have been disputes between the two countries with regard to natural gas sales. In 2009, Russia stopped supplying gas to Ukraine because of differences over the gas price between the two. However, gas supplies were resumed after Ukraine agreed to pay about US$400 per thousand cubic metres of gas to Russia.[86] Russia had a navy base in the Crimean peninsula, and the lease for using the base was extended for twenty-five years in 2010 by the Kharkiv Agreement. The deal was made after Russia agreed to reduce the price of natural gas sold to Ukraine from the 2009 rate by US$100.[87] Again, in February 2014, after the removal of President Viktor Yanukovych, known to be close to Moscow, Russia in a bid to pressurise Ukraine substantially increased the price of natural gas to be sold to Ukraine. As against Ukraine's demand of US$268.5 per thousand cubic meters of gas, Russia charged US$485 per thousand cubic meters.[88] Ukraine signed the EU Association Agreement at Brussels on 21 March 2014. Petro Poroshenko became the new President of Ukraine on 25 May 2014 and immediately the new government signed the Association Agreement on 27 June 2014.

In order to reduce its dependence on Ukraine, Russia has been diversifying its gas supply routes to the European market, bypassing Ukraine. Three new gas pipelines serve this purpose. The Yamal-Europe Pipeline runs for more than 4,000 kilometres carrying Russian gas from the Yamal Peninsula in Russia's Arctic region to Frankfurt-on-Oder on the Polish-German border.[89] In 2006, the Yamal-Europe gas pipeline reached its total capacity of 32.9 billion cubic meters.[90] Another pipeline, the Nord Stream pipeline, carries Russian gas to northern Germany through the Baltic Sea, which was started in November 2011.[91] Russia through this pipeline is already transporting about 55 billion cubic meters of gas to Germany.[92] The South Stream pipeline, which is under construction, would pass through the Black Sea in the Turkish part to Europe. The construction of the pipeline began in 2012, and was expected to be completed by 2015. However, due to the Ukrainian crisis, the work on the south stream has been stalled by Bulgaria since June 2014. It would transport about 63 billion cubic meters of Russian gas to Europe.[93] Another significant development is the signing of the thirty-year agreement on natural gas supply between Russia and China on 21 May 2014. It was agreed that Russia would supply 38 billion cubic meters of gas annually at US$350 per 1,000 cubic metres to China from its eastern Siberian gas fields, which will begin in 2018.[94]

If Ukraine had joined the EAEU, the country would have enjoyed a few benefits. It is dependent on Russia for its domestic natural gas needs. By joining the EAEU, it would have received gas at a lower price and crude oil without export duties. It would have helped Ukraine save US$5–6 billion annually and increase its exports to other countries to about US$4–9 billion annually.[95] There are many in Ukraine who, however, believe that Ukraine would lose its economic sovereignty by joining the EAEU, which would gradually erode its political sovereignty.[96] Russia had earlier shown interest in including Ukraine in the EAEU. It had offered a number of concessions to Ukraine to join the EAEU but it refused to offer a very low price for gas. In a survey conducted by the Democratic Initiatives Foundation and the Razumkov Centre in December 2012, only 40 percent of the population supported Ukraine's membership in the Customs Union.[97]

Ukraine did not sign the Association Agreement (AA) and Deep and Comprehensive Free Trade Agreement (DCFTA) with the EU in Eastern Partnership Programme (EPP) meeting at Vilnius on 28 November 2013. Since then Ukraine has been witnessing a major political unrest. Here, it is important to take a deeper look into EU membership of Ukraine. It has several conditionalities, like introducing a number of legal and political reforms, adopting anti-corruption measures, bringing transparency and reforms in the economy, particularly the energy and trade sector and so forth.[98] The signing of EU's DCFTA gives Ukraine a privileged access to the European single market, however, it needs to restructure the economy to meet EU standards.

Some analysts see Ukraine opting out of the EAEU as a major blow to the Eurasian integration process. Without Ukraine, the EAEU would lose a huge market, but would not stall the economic integration process that has begun in Eurasia.

With the signing of the agreement with the EU, Moldova is also no longer a prospective member of the EAEU. Moldova is dependent on Russia for its gas requirements and has a sizeable number of migrant workers going to Russia for work. Russia has been protecting Transnistria, the breakaway territory of Moldova, since 1991. It is also argued that Russia has put pressure on Moldova to join the EAEU, like imposing ban on import of Moldovan agricultural products, Moldovan wine and so forth. Earlier, a ban on Moldovan wines hit the Moldovan economy. Wine is the prime export item of Moldova, and Russia is its largest market. Despite having close economic linkage with Russia, Moldova signed the agreement with the EU.

There are also talks of including members from outside the former Soviet Union. Vietnam and Turkey are two possible countries outside the CIS that may be included in the group. Negotiations over the Free Trade Agreement (FTA) with Vietnam are in progress. Vietnam does not share a border with the present members of the EAEU, but can access Russia by sea without crossing any other country and from there to other members of the EAEU. Another development has been the member countries' readiness to cooperate with China, which includes exchange of customs information on goods and services, and intention to create expert groups on developing preferential trade agreements with Israel and India.[99]

Indian and Eurasian economic union

India has shown greater willingness to play a stronger role in the Eurasia region. India's Connect Central Asia Policy in 2012 reflects India's interest in building stronger ties with the region. The policy aims at setting up IT centres, e-network for telemedicine, joint commercial ventures, universities, hospitals, developing banking and pharmaceutical industries, improving air connectivity to facilitate trade and tourism, joint scientific research and strategic partnership in defence and security affairs.

India has a strategic partnership with Russia and Kazakhstan, two important members of the EAEU. India and Russia have close ties in diverse areas like defence, science and technology, nuclear and space sectors. India has invested in the Sakhalin I project in Russia and has acquired Imperial Energy. India and Kazakhstan relations have consistently grown since 1991. Both have signed various agreements to fight terrorism, cooperate in joint production of military hardware, space programme, pilot training and so forth. Kazakhstan is India's largest trade partner in Central Asia. There is need for India to look at the Eurasian region as a whole, which is much beyond Central Asia: "Eurasian integration is picking up speed, India should be ready with infrastructure and transportation linkages as well as special multilateral arrangements to play a larger economic role in the Eurasia region".[100] Through the EAEU, India would have access to the huge Eurasian market. Lack of direct access to the region has been India's major weakness in establishing strong economic linkages with the region. India could address the issue by speeding up the work on two routes: the International North-South Transport Corridor (INSTC) through Iran, and from the Chabahar port in Iran to Afghanistan and then to Central Asia. US sanctions on Iran have been a major hurdle in operationalizing these routes, but now with the removal of sanctions on Iran, things look brighter and India needs to utilise the opportunity.

India's total trade in 2014–2015 and 2015–2016 with the nine countries of the former Soviet Union in the Eurasian region (excluding Ukraine, Georgia, Moldova, Estonia, Latvia and Lithuania) was about US$8.4 billion and US$7.3 billion, respectively.[101] Talks are in process between India and the EAEU members for Free Trade Agreement (FTA) and Comprehensive Economic Partnership Agreement (CEPA). Once India is included, India could use any of the entry points of the common space to export its products to other countries of the EAEU without paying additional tariffs.

Conclusion

Economic integration in the Eurasian space is gaining momentum through the CAREC initiative, EurAsEC, EurAsEC Customs Union, EurAsEC Common Economic Space and EAEU. The wide transport network under the CAREC programme aims to bring these countries closer to each other and promote economic linkages in the Eurasian region. The EAEU, despite challenges, gives hope for better prospects of economic integration in the region. Expanding cooperation and allaying fears among the member countries would go a long way in the success of the EAEU, which if properly harnessed would be mutually beneficial. Time would determine the achievements or failure of the Eurasian economic integration initiatives. Willingness shown by the countries of the region indicates the transformation taking place in the region, which reflects the needs of the changing time. Coordination between EAEU and CAREC would facilitate in realizing the Eurasian economic integration in a more effective way. Speedy implementation of the CAREC projects, particularly the infrastructure projects, would boost the economic integration level in the region.

The EAEU is one of the largest common markets in the world, having deep regional as well as international implications. Russia's economic engagement with the post-Soviet states remains strong, and hence closer economic cooperation through a common space is seen to be mutually beneficial. The smaller states would get a number of concessions from Russia, which is attractive for these states. Geopolitics behind the integration process cannot be ignored. EU's engagement with the six CIS countries and China's growing economic engagement in Central Asia have influenced Russia in pushing for the EAEU, in the hope that the organization would give Russia a more bargaining power in the region. However, economic considerations need to take pre-eminence over politics to make economic integration a success. Also addressing the fears of the smaller countries over Russian dominance and preserving their sovereignty would be crucial for the effective functioning of the group.

For India, the Eurasian region remains significant. India desires to promote greater economic links with the region. Joining the EAEU would help India in developing robust economic ties with the region. It would give India access to the huge market of the region. Speeding up the negotiations on FTA and CEPA, and resolving other trade barriers with the EAEU is important. During the Soviet era, the Odessa port in Ukraine was used to access the region. If Ukraine would have joined the group, India would have benefited from this route. However, the port today is in bad shape and requires renovation. If India's connectivity with the region through INSTC or Chabahar materialises, the connectivity issue for India would be addressed. India is also keenly watching China's growing economic presence in Central Asia. Can the creation of Customs Union and then the EAEU address this common concern of Russia, Central Asian states and India? It is too early to suggest anything, but India needs to prepare to meet the challenges.

Notes

1 Asian Development Bank, *CAREC Ministers Agree on $23 Billion Action Plan to Boost Central Asia Links*, 30 October 2012. www.adb.org/news/carec-ministers-agree-23-billion-action-plan-boost-central-asia-links?ref=countries/subregional-programs/carec (Accessed on 16 June 2014).
2 Ibid.
3 Asian Development Bank, *Central Asia Regional Economic Cooperation Program: Twelfth Ministerial Conference*, 3 December 2013, IN.403–13. www.adb.org/sites/default/files/in403-13.pdf (Accessed on 16 June 2014). The TTFS 2020 calls for a more integrated approach to transport and logistics infrastructure focusing on multi-modal transport, logistics services to support value chains, improved and expanded corridor alignments to link to gateway ports, and improvements from border crossing services resulting from customs automation and modernization. The TPSAP 2013–2017 focuses on non-tariff measures and the removal of quantitative restrictions that are not World Trade Organization compliant, and the expansion of trade in services.
4 Asian Development Bank, *CAREC to Support Key New Routes to Boost Regional Trade*, 24 October 2013. www.adb.org/news/carec-support-key-new-routes-boost-regional-trade?ref=countries/subregional-programs/carec (Accessed on 16 June 2014).
5 Ibid.
6 Ibid.
7 Ibid.
8 Central Asia Regional Economic Cooperation (CAREC), *Projects Supported by the CAREC Program*. www.carecprogram.org/index.php?page=carec-projects-list (Accessed on 16 June 2014).
9 Central Asia Regional Economic Cooperation (CAREC), *Linking Europe and East Asia*. www.carecprogram.org/index.php?page=corridor-1 (Accessed on 16 June 2014).
10 Central Asia Regional Economic Cooperation (CAREC), *Linking the Mediterranean and East Asia*. www.carecprogram.org/index.php?page=corridor-2 (Accessed on 16 June 2014).

11 Central Asia Regional Economic Cooperation (CAREC), *Linking the Russian Federation With the Middle East and South Asia*. www.carecprogram.org/index.php?page=corridor-3 (Accessed on 16 June 2014).
12 Central Asia Regional Economic Cooperation (CAREC), *Linking the Russian Federation and East Asia*. www.carecprogram.org/index.php?page=corridor-4 (Accessed on 16 June 2014).
13 Central Asia Regional Economic Cooperation (CAREC), *Linking East Asia With the Middle East and South Asia*. www.carecprogram.org/index.php?page=corridor-5 (Accessed on 16 June 2014).
14 Ibid.
15 Asian Development Bank, *15th CAREC Ministerial Conference*, Islamabad, Pakistan, 26 October 2016. http://carecprogram.org/index.php?page=15th-carec-ministerial-conference (Accessed on 30 November 2016).
16 Asian Development Bank, *CAREC 2020 Strategic Framework*. www.carecprogram.org/index.php?page=carec2020-strategic-framework (Accessed on 30 November 2016).
17 Musafirbek Ozod, "Why Uzbekistan Suddenly Decided to Withdraw from the Eurasian Economic Community", *Ferghana Information Agency*, Moscow, 15 November 2008. http://enews.ferghana.ru/article.php?id=2477 (Accessed 20 May 2014).
18 *Integration Committee Secretariat of the Eurasian Economic Community (EurAsEC), EurAsEC Today*, Moscow, 2011, p. 3. www.evrazes.com/i/other/EurAsEC-today_eng.pdf (Accessed on 5 November 2013).
19 Ibid., p. 4.
20 Ibid.
21 Sergei Blagov, "Moscow Signs Series of Agreements within Eurasian Economic Community Framework". *Eurasia Daily Monitor*, Vol. 5, No. 22, 5 February 2008. www.jamestown.org/single/?tx_ttnews%5Btt_news%5D=33353&no_cache=1#.U60eqJSSwRM (Accessed on 27 June 2014).
22 *Integration Committee Secretariat of the Eurasian Economic Community (EurAsEC), EurAsEC Today*, Moscow, 2011, pp. 4–5.
23 Ajay Patnaik, "Customs Union and Eurasian Union: Implications for India". In: *Perspectives on Bilateral and Regional Cooperation: South and Central Asia*. Edited by Rashpal Malhotra, Sucha Singh Gill and Neetu Gaur. Chandigarh, Centre for Research in Rural and Industrial Development (CRRID), 2013. p. 80.
24 Gulshan Dietl, "Eurasian Union: Substance and the Subtext." In: *Perspectives on Bilateral and Regional Cooperation: South and Central Asia*. Edited by Rashpal Malhotra, Sucha Singh Gill and Neetu Gaur. Centre for Research in Rural and Industrial Development (CRRID), Chandigarh, 2013. p. 70.
25 Gleb Bryanski, "Putin, Medvedev Praise Values of Soviet Union". *Reuters*, Moscow, 17 November 2011. http://in.reuters.com/article/2011/11/17/idINIndia-60590820111117 (Accessed on 5 November 2013).
26 Arun Mohanty, "Eurasian Economic Integration: Challenges and Opportunities". In: *Perspectives on Bilateral and Regional Cooperation: South and Central Asia*. Edited by Rashpal Malhotra, Sucha Singh Gill and Neetu Gaur. Centre for Research in Rural and Industrial Development (CRRID), Chandigarh, 2013, p. 93.
27 Ibid., pp. 93–4.
28 *Integration Committee Secretariat of the Eurasian Economic Community (EurAsEC), EurAsEC Today*, p. 33.
29 Vladimir Radyuhin, "Russia, Kazakhstan, Belarus Launch a Customs Union". *The Hindu*, 6 July 2010. www.thehindu.com/news/international/russia-kazakhstan-belarus-launch-a-customs-union/article501602.ece.
30 Mohanty, "Eurasian Economic Integration: Challenges and Opportunities", p. 90.
31 Ibid., p. 92.
32 Christopher A. Hartwell, "Will Ukraine Become a Roadblock to Eurasian Integration?". *Russia Direct*, 20 March 2014. www.russia-direct.org/content/will-ukraine-become-roadblock-eurasian-integration (Accessed on 25 May 2014).

33 Ibid.
34 Patnaik, "Customs Union and Eurasian Union: Implications for India", p. 81.
35 Mohanty, "Eurasian Economic Integration: Challenges and Opportunities", p. 93.
36 Ibid.
37 Jeffrey Mankoff, "Eurasian Integration: The Next Stage". *Central Asia Policy Brief*, Elliot School of International Affairs, George Washington University, No. 13, December 2013, p. 2. http://origin.library.constantcontact.com/download/get/file/111034763 5144-129/Policy+Brief+13,+December+2013.pdf (Accessed on 20 March 2014).
38 Mohanty, "Eurasian Economic Integration: Challenges and Opportunities",p. 94.
39 Olga Shumylo-Tapiola, "Ukraine and Russia: Even Closer Neighbours?". *Policy Outlook*, Carnegie, 08 June 2011. p. 5. http://carnegieendowment.org/files/ukraine_ russia_2.pdf (Accessed on 20 March 2014).
40 Patnaik, "Customs Union and Eurasian Union: Implications for India", p. 81.
41 Ibid.
42 Mohanty, "Eurasian Economic Integration: Challenges and Opportunities", p. 94.
43 Ibid., p. 92.
44 Ibid.
45 Hartwell, "Will Ukraine Become a Roadblock to Eurasian Integration?"
46 Mohanty, "Eurasian Economic Integration: Challenges and Opportunities", p. 92.
47 Ibid., p. 95.
48 Ibid., p. 96.
49 Kambiz Behi and Daniel Wagner, "Russia's Growing Economic Influence in Europe and Beyond". *WorldPost*, 23 July 2012. www.huffingtonpost.com/kambiz-behi/russias-growing-economic-influence_b_1696304.html (Accessed on 16 June 2014).
50 Ibid.
51 Olga Shumylo-Tapiola, "Ukraine and Russia: Another Gas War?" *Carnegie Europe*, 21 February 2012. http://carnegieeurope.eu/2012/02/21/ukraine-andrussia-another-gas-war/b8wp (Accessed on 27 March 2014).
52 Mohanty, "Eurasian Economic Integration: Challenges and Opportunities", p. 95.
53 Mankoff, "Eurasian Integration: The Next Stage", p. 2.
54 Neil Mac Marquhar, "Russia and 2 Neighbors Form Economic Union that Has a Ukraine-Size Hole". *New York Times*, 29 May 2014. www.nytimes.com/2014/05/30/world/europe/putin-signs-economic-alliance-with-presidents-of-kazakhstan-and-belarus.html?_r=1 (Accessed on 29 May 2014).
55 Eurasian Economic Commission, *Implementation of EAEU's Members WTO Commitments*, August 2016. www.eurasiancommission.org/ru/act/trade/siteAssets/Presentation_2016%20eng.pdf (Accessed on 9 December 2016).
56 Alexander Panin, "For Russia, Eurasian Union Is About Politics, Not Economy". *Moscow Times*, 29 May 2014. www.themoscowtimes.com/business/article/russia-kazakhstan-and-belarus-sign-eurasian-union-agreement/501126.html (Accessed on 29 May 2014).
57 Eurasian Economic Commission, *Gas Production and Oil Extraction*. www.eurasian commission.org/en/Pages/ses.aspx (Accessed on 9 December 2016).
58 Dietl, "Eurasian Union: Substance and the Subtext", p. 70.
59 Tengri News, "Kazakhstan to Greatly Benefit from the Eurasian Economic Union: President Nazarbayev", 29 May 2014. http://en.tengrinews.kz/politics_sub/Kazakhstan-to-greatly-benefit-from-the-Eurasian-Economic-Union-President-253824/ (Accessed on 29 May 2014).
60 Mohanty, "Eurasian Economic Integration: Challenges and Opportunities", p. 96.
61 Panin, "For Russia, Eurasian Union Is About Politics, Not Economy".
62 Ibid.
63 Marquhar, "Russia and 2 Neighbors Form Economic Union that Has a Ukraine-Size Hole".
64 Mankoff, "Eurasian Integration: The Next Stage", p. 4.
65 Panin, "For Russia, Eurasian Union Is About Politics, Not Economy".

66 Marquhar, "Russia and 2 Neighbors Form Economic Union that Has a Ukraine-Size Hole".
67 Altair Nurbekov, "Eurasian Economic Integration 'Will Continue', Nazarbayev Says". *Astana Times*, 2 April 2014. www.astanatimes.com/2014/04/eurasian-economic-integration-will-continue-nazarbayev-says/ (Accessed on 24 April 2014).
68 Artur Abubakirov, "Public Perception Largely Positive for Eurasian Integration, Says Panel". *Astana Times*, 22 May 2014. www.astanatimes.com/2014/05/public-perception-largely-positive-eurasian-integration-says-panel/ (Accessed on 14 June 2014).
69 Ministry of Foreign Affairs, Republic of Kazakhstan, "Kazakhstan, Belarus and Russia Sign Eurasian Union Treaty". *Astana Calling*, A Weekly Online Publication, Issue No. 356, 30 May 2014. www.mfa.gov.kz (Accessed on 14 June 2014).
70 Tengri News, "Kazakhstan to Greatly Benefit from the Eurasian Economic Union: President Nazarbayev", 29 May 2014, *Op. cit.*
71 Ministry of Foreign Affairs, Republic of Kazakhstan. "Kazakhstan, Belarus and Russia Sign Eurasian Union Treaty". *Astana Calling*, A Weekly Online Publication, Issue No. 356, 30 May 2014. www.mfa.gov.kz (Accessed on 14 June 2014).
72 Ibid.
73 Ibid.
74 Ibid.
75 Ibid.
76 "Eurasian Economic Union Treaty signed in Astana", *Tengri News*, 29 May 2014. http://en.tengrinews.kz/politics_sub/Eurasian-Economic-Union-Treaty-signed-in-Astana-253845/ (Accessed on 29 May 2014).
77 Ibid.
78 Marquhar, "Russia and 2 Neighbors Form Economic Union that Has a Ukraine-Size Hole".
79 Panin, "For Russia, Eurasian Union Is About Politics, Not Economy".
80 Ibid.
81 Vladimir Socor, "Armenia Chooses Russia and Eurasia over the European Union". *Eurasia Daily Monitor*, Vol. 10, No. 156. 5 September 2013. www.jamestown.org/regions/russia/single/?tx_ttnews%5Bpointer%5D=4&tx_ttnews%5Btt_news%5D=41319&tx_ttnews%5BbackPid%5D=655&cHash=e7f11c932242d2c9bfc666eb8104ee28#.U61ieJSSwRM (Accessed on 20 March 2014).
82 Panin, "For Russia, Eurasian Union Is About Politics, Not Economy".
83 Gulnura Toralieva, "Kyrgyz Government Upbeat Before Grilling on Economy". *Central Asia, Asia Times*, 23 May 2013. http://atimes.com/atimes/Central_Asia/CEN-01-230513.html (Accessed on 20 March 2014).
84 Dmitry Solovyov, "Ukraine Crisis Fallout Threatens Caucasus, Central Asian Economies – ADB". *Reuters*, 2 May 2014. www.reuters.com/article/2014/05/02/ukraine-crisis-centralasia-growth-idUSL6N0NO1BE20140502 (Accessed on 20 June 2014).
85 Charles Recknagel, "Explainer: Is South Stream the Latest Victim of the Ukraine Crisis?" *Radio Free Europe*, 11 June 2014. www.rferl.org/content/ukraine-south-stream-halted-bulgaria/25418146.html (Accessed on 14 June 2014).
86 Shumylo-Tapiola, "Ukraine and Russia: Another Gas War?"
87 Ibid.
88 Radio Free Europe, "Bulgaria Suspends Work on South Stream Pipeline", 08 June 2014. www.rferl.org/content/bulgaria-suspends-work-on-south-stream-pipeline/25414739.html (Accessed on 14 June 2014).
89 Radio Free Europe, "Factbox: Russian Gas Export Pipelines, Projects". 06 January 2009. www.rferl.org/content/Russian_Gas_Export_Pipelines_Projects/1366873.html (Accessed on 14 June 2014).
90 Gazprom, "Yamal–Europe". www.gazprom.com/about/production/projects/pipelines/yamal-evropa/ (Accessed 14 June 2014).

91 Shumylo-Tapiola, "Ukraine and Russia: Another Gas War?"
92 Radio Free Europe, "Serbia Says It Will Be Forced to Suspend South Stream Construction", 09 June 2014. www.rferl.org/content/serbia-says-it-will-be-forced-to-suspend-south-stream-construction/25415286.html (Accessed on 14 June 2014).
93 Recknagel, "Explainer: Is South Stream the Latest Victim of the Ukraine Crisis?"
94 Alexei Lossan, "Russia-China Talks Yield 30-Year Gazprom Contract Worth $400 Billion". *Russia Direct*, 21 May 2014. www.russia-direct.org/content/russia-china-talks-yield-30-year-gazprom-contract-worth-400-billion (Accessed on 14 June 2014).
95 Shumylo-Tapiola, "Ukraine and Russia: Another Gas War?", p. 5.
96 Ibid., p. 7.
97 Kyiv Post, "Poll: Almost Half of Ukrainians Back Ukraine's Accession to EU", 10 January 2013. www.kyivpost.com/content/ukraine/poll-almost-half-of-ukrainians-back-ukraines-accession-to-eu-318650.html (Accessed on 14 June 2014).
98 Judy Dempsey, "The Long Hard Road to Reforming Ukraine". Carnegie Europe. http://carnegieeurope.eu/strategiceurope/?fa=55064 (Accessed on 27 March 2014).
99 Ministry of Foreign Affairs, Republic of Kazakhstan. "Kazakhstan, Belarus and Russia Sign Eurasian Union Treaty". Astana Calling, A Weekly Online Publication, Issue No. 356, 30 May 2014. www.mfa.gov.kz (Accessed on 14 June 2014).
100 Patnaik, "Customs Union and Eurasian Union: Implications for India", p. 83.
101 Department of Commerce, "Export Import Data Bank", 2014. http://commerce.nic.in/eidb/default.asp (Accessed on 19 June 2014).

Bibliography

Abayev, N. V., *Early Forms of Religion and Ethnic and Cultural Genesis of Turkic-Mongolian Peoples*. Kyzyl, 2005. (In Russian).
Aitken, J., *Nazarbayev and the Making of Kazakhstan*. London and New York, Continuum, 2009.
Akihiro, I., ed., *Siberia and the Russian Far East in the 21st Century: Partners in Community of Asia*. 2 vols. Sapporo, Slavic Research Centre, 2005.
Anzhiganova, L. V., *Traditional World View of the Khakass: Reconstruction Experience*. Abakan, 1997.
Asov, A., *Russkie Vedy: Zvezdnaia Kniga Koliady*. 1996. (In Russian).
Asov, A., *Slavic Gods and the Birth of Russia*. Moscow, Veche, 2000. (In Russian).
Bassin, M. and Gonzalo, P. *The Politics of Eurasianism: Identity, Popular Culture and Russia's Foreign Policy*. Washington, DC, Rowman & Littlefield, 2017.
Bhardwaj, O. P., *Studies in the Historical Geography of Ancient India*. Delhi, Sundeep Prakashan, 1986.
Bongard-Levin, G. and Vigasin, A., *The Image of India: The Study of Ancient Indian Civilisation in the USSR*. Moscow, Progress, 1984.
Brobst, P. J., *The Future of the Great Game, Sir Olaf Caroe, India's Independence and the Defense of Asia*. Akron, University of Akron Press, 2005.
Bryant, E., *The Quest for the Origins of Vedic Culture*. New Delhi, Oxford University Press, 2001.
Brzezinski, Z., *The Grand Chessboard: American Primacy and Its Geostrategic Imperatives*. New York, Basic Books, 1997.
Butanaev, V. Ya, *Burkhanism of Sayan-Altai Turks*. Abakan, Khakas State University Publishing House, 2003. (In Russian).
Chandra, L., *Buddhism across the Grasslands of Chinggis Khan*. New Delhi, Aditya Prakashan, 2013.
Chebodaev, P. I., *History of Khakassia*. Abakan, Khakas Book Publishing House, 1992.
Dawan, E. H., *Chinghiz-Khan as the Commander-in-Chief and His Legacy*. Almaty, 1992.
Demin, V. N., *Secrets of the Russian People*. Moscow, Veche, 2006. (In Russian).
Diment, G. and Slexkine, Y., *Between Heaven and Hell: The Myth of Siberia in Russian Culture*. New York, St. Martin's Press, 1993.
Dolgoliuk, A., Ilyin, V., Lamin, V., Plenkin, V. and Timoshenko, A., *Siberia: The Projects of the Twentieth Century (the Beginnings and the Reality)*. Novosibirsk, Publishing House of SB RAS, 2002. (In Russian).
Dugin, A., *Eurasian Mission: An Introduction to Neo-Eurasianism*, 2014.

Eastern, Vector, *Russia's Foreign Policy*. Moscow, Mezhdunarodnye Otnosheniya, December 2015.
Elaev, A.A., *Buriatskii narod: stanovlenie, razvitie, samoopredelnie* [*The Buriat People: Making, Development and Self-determination*]. Moscow, 2000. (In Russian).
Elverskog, J., *Buddhism and Islam on the Silk Road*. Philadelphia, University of Pennsylvania Press, 2010.
Erasov, B.C., *Russia and East: Geopolitical and Civilizational Relations*. Moscow, 1996.
Frank, A., *The Siberian Chronicles and the Taybughid Biys of Sibir*. Bloomington, Indiana University Press, 1994.
Gorenburg, D., *Minority Ethnic Mobilization in the Russian Federation*. Cambridge: Cambridge University Press, 2003.
Gorodetsky, G., *Russia between East and West: Russian Foreign Policy on the Threshold of Twenty-First Century*. London, Frank Cass, 2003.
Gumilev, L., *Drevnyaya Rus I Velikhaya Step* [*Ancient Rus and the Great Steppe*]. http.//www.litmir.co/br/?b=55848.
Halemba, A.E., *The Telengits of Southern Siberia: Landscape, Religion and Knowledge in Motion*. London, Routledge, 2006.
Hamburg, G.M. and Poole, Randall A., *A History of Russian Philosophy 1830–1930: Faith, Reason, and the Defense of Human Dignity*. New York, Cambridge University Press, 2010.
Harris, I., ed., *Buddhism and Politics in Twentieth-Century Asia*. London and New York, Continuum, 1999.
Hauner, Milan, *What Is Asia to Us? Russia's Asian Heartland Yesterday and Today*. London, Unwin Hyman, 1990.
Haywood, A.J., *Siberia: A Cultural History*. New York, Oxford University Press, 2010.
Humphrey, C. and Thomans, N., eds., *Shamanism, History and the State*. Ann Arbor, University of Michigan Press, 1994.
Huntington, S., *Clash of Civilizations and the Remaking of World Order*. New Delhi, Viking, 1997.
Kak, M., ed., *Nicholas Roerich: A Quest and a Legacy*. New Delhi, Niyogi Books, 2013.
Khodarkovsky, M., *Russia's Steppe Frontier: The Making of a Colonial Empire, 1500–1800*. Bloomington, Indiana University Press, 2002.
Kitinov, B., "Shakur Lama: The Last Attempt to Build the Buddhist State". In: *Buddhism in Mongolian History, Culture, and Society*. Oxford, Oxford University Press, 2015.
Krausse, A., *Russia in Asia: A Record and a Study, 1558–1899*. London, Grant Richards, 1899.
Kyzlasov, L.R., *The Oldest Khakassia*. Moscow, 1986. (In Russian).
Laruelle, M., *Russian Eurasianism: An Ideology of Empire*. Washington, DC, Johns Hopkins University Press, 2012.
Laruelle, M., Bassin, M. and Glebov, S., eds., *Between Europe and Asia: The Origins, Theories and Legacies of Russian Eurasianism*. Pittsburgh, University of Pittsburgh Press, 2015.
Levin, T. and Suzukei, V., *Where Rivers and Mountain Sing: Sound, Music and Nomadism in Tuva and Beyond*. Bloomington, Indiana University Press, 2010.
Machinskiyj, D.A., *Minusinsk "Three-Eyed" Images and their Place in the Esoteric Tradition*. St. Petersburg, 1995. (In Russian).
Mackinder, H., "The Geographical Pivot of History". *Geographical Journal* Vol. 23, No. 4, April 1904, pp. 421–37.

Bibliography

Marks, S. G., *Road to Power: The Trans-Siberian Railroad and the Colonization of Asian Russia*. Ithaca, Cornell University Press, 1991.

Mizyn, Y. and Yuriy, *Rus Vedicheskaya* [*Vedic Russian*]. Moscow, 2004. (In Russian).

Nazarbayev, N. A., *On the Eve of the XXI Century*. Almaty, 1996.

Oganovskii, N. P., *Narodnoe khozyaistvo Sibiri*. Moscow, 1921. (In Russian).

Okladnikov, A. P., ed., *Istoria Sibiri s drevneishikh vremyon do nashikh dnei*. Leningrad, Nauka, 1968–69. 5 Vols. (In Russian).

Popkov, Yu V., ed., *Everazisky mir: cennosti, konstanty, samoorganzaciyas* [*The Eurasian World: Values, Constants and Self-Organization*]. Novosibirsk, Parallel, 2010. (In Russian).

Potapov, L. P., *Altaian Shamanism*. Leningrad, 1991.

Rasputin, V., *Siberia, Siberia*. Translated by Margaret Winchell and Gerald Mikkelson. Evanston, IL, Northwestern University Press, 1997. (First published in Russian in 1991.)

Riha, T., ed., *Readings in Russian Civilization*. Chicago, University of Chicago Press, 1969.

Rishi, W. R., *India i Rossiya: Altay – Gimalai*. Novosibirsk, Conference materials, 1992.

Rishi, W. R., *India and Russia: Linguistic and Cultural Affinity*. Chandigarh, Roma, 1982.

Roerich, N. K., *Altayj–Gimalai; Travel Diary*. Riga, 1992. (In Russian).

Roerich, N., *Altai-Himalaya: A Travel Diary*. Stokes, 1929.

Roerich, N., *Trails to Inmost Asia: Five Years of Exploration With the Roerich Central Asian Expedition*. New Delhi, Book Faith India, 1996.

Rupen, R. A., *Mongols of the Twentieth Century*. Bloomington, Indiana University Press, 1964.

Rybakov, B. A., *The Paganism of the Ancient Slavs*. Moscow, Nauka, 1994. (In Russian).

Rybnikov, V., *Vedicheskaya Kultura Rusi* [*Vedic Culture of Russia*]. Moscow, 2005. (In Russian).

Sahai, P. S., ed., *India-Eurasia: The Way Ahead*. Chandigarh, CRRID, 2008.

Sankrityayan, R., *History of Central Asia: Bronze Age (2000 BC) – Chengiz Khan (1227 AD)*. Calcutta, New Age, 1964.

Sankrityayan, R., *Madhya Asia ka Itihas* [*History of Central Asia*]. 2 Vols. Patna, Rashtra Bhasha Parishad, 1956.

Shlapentokh, D., ed., *Russia between East and West: Scholarly Debates on Eurasianism*. London, Brill, 2007.

Shodoev, N., *Spiritual Wisdom from the Altai Mountains*. UK, Moon Books, 2012.

Smolyak, A. V., *Shaman: Personality, Functions, World View (Peoples of Nizhny Amur)*. Moscow, 1991.

Snelling, J., *Buddhism in Russia: The Story of Avgan Dorzhiev, Lhasa's Emissar to the Tsar*. Brisbane, Lelement Books, 1993.

Thubron, C., *In Siberia*. London, Vintage Books, 2008.

Tilak, Ba. G., *The Arctic Home of the Vedas*. Poona, Tilak Bros., 1903.

Tokarev, S. A., *Early Forms of Religion*. Moscow, 1990.

Trenin, D., *The End of Eurasia: Russia on the Border Between Geopolitics and Globalization*. Moscow, Carnegie, 2013.

Trenin, D., *Post-Imperium: A Eurasian Story*. Washington, DC, Carnegie Endowment, 2011.Trubetskoy, N. S., *We and Others: Russian Network of Eurasianism*. Moscow, 1997. (In Russian).

Vainshtein, S. I., *Zagadochnaya Tuva* [*Mysterious Tuva*]. Moscow, 2009. (In Russian).

Valdiya, K. S., *Geography, Peoples and Geodynamics of India in Puranas and Epics*. New Delhi, Aryan Books, 2012.

Vinokurov, E. and Libman, A. *Eurasian Integration: Challenges of Transcontinental Regionalism*. Basingstoke, Palgrave Macmillan, 2012.
Warikoo, K., ed., *Afghanistan: The Challenge*. New Delhi, Pentagon Press, 2007.
Warikoo, K., ed., *The Afghanistan Crisis: Issues and Perspectives*. New Delhi, Bhavna Books, 2002.
Warikoo, K., ed., *Afghanistan Factor in Central and South Asian Politics*. New Delhi, Trans Asia Informatics, 1994.
Warikoo, K., ed., *Bamiyan: Challenge to World Heritage*. New Delhi, Bhavna Books, 2002.
Warikoo, K., ed., *Central Asia: Emerging New Order*. New Delhi, Har Anand, 1995.
Warikoo, K., *Central Asia and Kashmir: A Study in the Context of Anglo-Russian Rivalry*. Delhi, Gian Publishing House, 1989.
Warikoo, K., ed., *Himalayan Frontiers of India: Historical, Geo-Political and Strategic Perspectives*. London and New York, Routledge, 2009.
Warikoo, K., ed., *The Other Kashmir: Society, Culture and Politics in the Karakoram Himalayas*. New Delhi, IDSA, Pentagon, 2014.
Warikoo, K., ed., *Religion and Security in South and Central Asia*. London and New York, Routledge, 2011.
Warikoo, K., ed., *Society and Culture in the Himalayas*, New Delhi, Har Anand, 1995.
Warikoo, K. and Norbu, D., eds., *Ethnicity and Politics in Central Asia*. New Delhi, South Asian Publishers, 1992.
Warikoo, K. and Umarov, Khojamahamad, eds., *Tajikistan in the 21st Century: Society, Politics and Economy*. New Delhi: Pentagon, 2015.
Wood, A., ed., *The History of Sibiri: From Russian Conquest to Revolution*. London, Routledge, 1991.
Zhernosenko, I.A., *Russian Veda – "The Secret Doctrine" of the Ancient Slavs*. Barnaul, 2003. (In Russian).

Index

Afghanistan Problem 98–100
Ajna Chakra 29
Ak-kem-white water river 31
Altai 30, 31, 32, 40–9, 63, 84
Altai-Himalayas 21
Altai music 63
Animal Book 22
Arkaim 25, 26, 27
Aryans 2, 3, 21, 25, 27, 32
Ashoka 14, 15, 66, 67
Avesta 2, 25, 29, 30

Baikal-Amur Railway 129, 131
Belarus and Customs Union 142–3
Belovodye 31
Belukha 31, 41, 42, 44
Boddhisattva 13, 14
Bodh Gaya 38, 56, 71
Book of Doves 22
Book of Veles 22, 23
Boyan's Anthem 22
Brzezinski, Zbigniew 94
Buddhism 34, 35, 36, 61
Buddhism and Mongols 68–70
Buddhism in Central Asia 66–76
Buddhist Civilization 13–19
Burgan Daa Buddhist shrine, Tuva 51
Buryatia 34–40
Buryatia, Dalai Lama 37
Bush, George W. 7, 8

Central Asia Regional Economic Cooperation (CAREC) 134, 135–7
Chakras 29, 44
Chakravartin 15, 15, 74, 75
China and Kazakhstan 115–16
CICA 114
Collective Security Organization (CSTO) 95, 114, 137
Customs Union (CU) 118, 119, 139–41

Customs Union and Belarus 142–3
Customs Union and Kazakhstan 141–2
Customs Union and Russia 141
Customs Union Commission (CUC) 119

Dalai Lama in Buryatia 37
Dalai Lama in Tuva 50
Derzhavin, G.R. 22
Dharma 15, 16, 71
Dharmshala 37, 56
Dugin, Alexander 5, 112

Egitui Datsan 71, 73
EurAsEc Common Economic Space (CES) 119, 143
EurAsEc Customs Union 139–43
Eurasia, International Transport Corridors 126–33
Eurasia, Shamanism 39, 50, 52, 88–92
Eurasia, Vedic Constants 21–33
Eurasia: Regional economic cooperation 134–55; religions 81–2
Eurasia and India: historical-cultural linkages 34–57
Eurasia and Roerich 78–87
Eurasian Commission 119
Eurasian Economic Community (EurAsEc) 119, 134, 137–9
Eurasian Economic Union (EAEU) 119, 120, 121, 134, 143–51
Eurasian Economic Union and Armenia 146
Eurasian Economic Union and India 149–50
Eurasian Economic Union and Moldova 149
Eurasian Economic Union and Tajikistan 147
Eurasian Economic Union and Ukraine 147–9
Eurasian Factor in Russian Foreign Policy 93–100
Eurasian Integration Project and India 121–2

Index

Eurasianism 5, 78–80, 111–13, 117–21; Kazakhstan's foreign policy 111–25
Eurasianism and Kazakhstan 111–22
Eurasian Regional Economic Cooperation 134–51
Eurasian Union 95, 113, 118
Eurasian Vector in Kazakhstan's Policy 101–10
European Union and Kazakhstan 116–17

flutes 62

Genghis Khan 14, 15, 88, 89
Gesar 13, 36, 29, 39
Golden Light Sutra 34, 73, 74
Gorno Altai 21, 40–9, 58, 59
Gumilev, L.N. 111, 112

Harappan settlements 1
Hinayana 71

India and Eurasia: historical-cultural linkages 34–57
India and Eurasian Economic Union 149–50
India and Eurasian Integration Project 121–2
India and Kazakhstan 102–10
India and Siberia: cultural links 58–64
International Transport Corridors in Eurasia 126–33

Kalmyks 71, 72, 73
Karakolsky culture 32
Karakol Valley 32, 44, 45
Kazakhstan and China 115–16
Kazakhstan and Customs Union 141–2
Kazakhstan and Eurasianism 101–10, 111–22
Kazakhstan and European Union 116–17
Kazakhstan and India 102–10
Kazakhstan and Russia 115
Kazakhstan and United States 116
Khakassia 28, 29, 52–4, 58–64; Fine arts and music 58–64; Shamanism 89–91
Khakassko-Minusinskaya Trough 28
Khors-the Sun God 23
Kozyrev 6
Kublai Khan 15, 68, 74, 75
Kucha 71
Kumarajiva 71, 74
Kumarayama 71
Kushan empire 1
Kyzyl 50, 51

Mackinder, Halford 4, 5
Mahabharata 29, 30

Mahayana Buddhism 15, 16, 49, 68, 71, 73
Maitreya 13, 14, 19
Mandala 27
Mitra 13, 14
Moldova and Eurasian Economic Union 149
Mongols and Buddhism 68–70
Mother stone, Abakan 53
Mount Meru 13, 30, 31

Nazarbayev, Nursultan 10, 11, 113, 117–21, 144, 145
Nazarbayev and Eurasianism 117–21
Nikitin, Afanasy 1
Nomads: heritage 66–77
North-South Transport Corridor 127, 128, 150

OIC 114
OSCE 114

Panchtantra 2
Primakov 6
Puranas 22, 43
Putin, Vladimir 5, 6, 7, 8, 93, 94, 144

Rigveda 22, 25
Roerich: expeditions 80–1
Roerich, Nicholas 21, 30, 31, 41, 42, 44, 45, 54–5, 78–87
Roerich and Eurasia 78–87
Roerich Pact 85–6
Russia and Customs Union 141
Russia and Kazakhstan 115
Russian foreign policy, Eurasian factor 93–100
Rus Vedicheskaya 2

Sagaalgan 36
Sankrityayan, Rahul 3
Savitsky, Peter 78, 80, 111
Secret Book 22
Selenga River 35
Shamanism in Eurasia 39, 50, 52, 88–92
Shamanism in Khakassia 89–91
Shamanism in Mongolia 91
Shamanism in Tuva 90
Shambhala 13, 14, 41
Shanghai Cooperation Organisation (SCO) 3, 95, 96, 97, 99, 107, 114, 135
Siberia and India: fine arts and music links 58–65; historical and cultural kinship 21–33
Sumeru Parvat 30, 31, 42–5; *see also* Mount Meru

Svarog 24
Swastika 24, 25, 46

Tajikistan and Eurasian Economic Union 147
Tilak, Bal Bangadhar 2, 3, 25, 43
Trans-Siberian Railroad 127, 129, 130, 131, 132, 133
Tsadan Jo wo statue 71, 72
Tuva 49–51, 63
Tuva, Dalai Lama 50
Tuva, Burgan Daa Buddhist shrine 51

Ukraine and Eurasian Economic Union 147–9
Ulaan-Baatar 37
Ulaan-Hongor 37
Ulan-Ude 35, 37

United States and Kazakhstan 116
Urals 27, 28

Vanyukov 4
Vedas 21
Vedas of the Slavs 22
Vedic Constants in Eurasia 21–33
Vedic Rus 2
Verkhniy Oymon 45–6
Vernadski, G.V. 4, 5, 10, 111
Vostochniki 4

Word about Igor's Regiment 22

Yenisie river 50
Yuan empire 14

Zyuganov, V. 5